THE LAST PROFESSORS

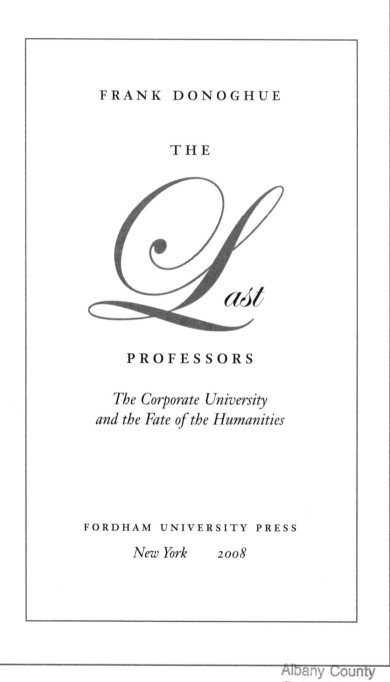

FRANK DONOGHUE

THE

Last

PROFESSORS

*The Corporate University
and the Fate of the Humanities*

FORDHAM UNIVERSITY PRESS

New York   2008

Library of Congress Cataloging-in-Publication Data

Donoghue, Frank, 1958–
  The last professors : the corporate university and the fate of the humanities / Frank
Donoghue. — 1st ed.
     p.   cm.
  Includes bibliographical references and index.
  ISBN 978-0-8232-2859-1 (cloth : alk. paper) —
  ISBN 978-0-8232-2860-7 (pbk. : alk. paper)
   1. Universities and colleges—United States—Faculty.   2. College teachers—
Professional relationships—United States.   3. College teachers—United
States—Tenure.   4. Humanities—Study and teaching (Higher)—United States.
I. Title.
LB2331.72.D   2008
378.1'21—dc22

                                                                    2008003062

Printed in the United States of America
10 09   5   4
First edition

To My Students in English 890

CONTENTS

Acknowledgments   ix

Preface   xi

1. Rhetoric, History, and the Problems of the Humanities   1

2. Competing in Academia   24

3. The Erosion of Tenure   55

4. Professors of the Future   83

5. Prestige and Prestige Envy   111

Notes   139

Bibliography   161

Index   171

ACKNOWLEDGMENTS

I owe my longest-standing debt of gratitude to the Ohio State graduate students in various incarnations of my seminar on academic labor. They helped me to work out the ideas and arguments expressed here, and dedicating the book to them seems the least I can do to repay them for their interest and their effort. I don't have space to name all of them, but Ken Petri, Chris Mannion, Sarah Adams, and Adrien Ardoin stayed interested and stayed in touch. My department chair, Valerie Lee, and College of Humanities Dean, John Roberts, came through with a crucial year of funding that allowed me to complete the book. Helen Tartar provided invaluable support for the project from the moment that I described it to her. The readers of the manuscript for Fordham University Press, in particular J. Hillis Miller, offered valuable advice, almost all of which I have taken. Thanks to Stanley Fish, who long ago introduced me to academic labor as a subject worth studying, and who still influences my standards for argument and my prose style. Thanks to W. B. Carnochan and Richard Ohmann for their helpful feedback on early versions of parts of the book. I've been especially fortunate to have so many generous colleagues at Ohio State. Jim Phelan and David Brewer offered insightful and supportive suggestions. Harvey Graff was an inexhaustible source of new ideas and references. Elizabeth Renker was the single most important influence on the shaping of this study. She was my first reader at every stage of composition and always struck the perfect balance between rigor and enthusiasm.

Two small sections of the book have previously appeared in print. Part of Chapter one appeared in the inaugural issue of *American Academic*, and I'm grateful to Larry Gold and the American Federation of Teachers for giving me access to an audience that I might otherwise not have reached. Part of Chapter five appeared in *Profession* 2006 and thus, for better or worse, has the imprimatur of the MLA.

Universities are timeless. A Carnegie Foundation study forty years ago counted sixty-six institutions that have been in continuous operation since 1530: the Roman Catholic Church, the Lutheran Church, the parliaments of Iceland and the Isle of Man, and sixty-two universities. Professors are a different story. As we know them—autonomous, tenured, afforded the time to research and write as well as teach—professors have only been around for the last eighty years. Yet, as the American university took shape in the twentieth century, the professor became one of its defining features. *The Last Professors* argues that they are now disappearing from the landscape of higher education. The university is evolving in ways that make their continued presence unnecessary, even undesirable. Over the course of the last century, the American university has risen to prominence both alongside and in opposition to corporate logic and corporate values. Important recent studies such as Derek Bok's *Universities in the Marketplace* and David Kirp's *Shakespeare, Einstein, and the Bottom Line* have elaborated on this development.[1] My book focuses squarely on the figure of the professor. I exclude from my study those academics whose work is subsidized by government or corporate funding or is supplemented by extensive consulting contracts. This leaves professors of humanities. I take a dispassionate look at how our jobs have evolved and how they have come to be assessed (and devalued) by corporate standards. I speculate on why those jobs are likely to vanish in the not-too-distant future and on what universities might look like without professors.

I have written a book that I suspect will be unpleasant for professors and Ph.D. students to read, since I have not only pointed out but also foregrounded the market forces and the deeply entrenched institutional practices that will, I believe, eventually overwhelm us. I paint what could be called an unremittingly bleak picture of what the future holds in store for humanities professors, and I offer nothing in the way of uplifting solutions to the problems that I describe. I think that professors of the humanities have already lost the power to rescue themselves.

Clearly, mine is not the standard approach to the problems of the humanities, a topic that has recently been so richly debated that I only hope that I have done justice to my many interlocutors. This is a different kind of book for two reasons: first, my narrative's historical sweep goes from the Gilded Age to the digital age. Some might argue that this history is a fitter subject for a series of books and, indeed, I intend to write more. However, I wanted to make this book's narrative a unified and, I hope, memorable story. Second, the book is more directly personal than many of the contributions to this subject. Certainly, I make the requisite acknowledgments and apologies that one always finds in the prefaces to books on the academy; I am a professor in an English department at a doctoral-granting state university, so of course my whole outlook is colored by my place in a specific discipline in the humanities and at a specific kind of school. My position in the academy thus makes it difficult for me to do justice to the community college, the comprehensive commuter university, and the small liberal-arts college, places where professorial life is defined very differently than it is at the institutions—Brandeis, Johns Hopkins, Stanford, and Ohio State—where I have spent my time both as a student and as a professor. Nevertheless, my decision to focus on the figure of the professor has brought my narratives and arguments even closer to home. In the course of writing sections of this book about graduate school, going on the job market, academic publishing, tenure, and institutional and individual prestige, I have had to revisit every phase of my own professional life. In the process of researching and writing this book, I have had to step away from my original field of training, eighteenth-century British literature, and this has ultimately made me feel like an outsider looking in, both on my area of specialty and on the profession at large. This has happened even though I have never ceased being a humanities professor, nor could I be mistaken for anything else. Writing about the last professors as opposed, say, to the university in ruins, has forced me into an intimate and not always comfortable relationship with my subject.

Let me say more about writing a brief book with a long historical sweep. I have refrained from characterizing the problems currently facing the humanities as a "crisis," a suddenly looming emergency for which we need to find a dramatic and immediate solution. Presumably, after the crisis has passed, we can all go back to practicing in our humanistic disciplines such as English, languages, and philosophy, just as we have always done. In my view, such a vision of restored stability is a delusion, yet the word "crisis" is ubiquitous in professors' discussions of their institutional predicament. I elaborate my disdain for the word and the scenario that it implies in Chapter one, but my attitude about how to characterize our problems in fact shapes the entire book. For I believe that if we set aside the rhetoric of crisis and first look back at our situation as it existed a century ago and then forward from the present as far as we can see, our problems take on a wholly new complexion. They may, in my account, seem more ominous than they do in narratives about the humanities in crisis, but I think we ultimately benefit by looking at them through the widest possible lens, and by extending our attention to texts that fall outside the bounds of our intramural conversations.

The first chapter frames the corporate world's hostility toward higher education as a century-old problem. Attacks on the academy, I argue, originated as attacks on the humanities, on the grounds that disciplines such as philosophy and literary studies are useless to success in business. I examine the rhetoric of these early attacks, mounted by industrialists such as Andrew Carnegie and Richard Teller Crane and critiqued by early twentieth-century defenders of the university such as Thorstein Veblen and Upton Sinclair. Carnegie famously declared that the traditional college education of the late nineteenth century left graduates "adapted for life on another planet," and that time spent studying Shakespeare and Homer was wasted. Richard Teller Crane, founder of a Chicago-based company that is part of the S&P 500 today, made the case in 1909 that no man who has "a taste for literature has the right to be happy" because "the only men entitled to happiness in this world are those who are useful."[2]

The excavation of attacks such as these reveals that the humanities has been on the defensive ever since the emergence of America as an industrial power. Constantly judged by a standard in which usefulness, defined strictly in economic terms, stands as the ideal, the humanities has long struggled to justify its own existence in a way that vocational learning never has had to do. Veblen, in *The Higher Learning in America* (1916), and Sinclair in *The Goose-Step: A Study of American Education* (1923), protested that these applications of commercial standards to higher education were crude and unfair, but corporate logic and corporate values already had such firmly entrenched popular support that their responses to it had little effect.

I intend this first chapter as an emblem of the relationship between corporate America and academia, since, clearly, a single chapter cannot capture the many developments and nuances in that relationship that the last century has witnessed. Unregulated monopolistic capitalists such as

Carnegie and Crane simply thought of the humanities as, literally, worthless. The mature industrialists of the 1940s, 1950s, and early 1960s in some ways embraced the humanities as an ideological bulwark against the putatively soulless Soviet Union. This is, perhaps, small consolation, since no one who lived through or even studied the encroachments on academic freedom during the Cold War would look back on this period as the salad days of the humanities. Corporate America did, however, see our traditional message as useful during that era, and the post–Second World War boom in the humanities is in part due to corporate and government goodwill, however vague and unexamined was the impulse to support us.

Since the beginning of the Reagan era, I would argue, corporate America has largely viewed higher education as a consternating labor problem. The dismantling of the American professoriate is part and parcel of the casualization of labor in general, a phenomenon that began in earnest in the 1980s and has accelerated since then.[3]

Paradoxically, the trend has coincided with a steady and significant increase in college enrollments and the valorization of the idea that a college degree is the key to success in the new high-skills, high-wage economy. Thus, while the traditional professor—with tenure, benefits, and a remarkable amount of autonomy and stability in the workplace—proves a constant source of irritation to those who wish that universities would operate like businesses, universities nevertheless need a constantly increasing supply of classroom teachers. The phases of the relationship between corporate America and higher education that I have touched on are treated in depth and persuasively by other scholars. I have benefited in particular from the work of Christopher Newfield, Clyde Barrow, Roger Geiger, and Stephen Brint. Furthermore, I could not have imagined the broadest parameters of this relationship without the pioneering work of Richard Ohmann and the historical narrative provided by Gerald Graff in *Professing Literature*. Reworking the ground that they have so admirably covered is beyond the scope of this book and, indeed, would have turned it into a different kind of project.

I am, though, interested in making one set of connections that link the old and the new forms of American capitalism in an uncomfortable interaction with the humanities in particular. I am convinced that the repertoire of techniques by which business denigrates the humanities has remained largely unchanged. At the very least, that repertoire has been revived after a hiatus encompassed by the Great Depression, the Second World War, and the prolonged ideological standoff with communism. In other words, the terms in which Carnegie and Crane attacked the humanities are being reiterated today. More particularly, the legacy of Frederick W. Taylor, the architect of modern capitalist labor management, figures as centrally in present-day universities as it did in the factories of the teens and 1920s. This recurrence not only of management philosophy and techniques, but also of vocabulary—the very language in which the humanities is dismissed—seems crucial to me. It speaks, I believe, to the persistence and durability of those aspects of corporate capitalism that most threaten the place of the humanities in higher education as well as what we might broadly call the academic way of life.

In deciding to emphasize the oppressive significance of the corporate vocabulary of efficiency, productivity, and usefulness, I am deliberately sidestepping the Culture Wars of the late 1980s and 1990s. I do not mean to underestimate the influence of this phenomenon, which I trace to (then Secretary of Education) William Bennett's 1984 report, *To Reclaim a Legacy*. This essay spawned a demand among conservative journalists, most notably Charles Sykes, Dinesh D'Souza, and Roger Kimball, that the academy, the humanities in particular, return to the task of preserving and expounding on "the best that has been thought and said" in literature and philosophy. This is the legacy that Bennett felt needed to be reclaimed. The rhetoric of this critique has proven widely popular and still exercises considerable influence over everyday public opinion about higher education. Its message to professors is simple and readily understandable: "Literature and contemporary political debate occupy separate spheres; combining them in the college classroom, especially to promote a liberal agenda, can corrupt impressionable young minds. So don't do it. Instead, continue to celebrate the Western cultural tradition as humanities professors have done in generations past." This message is the driving idea behind conservative movements such as Students for Academic Freedom, and for David Horowitz's published list of the country's 100 most dangerous professors, all of whom stand accused of subverting rather than reclaiming the legacy.[4]

For all of its notoriety, I see the Culture Wars as largely played out, and as a phenomenon that never posed a danger to the humanities that humanists could not ably and even eloquently fend off. A far graver danger to the humanities, in my opinion, is posed instead by someone like Robert Zemsky, whose whole body of work relentlessly poses the following question: Businesses and markets have always proven successful, so why don't universities operate more like businesses? Why can't they be, in the words of Zemsky's latest title, "market-smart"?[5] Disarming in its simplicity, this question is, I fear, one that humanists will prove unable to answer. Acceding to it would mean agreeing to wholesale changes in the way that universities are organized and in the way that the higher-education teaching force is managed and compensated. It might likely mean the end of research culture altogether. All of these developments have already been implemented in the growing number of universities that *are* businesses, the for-profit, postsecondary institutions that I deal with in Chapter four. Yet Zemsky's basic question applies to all of us, especially those of us in the humanities, and we do not seem to have a good comeback. Moreover, Zemsky's question is in essence no different from the one posed by Carnegie, Crane, and others a hundred years ago.

The middle section of the book traces the defensive posture of the humanities and its concessions to corporate values in present-day academia, as illustrated in the professional lives of graduate students and professors. My overarching argument in Chapters two and three is that the market categories of productivity, efficiency, and competitive achievement, not intelligence or erudition, already drive professional advancement in the academic world, even in the humanities. Today's professors have, in other words, internalized the very standards that have traditionally been used to attack them. The most crucial aspects of academic careers—surviving graduate school, finding an academic job in the humanities, and running in the publication race that now determines tenure decisions—have the effect of turning budding scholars into salespeople. Chapter two brings under a single umbrella an assortment of topics such as Ph.D. attrition, the perennially weak humanities job market, and the unhealthy state of scholarly publishing. Scholars such as Cary Nelson, Marc Bousquet, Michael Bérubé, and Lindsay Waters have insightfully studied these phenomena individually, but not discussed them as part of the same continuum. In each of these areas, scholars in the humanities have been pushed to compete for shrinking resources. Competition, I argue, is currently as central to academic culture as it is to corporate culture. Competition creates the need for uniform standards of achievement, metrics by which very different kinds of intellectual work can be measured against one another. Preoccupation with these standards of achievement, whether the Ph.D., the publication of a scholarly monograph, or tenure, have given rise to the peculiar academic culture that prevails today. The immediate and urgent motivation for research now is institutional reward, and published research is now obligatory rather than elective. Since the fruits of research projects must be comparable in order for institutions to assess their competition with each other, the dissertations, articles, and monographs that emerge from the process adhere to the strictest code of uniformity. Thus, in an ironic turn, professors, who like to think of themselves as autonomous intellectuals, find that their work tends, because it is constantly evaluated and managed, toward narrow conformity and standardization.[6]

Chapter three takes up both the rhetoric and the reality of tenure in today's universities. The reality—the inexorable casualization of the college teaching workforce—is widely acknowledged as a serious problem and has yielded several compelling interventions. I argue that professors have been both unwittingly complicit in that process of casualization and oblivious to its likely long-term consequences. In the present-day academy, though, tenure has acquired an odd, totemic status. Professors cling to it tenaciously, idealizing it as the guarantor of academic freedom; critics of academia invariably begin by singling out tenure for special abuse. In other words, I ask and try to answer the question of why the idea of tenure remains central to all discussions of higher education, even as the practice itself becomes increasingly rare.

My fourth and fifth chapters look ahead to a future in which professors do, in fact, lose their distinct professional identity. Like James Fenimore Cooper's last Mohicans, professors will not become extinct per se; instead, they will be absorbed into broader categories of professionals and service workers. The fate of the traditional professor is tied to that of the liberal-arts curriculum and the educational goals that it supports.[7] I argue that the liberal arts model of higher education, with the humanities at its core, is crumbling as college credentials become both more expensive and more explicitly tied to job preparation. With every passing decade, the liberal arts education will increasingly become a luxury item, affordable only to the privileged.

Accordingly, universities of the future will develop, as they have already begun to do, along two divergent paths. In Chapter four, I predict that a great many will follow the example of the for-profit colleges. These have become the only growth sector in higher education. They are pioneers in such areas as online instruction and convenience-driven scheduling. They have eliminated tenure, reallocating money to aggressive advertising and recruiting programs, and to job placement for their graduates. Although an increasing number of for-profits offer Bachelor's, Master's, and even Ph.D. degrees, they emphasize employment-ready, on-demand certification rather than traditional diplomas. The traditional professor, especially the humanities professor, is already absent from the for-profit university, in which higher learning has been transformed into streamlined and efficient vocational training. A growing number of financially straitened traditional universities are now marketing themselves in the image of the for-profits, embracing the only business model that will allow them to survive. Thus, the transformative influence of the for-profit college model will continue to expand. Their aggressive innovations, though, leave no room for the humanities.

At the other end of the spectrum from the for-profits and their growing number of imitators is the dwindling number of elite institutions still devoted to the liberal arts model. This model, too, though, has been in the midst of a significant redefinition since the 1980s. Specifically, it has come under the domain of *U.S. News & World Report*, whose *America's Best Colleges* issue debuted in 1983, and has since exerted enormous influence over the popular assessment of higher education. Unlike earlier, more general ranking schemes, such as the Carnegie classification, *U.S. News* implies that the prestige generated by any university can be quantified and compared, a move that goes far beyond recognizing the cachet of a handful of institutions—Harvard, Yale, and Princeton. Its circular logic suggests that credentials (B.A., M.B.A., Ph.D.) derive their value from the numerical rankings of the institutions that grant them. The universities most active in this new competition for quantified and commodified prestige are those still committed to traditional liberal-arts curricula, those that emphasize the humanities rather than vocational training. I argue that in this competitive, prestige-driven environment, the humanities has had to abandon the traditional rationales for its own existence, most notably its claims to intellectual self-improvement and preparation for citizenship. Already relegated to the periphery of the corporate university, the humanities now lack a persuasive mission in the prestige-hungry universities as well. Humanists at such institutions now find themselves in an impossible position: participating in the frenzied pursuit of prestige, even though doing so undermines their distinctive contribution to higher learning.

As I was finishing this book, a colleague familiar with its, dare I say, sepulchral tone, forwarded me an article on columbaria, or on-campus tombs. It seems that universities are starting to cater to the demand of some professors to remain at their institutions forever, in a kind of logical extension, perhaps, of the abolition of mandatory retirement at many schools.[8] My colleague's reasoning, presumably, was that if we are indeed the last professors, the least we deserve is a decent burial that pays tribute to the jobs we once did. However much my title and some of my major claims may suggest morose delectation, though, I am not scouting out peaceful, shaded plots near Ohio State's Mirror Lake and waiting in abject resignation. Indeed, I intend never to retire, and I couldn't imagine doing anything else for a living.

In fact, I've always been disappointed by the conclusion of Kingsley Amis's *Lucky Jim*. I've long considered it the greatest academic novel ever written, and for years have been pushing it on my graduate students (and anyone else entertaining thoughts of an academic career). Amis's hero, Jim Dixon, inhabits a British redbrick university, not a corporate American one, but he experiences several of the academy's institutional horrors that I describe here. He struggles to remain sane despite not having tenure. Not only his worklife, but also his whole relationship to high culture is managed and judged by a tyrannical administrator, his department chair, Professor Welch. He's victimized by the frenzy of academic competition when another scholar plagiarizes an article that he has written. In the end, he is fired after delivering a drunken public lecture that can only be described as an act of self-immolation.

I cannot help feeling, though, that Dixon should have found a means of coping with professorial life because the academy is in a way worse off without him. Sure, he is misogynist, feckless, shallow, and anti-intellectual, but he is also a self-declared "boredom detector" with a gift for identifying the whole range of arcane and pretentious behavior that alienates universities and their denizens from the rest of society. Amis invested his hero with the same alertness that he himself demonstrated during his first glimpse of professors in their natural habitat. He accompanied his friend Philip Larkin to the faculty common room at the college in Leicester where Larkin was teaching and was inspired to write *Lucky Jim* by what he took in: "I looked round a couple of times and said to myself, 'Christ, somebody ought to do something with this.' Not that it was awful—well, only a bit; it was strange and sort of developed, a whole mode of existence no one had got at from the outside, sort of like the SS in 1940."[9] If only Jim Dixon could have hung in there and endured the university, he might have written his own version of *The Last Professors*.

CHAPTER I

Rhetoric, History, and the Problems of the Humanities

Too many observers now describe the current state of higher education, particularly of the humanities, as a crisis. I wish instead to characterize it as an ongoing set of problems, a distinction that might at first appear only to be semantic. The terms of the so-called crisis, from the academic humanist perspective, are always the same: corporate interests and values are poised to overwhelm the ideals of the liberal arts and to transform the university into a thoroughly businesslike workplace. Humanists have perhaps always waxed histrionic on this topic. In an address at the Modern Language Association's annual convention in December 1952, Hayward Keniston proclaimed: "Ladies and gentlemen: it is time for an awakening . . . for a restoration of the relevance of our discipline to the life of our day. For our day is a day of crisis."[1] I don't dispute this depiction of the opposing camps, but rather I begin my own account by observing that it has been like this for a very long time.

Crisis is a dramaturgic term, suggesting urgent problems that require immediate heroic solutions. If we recognize that the antagonism between corporate America and American universities reaches back more than a century, though, we are compelled to give up the notion of crisis, and to think of that contest very differently than is usually done today. We will realize that the terms of today's hostilities are the product of a long evolution, and that the battle will not end abruptly any time soon. This chapter is, then, largely a matter of excavation, of recovering the emblematic features of a fascinating historical narrative, in which legendary capitalists, famous journalists, and academics all played an important part. Corporate dissatisfaction with higher education in fact *originated* as dissatisfaction with the liberal arts and the humanistic fields of learning that were central to universities a century ago. We need to look closely at these origins if we are to make sense of the humanities' present-day predicament.

As this chapter will make clear, the great capitalists of the early twentieth century saw in America's universities a set of core values and a management style antithetical to their own. Not only did they attack higher education, but, perhaps more surprisingly, even a hundred years ago they had already forced academics onto the defensive. That is, early twentieth-century defenders of the university, such as Thorstein Veblen and Upton Sinclair, already worried about the significant encroachment of business models into the operations of the academy and the work lives of professors and held out little hope of preserving the academy's core values.

If the history of corporate hostility toward the humanities has been imperfectly understood, so too have the motives driving it and the elements that make it up. Among defenders of the university today, the ruling metaphor for the relationship between capitalism and academia is metastasis. Somehow, in other words, the assumptions by which corporations operate have stealthily and perniciously spread into the realm of higher education. Stanley Aronowitz, for example, claims that since the late 1980s universities have aggressively "adopted the ideology of the large corporation." J. Hillis Miller's (1996) account dovetails with Aronowitz's. He points to the post–Cold War years as a period of stark disinvestment and argues that "the university in response to these radical changes became more and more like a bureaucratic corporation."[2] Note that both examples embrace the foreshortened timeline of the crisis model, tracing the problems of higher education back no farther than the end of the Cold War.[3] Inasmuch as they perceive our current situation to be a crisis, they assume that our problems must be of recent origin, and thus they look back only so far for explanations. These scholars also present *the* corporate ideology as monolithic, never pausing to describe that ideology's component parts. Moreover, they imply that universities and corporations were once entirely separate spheres before corporate thinking began to pollute academic organizations. They seem to imagine that our nation's universities came to be corrupted not by actual companies, but by a kind of organizational thinking that they simply posit as alien to academia.[4]

In fact, corporations and universities have been prominent features of American society since the aftermath of the Civil War, when both kinds of institutions were born. They have always intersected, sometimes in very concrete ways: businessmen began serving on university boards of trustees as early as the 1870s; the University of Pennsylvania's Wharton School first offered an academic credential in business administration in 1881. Perhaps not surprisingly, the nature of their antagonism has changed very little over the last one hundred years. We might expect the disagreements to focus on money and assume that early twentieth-century capitalists complained that universities are unprofitable. They *did*, but these complaints do not account for the intensity, bordering on outrage, of their critiques. Instead, America's early twentieth-century capitalists were motivated by an ethically based anti-intellectualism that transcended interest in the financial bottom line. Their distrust of the ideal of intellectual inquiry for its own sake led them to insist that if universities were to be preserved at all, they must operate on a different set of principles from those governing the liberal arts. An important task of this and subsequent chapters will be to figure out exactly what aspects of business thinking are at odds with academia, to move beyond the notion of an undifferentiated corporate ideology. In doing so, I hope to move *toward* a better understanding of the mechanics of the corporate university, an institution that has been with us since for generations.

I begin at a dynamic and critical point, the late nineteenth and early twentieth century. During that period, both universities and the nation's economy grew at an unprecedented rate. Driven by booming and largely unregulated industrial growth, the total national wealth of the United States nearly doubled—from $87.9 billion to $165.4 billion from 1900 to 1910, and nearly doubled again, to 335.4 billion by 1920. No subsequent increases have ever approached these rates. Higher education exploded in growth as well. The percentage of the country's population of 18- to 24-year-olds attending college rose from 2.3 percent in 1900 to 7.2 percent in 1930. Not until the post–Second World War era was there a comparable surge in enrollment. The number of America's universities grew vigorously (increasing from 977 institutions in 1900 to 1,409 in 1930); the number of faculty increased even more, from 23,868 in 1900 to 82,386 in 1930.[5] During these decades, then, although no one acknowledged it in just these terms, both attackers and defenders of universities spoke from a position of strength that is reflected in energetic polemics.

During this era of intense rivalry, prominent industrialists spoke out against America's universities. Andrew Carnegie, the meagerly educated, self-made multimillionaire, was perhaps the earliest and certainly one of the sharpest critics of traditional liberal arts education and curricula that foreground the humanities. He had the following to say in an 1891 commencement address at the Pierce College of Business and Shorthand of Philadelphia:

> In the storms of life are they [traditional graduates] to be strengthened and sustained and held to their post and to the performance of duty by drawing upon Hebrew or Greek barbarians as models . . . ? Is Shakespeare or Homer to be the reservoir from which they draw? . . . I rejoice therefore, to know that your time has not been wasted upon dead languages, but has been fully occupied in obtaining a knowledge of shorthand and typewriting . . . and that you are fully equipped to sail upon the element upon which you must live your lives and earn your living.[6]

After this flurry of mixed metaphors, Carnegie concludes that "college education as it exists today seems almost fatal" in the business domain, and he starkly contrasts such traditionally educated students, "adapted for life on another planet," to "the future captain of industry . . . hotly engaged in the school of experience, obtaining the very knowledge required for his future triumphs." He lauds the relatively new practice of populating university boards of trustees with businessmen, noting what he perceives to be the intransigence of academics, "professors and principals [college presidents] who are bound in their set ways and have a class feeling about them which makes it impossible to make reforms." Though he allows that graduates of polytechnic and scientific schools have an advantage over traditional apprentices in that they are likely to be "open-minded and without prejudice," he uses that exception to justify his conviction that the only worthwhile education is that which has "bearing on a man's career if he is to make his way to fortune." As a philanthropist, Carnegie was true to his word. He founded the technical school that bears his name, and the terms of the Carnegie Trust for the Universities of Scotland (his native country) provide for money for "English Literature and Modern Languages, and such other subjects *cognate* to a technical or commercial education" (emphasis mine).[7]

The generation following Carnegie witnessed more comprehensive and systematic critiques of higher education as it then existed. In 1907, Clarence F. Birdseye, lawyer, legal scholar, and father of the man who would revolutionize the frozen food industry, published *Individual Training in Our Colleges*. Birdseye, himself a college graduate (who in fact dedicated his book to his brothers in the Chi Psi fraternity), wrote not to denounce higher education outright, but to realign it with "business principles," which he repeatedly contrasts with "college standards."[8] Birdseye's central argument elaborates on this opposition:

> If they had to compete with our ordinary business establishments, the colleges would have been long since distanced and bankrupted. They have escaped this fate because, owing to the continuing force of our reverence for a college education, they have . . . had an unlimited public and private purse on which to draw, which never has asked for an accounting.
>
> (187–88)

At several points, he expresses a wish for a "panic" among our colleges that would winnow the lot of them, forcing the survivors to run their operations with businesslike efficiency (189, 367). In the absence of such a radical development, he urges an assortment of remedies consistent with and, indeed, indebted to Carnegie's ideas. He advises faculty to imitate "a good manufacturer" who "studies more carefully than almost anything the wastes of his factory and the points wherein he can avoid these. You should learn from him" (364). He also encourages alumni to "help introduce business methods into the work of your alma mater" (370).

Birdseye extends his rhetoric even further than Carnegie, though, claiming higher education as a corporate entity many decades before it became commonplace to do so. He states unequivocally that "our colleges have become a part of the business and commercial machinery of our country, and must therefore be measured by somewhat the same standards" (189). He thus discusses universities in corporate terms, referring to the college as the "factory" (363) and students as the "product" (189). He has high praise for the Carnegie Technical School, founded in Pittsburgh in 1900, particularly for its policy of hiring its faculty on the basis of extra-academic professional expertise, "men who are in close touch with the ordinary problems of business life, and not merely good instructors in nonpractical courses" (266). His book is also replete with warnings that unless he has taken a "technical course," the traditionally trained college graduate has undergone an experience that "unfits him for business" (273–74).

No one in the early twentieth century wrote more ferociously on the topic of college as a waste of time and money than Richard Teller Crane, president and founder of Crane Co., a Chicago-based company that once manufactured 95 percent of the country's elevators and that is still part of the S&P 500 today. From 1909 to 1911, Crane published three pamphlets,

"The Futility of Higher Schooling," "The Futility of Technical Schools," and "The Demoralization of College Life," and a book, *The Utility of All Kinds of Higher Schooling*, each expounding on the reasons why he felt "out of all sympathy with educational institutions, so-called."⁹ Though much of his writing may seem only of antiquarian interest today, it was a noteworthy issue in the 1912 presidential election, which pitted Yale B.A. William Howard Taft against Johns Hopkins Ph.D. and former Princeton president Woodrow Wilson. In light of Crane's attacks, the candidates issued a joint statement reassuring the American public that higher education was not "the great curse of the country."¹⁰

Crane began his research in 1902 by hiring a private investigator to spy on the comings and goings of Harvard undergraduates. After first deeming the findings of his P.I. "really too disgusting to print,"¹¹ he eventually published them, first in the August 1911 issue of one of his industry's leading trade journals, *Valve World*, and then as a pamphlet. *The Utility of All Kinds of Higher Schooling* collects the results of questionnaires that Crane circulated to a large number of university presidents, college alumni, and prominent businessmen and then redacted to suit the negative outlook outlined in his pamphlets. He thus presents his brutally anti-academic conclusions with an air of empirical certainty. His interprets the timeless adage, "money isn't everything" as an accountant's pie chart that minimizes any but the most profitable kinds of knowledge: "If money is not the whole thing, I think it is safe to say that it is seventy-five per cent of the whole thing."¹²

Though Crane affirms much of what Birdseye suspected about the tendency of college to unfit men for business, he extends his attack on liberal arts education far more broadly. His method in all of his writings is to praise knowledge of "things worth while" at the expense of "impractical, special knowledge of literature, art, languages or history."¹³ He argues that no man who has "a taste for literature has the right to be happy" because "the only men entitled to happiness in this world are those who are useful."¹⁴ He is even unwilling to grant an exception to technical courses, characterizing them as a belated and inadequate attempt on the part of traditional universities to remedy a long-standing curricular problem; in fact, he devotes a whole pamphlet to an attack on technical schools. Nor does Crane excuse Andrew Carnegie's softening opinion of higher education in his elder years. Crane mercilessly cites the anti-academic remarks in Carnegie's *The Empire of Business* (1902) against its author and asserts that the self-made multimillionaire's only motive for endowing the Carnegie Technical School was "to immortalize the name of 'Carnegie.' "[15]

If Carnegie, Birdseye, and Crane's attacks on higher education seem dated and their insistence on the primacy of business principles seem vague, management pioneer Frederick Winslow Taylor supplied tangible and enormously influential means of remaking the academy as a corporate workplace. Taylor, whose *Principles of Scientific Management* (1911) inaugurated comprehensive changes in America's work habits, essentially created modern scientific management. A wealthy Philadelphian, Taylor was bound for Harvard before poor eyesight forced him to go to work as a foreman at the Midvale Steel Company. Observing the routine operations at the plant led him to conclude that "the whole country is suffering through inefficiency in almost all of our daily acts" and to launch a crusade to systematize labor.[16] He uses the contrast between a surgeon and a frontiersman to illustrate his goal. The modern surgeon is trained to perform a limited number of tasks in a precise and standard way, while a frontiersman, with no specialized training, must always improvise, learning anew skills that have already been refined by others. He must be "surgeon . . . architect, housebuilder . . . farmer, soldier," and so forth, all in one, and must spend a great deal of time learning all of those skills. The surgeon's training is "almost identical in type with the teaching which is given to the workmen under scientific management." It is the preferred model not because the frontiersman lacks intelligence and creativity, but because, in Taylor's view, progress only occurs when we use *"originality and ingenuity to make real additions to the world's knowledge instead of reinventing things which are old."*[17]

Opinion about Taylor's contribution to labor theory is predictably split. For modern-day management theorists such as Peter Drucker, Taylor is a hero. Drucker marvels at the fact that within a few years of Taylor's innovations, productivity in the U.S. began to rise between 3.5 to 4.5 percent compounded per year, doubling every eighteen years. He touts the social benefits of this development, noting that in 1910 workers averaged 3,000 hours per year and today they average 1,600 to 2000.[18] Detractors point out that Taylor's theories erase any distinction between skilled and unskilled labor. Anyone who follows the scientifically prescribed work practices correctly is a "first-class man" who deserves a first-class wage, regardless of any distinct abilities he might have brought to the job. Thus, David F. Noble, in *America by Design*, partially blames Taylor for the deskilling of the American workforce.[19] Taylor's principles clearly transfer power in the workplace from the worker to management and privilege the organization over the individual. This shift, many have argued, opens the door to a host of abuses and creates the perfect conditions for a plutocracy. Taylor clung idealistically to the belief that "intimate friendly cooperation between the management and the men" was the real key to his philosophy.[20] His reputation among his contemporaries exposes this conviction as naively utopian. He was despised by labor unions because of his relentless quest for increased productivity; at the same time, he was bitterly attacked by factory owners as a socialist for advocating greatly increased wages and shorter work weeks (Taylor called the owners "hogs").[21] No one doubted the results of Taylor's experiments in efficiency, but everyone, it seems, worried deeply about how those results would be applied.

Academia didn't have to wait long to find out, and Taylor's philosophy still informs the plans of university reformers today. Inspired by Taylor's early work, Henry S. Pritchett, the president of MIT, wrote to him in 1909 seeking advice on how to do an "economic study" of education. Taylor personally recommended that Morris Llewellyn Cooke undertake the project. A year later, Cooke published *Academic and Industrial Inefficiency*, the first report sponsored by the newly endowed Carnegie Foundation for the Advancement of Teaching. Carnegie himself had been moved to create the foundation after reading an article by Pritchett, "Should the University Become a Business Corporation?"[22] Cooke's recommendations are very farsighted. They accurately anticipate the business model for today's for-profit universities, which I discuss in detail later. Not surprisingly, Cooke calls for the abolition of tenure, since tenure, the ultimate in worker autonomy, has no place in Taylor's system. Two of his other findings are far subtler. Cooke recommends that to maximize efficiency and organizational control, (1) textbooks and lecture notes for all of a university's "elementary and medium branches" of instruction should be standardized and (2) that those materials plus every professor's lectures and "pedagogical mechanisms" should be the property of the university.[23]

Cooke's recommended policies would eventually form the lines of battle between faculty who wish to preserve their professional individuality and university administrators eager to control the growing costs of multifaceted institutions of higher education. It is crucial to note as well, though, that Cooke's observations and recommendations have nothing to do with research, which even in 1910 was fast becoming associated with professional prestige. Cooke was in fact deeply suspicious of professors' research agendas, and had the following to say on the subject:

A man can become an acknowledged efficient teacher without adding materially to his professional reputation or earning value. To accomplish the latter he must, generally speaking, do research work and publish the results of it in at least fairly technical language and in fairly technical publications.[24]

This is a remarkable, if embryonic, critique of overspecialization and the pursuit of research at the expense of teaching, such as have become familiar anti-academic refrains in our own time. For Cooke, the business-like operation of a university, with its goal of maximum productivity in teaching and learning, stands independent of and implicitly opposed to research culture and the prestige that research culture generates for individual professors and (by association) for the universities that employ them.[25]

Entrepreneurs and their supporters, such as Carnegie, Birdseye, and Crane, and their master engineer, Taylor, did not speak unopposed. Career educators, of course, defended college training.[26] Some businessmen also either defended college or tacitly supported its importance. The self-educated entrepreneur and inventor of the automatic sprinkler system, Edward Atkinson, recommended college as something for which any young man should "make the utmost sacrifice possible."[27] At the five-year anniversary of the reopening of the University of Chicago, John D. Rockefeller, who had rescued the university from bankruptcy through the auspices of the Baptist Education Society in 1889, declared the university to be "the best investment I ever made in my life" and never meddled in its day-to-day affairs.[28] The enduring terms of the anti-higher-education rhetoric had been set, however, by Carnegie's speeches and the writings of such figures as Birdseye and Crane. This rhetoric owes its power to the American public's readiness to accept not just a monetary bottom line, but an ethic of productivity for its own sake as the irrefutable measure of success *of any kind*. Crane especially draws on his audience's unquestioning willingness to view higher education as an investment to be judged according to its return on the original outlay of money and time.

Richard Hofstadter, in his landmark study *Anti-Intellectualism in American Life*, argues that the opposition to higher education modulated as America's corporations came to depend on college graduates and had undergone a "conspicuous change" by the turn of the century. That is, as corporate entities became so large and complex that they required engineers, accountants, and lawyers in order to run smoothly, corporate executives were less likely to attack the universities that produced these professionals.[29] As Carnegie, Crane, and Birdseye's rhetoric makes clear, though, industrialists unanimously drew a key distinction between college as training in business-related expertise and college as cultivation in the liberal arts. They argued among themselves about whether college might be the appropriate place to become an expert, but they were united in viewing the liberal arts and the humanities as irrelevant and even danger-ous.[30] Thorstein Veblen recognized the significance of the new corporate attacks on the university, which serve as the immediate context of his book *The Higher Learning in America* (1916). Almost subtitled "A Study in Total Depravity," *The Higher Learning* was written in 1904 directly out of Ve-blen's experiences as a professor at the University of Chicago and pub-lished only after his employer, the president of the university, William Rainey Harper, had died. Veblen begins by admitting that any study of higher education in his time will necessarily focus on the harm done to "the ideals, aims and methods of the scholars and schools" by "an habitual pursuit of business." He further concedes that "those principles and stan-dards of organization, control and achievement, that have been accepted in . . . business will, by force of habit . . . reassert themselves as indispens-able and conclusive in the conduct of the affairs of learning."[31] These two assumptions—that business standards of organization rather than the pur-suit of profit per se harm academia and that much harm has been done already—shape the defensive tone of Veblen's entire study.

While readers of Veblen have often characterized his hopes for the fu-ture of higher learning as naively optimistic, Veblen himself is careful to separate his ideals from his sense of what is likely to happen. His ideal university is "a place of refuge and a place of meeting, confluence and dissemination for those views and ideas that live and move and have their being in the higher learning" (38). He believes that the pursuit of learning is properly defined as a "species of leisure," a form of activity that has no "economic, and more particularly no pecuniary, end or equivalence" (85). However, the governing boards of universities in his day and their hand-picked administrators are instead bent on "standardized erudition." While Veblen believes that higher learning is "not readily set out in statistical exhibits . . . and can ordinarily come to appraisal and popular appreciation only in the long run," he acknowledges that the need of "a businesslike showing is instant and imperative," particularly in an era of "large turn-over and quick returns." The corporate overseers of higher education thus value the expedient and immediately tangible above all else, even pander-ing to the popular conception of the university as an "aggregation of buildings and other improved real-estate" by spending more money to improve the appearance of their campuses than on any more abstract and purely intellectual needs (64).[32]

Most centrally, though, the governing boards and university presidents must capitulate to a "system of accountancy," which gives rise to the shape of the university we recognize today. It includes "semi-annual or quarterly periods of instruction . . . parcelment of credits . . . a system of grading the credits allowed for the performance of these units of task-work." Moreover, in "the most solicitously perfected schemes of control of this task-work, the percentages so turned in will then be further digested and weighed by expert accountants, who revise and correct these returns by the help of statistically ascertained index numbers that express the mean average margin of error to be allowed for each individual student or instructor." The system of accountancy has the ultimate effect of diverting "the interest of the student from the work at hand to the making of a passable record in terms of the academic 'miner's inch'" (76). The ultimate function of this system is that it offers a "detailed prestige of its personnel" largely for the benefit of the "laity" rather than for the "scholarly classes" (78).

The scheme of control that Veblen elaborately describes barely touches on profitability, but instead aggressively co-opts the entire university in pursuit of the more theoretical goal of measurable efficiency. In his picture, the university does operate like a business, but more radically, it serves as a comprehensive and uniform credentialing service for all business interests. The system of accountancy he describes anticipates Evan Watkins's claim that the most important products of universities are student transcripts. Describing the work of English professors, Watkins notes that "you don't report to the registrar that *Paradise Lost* is a revolutionary fusion of contradictory ethical claims, or even that John has a remarkable grasp of English history for a sophomore. You report that 60239 got a 3.8 in Engl 322, which in turn, in a couple of years, is then circulated to the personnel office at Boeing as 60239's prospective employer."[33] For Veblen, as for Watkins, higher learning is the casualty of this utilitarian remaking of the university.

Veblen concludes that the future of higher learning will rest on the resolution, by "adjustment, reconciliation or compromise" of the conflict between science and scholarship on the one hand and business principles and pecuniary gain on the other (35). Though he repeatedly insists that these two realms have nothing in common with each other—in particular reasserting that competition is alien to higher learning yet essential to business—he admits that they are increasingly brought into an uneasy co-existence that can only be harmful to scholarship. At times, Veblen over-simplifies the emergence of the corporate university: he claims that in the second half of the nineteenth century, businessmen came to be judged as "the safest and most competent trustees of the university's fiscal interests"; those trustees in turn appointed like-minded "captains of erudition" to oversee such matters as the hiring and promotion of faculty and the estab-lishment of standardized curricula; and those administrators in turn pro-moted the university as a center of vocational training, while underpaying and underappreciating its professors.

Such developments did not happen as programmatically as Veblen sometimes suggests. Yet his analysis of the state of higher learning is at its subtlest and most prescient when he writes about the popular sentiment that undergirds business principles and values. There he reluctantly con-cedes the basic assumption of Crane's screeds. He notes the tendency of the public to adduce business success as evidence of wisdom in all areas, including academia, or as he puts it, "the aphoristic wisdom that com-mands the faith of the business community" (53). A cornerstone of this wisdom is an unconditional reverence for practicality and usefulness. This reverence has, in Veblen's view, far-reaching consequences, the most sig-nificant of which is the redefinition of learning and instruction as a "spe-cies of skilled labour, to be hired out at competitive wages and to turn out the largest merchantable output that can be obtained" (85). Through the prism of the market, the university takes the shape of a large department store, with its "traffic in pageantry and ceremony," its "formal 'openings' to inaugurate the special trade of each of the four seasons, designed to put the patrons of the house on a footing of good-humoured familiarity with the plant and its resources, with the customs of the house, the personnel and the stock of wares in hand, and before all to arrest the attention and enlist the interest of those classes that may be induced to buy" (116–17).

Veblen's conclusions are as farsighted as they are discouraging to those who work in higher education. In light of the certain popular appeal of business axioms, he sees only two unappealing possible futures for "the common run of academic policy":

> either a short-sighted and headlong conformity to the vulgar prejudice that does not look beyond "practical" training and competitive expansion . . . or a

strategic compromise with the elders of the Philistines, a futile doing of evil in the hope that some good may come of it.

(176)

Because such values as practicality and usefulness are taken by the public as a "self-evident principle" (145), even that compromise will be made on the most unfavorable terms, with the ideals of scholarship "yielding ground, in an uncertain and varying degree, before the pressure of businesslike exigencies" (139). In response to the insistent question from the business world: "What is the use of this learning?" university administrators will be forced to "plead the merits of academic training as a business proposition." This predicament, Veblen adds, will be hardest, almost absurdly implausible for the humanities, the traditional academic discipline furthest removed from businesslike thinking. Scholars in the humanities will be at great pains to "satisfy the worldly-wise that this learning for which they speak is in some way useful for pecuniary gain" (146), and they are destined to fight a losing battle.

Veblen's balanced, incisive sociology of the academy is at first glance a sharp contrast to Upton Sinclair's vituperative exposé, *The Goose-Step: A Study in American Education* (1923), an intensely self-righteous text filled with incendiary anecdotes and innuendos. The two books, though, share the same perspective. Sinclair, most famous for his depiction of the Chicago meat-packing industry in *The Jungle* (1906), comes at American academia "with a bowie knife in his hand."[34] Like Veblen, he maintains that the country's universities have been made to serve as a proving ground for the rich and powerful. He asserts simply that "men die, but the plutocracy is immortal; and it is necessary that fresh generations should be trained to its service." Therefore, "the interlocking directorate [a phrase borrowed from Louis Brandeis's writings on monopoly capitalism] has need of an education system, and has provided it complete" (21). In a tone obviously different from Veblen's, he then systematically attacks this system, university by university, in a 500-page tour de force of muckraking.

He nicknames a score of universities in a way that highlights their corporate affiliations and loyalties: Columbia is the University of J. P. Morgan, Penn the University of United Gas Improvement, Minnesota the University of the Ore Trust, Chicago the University of Standard Oil, and so on. In the case of Columbia, he spells out in exhaustive detail how pervasive the relationship between corporate America and the university has become:

Whoever you are, and wherever you live in America, you cannot spend a day,
you can hardly spend an hour of your life, without paying tribute to Columbia
University. In order to collect the material for this book I took a journey of
seven thousand miles, and traveled on fourteen railroads. I observe that every
one of these railroads is included in the lists, so on every mile of my journey I
was helping to build up the Columbia machine. I helped to build it up when I
lit the gas in my lodging-house room in New York: for Columbia owns $58,000
worth of New York Gas and Electric Light and Power Company's 4 per cent
bonds; I helped build it up when I telephoned my friends to make engagements,
for Columbia University owns $50,000 of the New York Telephone Company's
4 1/2 per cent bonds; I helped to build it up when I took a spoonful of sugar
with my breakfast, for Columbia University owns some shares in the American
Sugar Refining Company, and also in the Cuba Cane Sugar Corporation.

(24)

He goes on to conclude that "you could not tell a chart of Columbia
trustees from a chart of the New York Central Railroad, or the Remington
Arms Company" (27).

Sinclair presents one grotesque instance after another of the corporate
grasp on American universities. He reserves perhaps his most intense
scorn for his home state's Stanford University, which, he notes, had once
employed Veblen. Sinclair's series of anecdotes captures a university
wholly bereft of any intellectual mission. Leland Stanford, railroad mag-
nate and former governor of California, frustrated at not being named a
trustee of the University of California, "decided to start a rival university"
on a farm in Palo Alto on which he raised standardbred racehorses (152).
His death during the economic panic of 1893 precipitated an onslaught of
creditors, along with politicians and newspapermen whom Stanford had
regularly bribed over the years, all of them wanting something from the
new university.

They were led by another of the Big Four of the Central Pacific Railroad, Collis P. Huntington, a virulent anti-intellectual who had taken
Stanford's decision to found a university as a personal "insult to his lack
of culture," and who had vowed to "stop that circus [i.e., higher education
at Stanford] some day." The university officials thwarted Huntington's
attempt to acquire its holdings in Central Pacific stock by reclassifying the
entire university as Mrs. Stanford's private property, listing all the faculty
as her personal servants. School officials even effectively deprived faculty
of their citizenship, decreeing that "no Stanford professor shall electioneer

. . . for the success of any political party or candidate in any political contest" (160).

Sinclair goes on to sketch a vignette of the Stanford museum, which predictably celebrates not the university's contribution to higher learning, but rather the personal opulence of the Stanford family. Sinclair is particularly offended by Leland Stanford's collection of twenty-four "elaborate and expensive canes" and by the meticulously preserved toys of his dead son, Leland Jr., to whom the university stands as a memorial:

> Poor, feeble lad, spoon-fed and coddled, he beat his little drum, but the drumsticks fell from his nerveless fingers. If he had grown up he would have wasted the Stanford fortune, as the Pullman boys, and the Goulds, and the Thaws, and the Crokers, and the Whitneys, and the McCormicks, and so many others. Instead, he died, and the world has a university!
>
> (155)

Perhaps the most telling vignette in Sinclair's discussion of Stanford is that of the university's second president, Ray Lyman Wilbur, recalling at an alumni dinner the scene at a dock in New York where he had gone to welcome then Secretary of Commerce and Stanford alumnus, Herbert Hoover, back from abroad. Sinclair quotes Wilbur: "I saw one of America's biggest bankers throw his arms around him [Hoover], and I said to myself, 'At last Stanford has arrived'!" (159)

Nor does Sinclair spare his bowie knife when discussing public universities. One of his many targets is James Oxley Thompson, president of The Ohio State University from 1899 to 1925, whose unlimited power and extensive ties to the business world made him little different from his counterparts at private colleges. Sinclair writes of Thompson: "here the president is a clergyman . . . also he is a coal merchant and farmer, vice-president of a bank and president of an insurance company, and faculty committees have to wait while he keeps his important business appointments. His professors are underpaid, and when they get into debt, he doesn't increase their salaries, but lends them money from his City National Bank at the prevailing rate of interest." Sinclair relates an anecdote about one such underpaid professor who was late in paying a bill at a local shoe store. The store sent the bill to Thompson, who peremptorily fired the professor, stating that he " 'lacked integrity' " (337).

While Sinclair instinctively reaches for the most outrageous examples, his characterizations are often validated by the words of the people he

attacks. Thompson himself, for example, in an address on land-grant universities, squarely places Ohio State at the disposal of Ohio's agribusiness.
He exclaims: "Let us thank our stars that the Land-Grant Act makes no
provision for a university. It provided for a college and only for a college.
In this college two things were always to be present . . . the teaching of
the sciences related to agriculture and the mechanic arts." He concludes
his essay with a contrast between the liberal arts professor, "arrayed in his
dressing gown, pipe in mouth, far removed from the scenes where the
clanging noise of the school bell would disturb him in his meditations
upon his favorite subject," and "the agricultural college professor," a
"field marshal and not ashamed to wear overalls or to have a little mud on
his boots." Exaggerated as the stereotypes are, they stand in Thompson's
mind for two incompatible sets of values, those of "the polite circles of
classical people" and the "spirit of life and progress in this great central
West." He emphasizes that, at Ohio State, "we are educating these boys
and girls by using the daily experiences of life as the basis of progress."[35]
These daily experiences exclude anything impractical, and progress is implicitly economic in nature.

Sinclair straightforwardly aims to prove that America's corporate pow-
ers have infiltrated and commandeered the country's university system for
their own ends. The battles he describes pit business-minded boards of
trustees and university presidents against professors and students. His
ideal vision of the university comes starkly into focus in a series of opposi-
tions he makes when he examines the impossibly conflicted role of the
college president:

> a man who procures money from the rich, and uses it for the spreading of
> knowledge; in fulfilling which two functions he places himself, not merely in
> the line of the warring forces of the class struggle, but between the incompati-
> ble elements of human nature itself—between greed and service, between hate
> and love, between body and spirit.

(383)

Unfortunately, corporate interests dictate that the college president can
only do this job "by being the most universal faker and most variegated
prevaricator that has yet appeared in the civilized world." He must explain
to businessmen the "eccentricities of the scholar; explaining the absurd
notion which men of learning have that they owe loyalty to truth and
public welfare," and he must beg professors to "realize the president's own

position, the crudity of business men who hold the purse-strings, and have no understanding of academic dignity" (386). Whenever the president is forced to make a decision, business interests inevitably win his favor, though he frames his choice always as an "administrative matter" posing no threat to academic freedom. These are the mechanics of the unfavorable compromise that Veblen had predicted.

Veblen and Sinclair's arguments converge again when they come to propose solutions to the permeation of the academy by corporations and corporate thinking. Having identified presidents and business-friendly boards of trustees as the root of the problem, both writers are drawn to the idea of dispensing with university administration altogether. Veblen raises this proposal only to withdraw it. He states that "it should be no difficult matter to show that these governing boards of businessmen commonly are quite useless to the university" (48). He adds that anything short of the abolition of the academic executive and of the governing boards "is bound to fail because the evils sought to be remedied are inherent in these organs, and intrinsic to their functioning" (202). However, he then despairs that "such an extraordinary proposal" will "doubtless seem suicidal to any professors who might contemplate it" (202). His critique thus stops short of a call to action.

Predictably, given his political animus, Sinclair's *The Goose-Step* does issue a call to action. He first points to "workers colleges" or "labor colleges," which sprang up in America in the 1920s, as encouraging alternatives to the traditional university. Students there paid dues rather than tuition, and the faculty consisted of "kicked-out college professors and school teachers" (450). There is an idyllic, utopian quality to Sinclair's characterizations of these colleges. They nostalgically replicate ideal sites of education unencumbered by administration or capital: "here you have students who really want to study. You are back in the twelfth century when five thousand men thronged to Paris to listen to Abelard and dispute with him. You are back in the old days in America, when a college was 'a student sitting at one end of a log and Mark Hopkins on the other end.'"[36] The practical call to arms with which he concludes his book is addressed to professors, whom he urges to unionize and strike. For Sinclair, the strike should have two goals: to secure tenure (which in 1923 was not formally part of university employment practices) and to secure "collective control of . . . how the college should be conducted, and what higher education should be. That means that we must take from the trustees, and from their hired man, the president, the greater part of their present functions" (460).

Although, since the 1980s, academic unionism has been, in Stanley Aronowitz's words, "one of the few growth fields in the labor movement," there has not been the progress that Sinclair might have hoped for.[37] Some 40 percent of faculty are unionized, but this percentage includes the expanded numbers of a very poorly compensated adjunct teaching workforce. The legal obstacles to broader unionization are as formidable as the diverse economic interests of academia's stratified teaching workforce. In 1980, the Supreme Court's decision in *National Labor Relations Board v. Yeshiva University* categorized private school faculty as managers, thus preventing them from unionizing. Faculty at public universities in some states are prevented from striking because they are classified, first and foremost, as state employees. According to Sonya Huber, only about half the states have in place legislation that "sets up a legal framework for organizing faculty and that requires university administration to sit down at the bargaining table. In Arizona, Texas, Indiana, Mississippi, and other states, there is no enabling legislation, so faculty unions don't have legal recourse if their rights to organize are violated."[38] Thus, Thorstein Veblen's estimate that the lowest-paid university instructors typically earn only one-twelfth to one-twentieth as much as the highest-paid professors is, sadly, as true today as it was in 1916 (118).

The legal climate notwithstanding, if we are to make sense of this relative lack of progress toward full unionization, we need to recognize that the gesture of self-definition entailed in forming or joining a union is one that professors are reluctant to make. Again, Veblen and Sinclair agree. Though each finds large problems with administrative policy and often oppressive working conditions in higher education, when it comes to unions, both raise questions about professors themselves. Veblen notes that salary increases, honorific titles, and better working conditions are always the "outcome of individual bargaining" rather than a collective effort. He speculates about professors as a group: "there appears to be a feeling prevalent among them that their salaries are not of the nature of real wages, and that there would be a species of moral obliquity implied in overtly dealing with this matter" (118). Sinclair is more pointed. He likens professors to temperamental "actors," explaining that "they have their individual idiosyncrasies, their jealousies and personal superiorities. They do not think of themselves as a class; each one thinks of himself as something impossible to duplicate" (458). He adds that "the college professor must do what the labor men are doing—agitate, educate, organize. The formula, 'In union there is strength,' applies to brain workers precisely as to hand workers. You would think that the brain workers ought to have the brains to realize this, but they do not, for the reason that their class prejudices stand in the way, the anarchist attitude which goes with the intellectual life. So it comes about that college professors are only two or three percent organized, while coal miners are sixty or seventy percent organized, and garment workers and railway men from ninety to a hundred percent organized" (454–55).

Professors' reluctance to unionize stems, according to both Veblen and Sinclair, from a reluctance to think of themselves as workers. The reasons for this odd act of self-displacement are both complex and crucial to the fate of the professor in the university of the future. David Damrosch, in *We Scholars*, argues that the capacity to thrive on solitude is essential to professional survival in academia. He describes what he calls the "scholarly personality": "Even if they are the best of friends and the most devoted of parents, prospective scholars are most likely to succeed in academia if they can construct a highly individualistic scholarly self; those who refuse or who fail to do so are more likely to turn to other careers, being eased out—or simply losing momentum—at one or another stage during the dozen or more years that will elapse between the start of graduate school and the achievement of tenure."[39] Clearly, if an academic, a "brain worker" is inclined to "agitate and organize," even to "educate" as Sinclair uses the term, he or she will not fit the profile that Damrosch sketches as necessary for individual success in academia. Aronowitz connects the resistance of professors to collective thinking to the function of higher education in the popular imagination. He theorizes that higher education is "one of the salient features of the doctrine according to which individuals may transcend the conditions of their birth, a hallmark of American ideology." However, he adds, this doctrine that we "make and remake ourselves through schooling has played an important part in discouraging collective action and expressions of social solidarity in favor of individual achievement."[40] Academics are, in other words, curators of America's strictest and most idealized meritocracy; unionizing would represent a fundamental conflict of interest, a move that seems to go against the very ethos in which professors succeed as individuals.

The debate between critics and apologists for the university at the turn of the last century raises enduring questions, setting the template for today's disagreements about the social role of higher education and, more specifically, about the place of the humanities and of professors who teach in that discipline. Humanists have never adequately been able to answer two objections raised by the early twentieth-century industrialists. The first, the one most familiar to students of the recent history of academia, has to do with the content of the curriculum. Figures such as Carnegie, Crane, and Birdseye asked what was the use of traditional academic studies to business? Veblen and Sinclair, even as they outline the corporate infiltration of higher education, offer little in the way of an answer to this question. Sinclair invokes images of unmediated teaching, such as disputations with Abelard and conversations with Mark Hopkins, ideals that are neither realizable nor specifically related to the kinds of institutions of higher learning that *The Goose-Step* describes. Veblen's definition of higher learning as a "species of leisure" is equally disconnected from the concerns of the modern American university, and he is utterly disdainful of much undergraduate education, including professional training and remediation, calling it a "public amusement" (11).[41]

Modern-day humanists defend their subjects differently, though with a rhetoric that has grown hackneyed and ineffective. Two examples will suffice to illustrate this rhetorical rut. The 1964 *Report of the Commission of the Humanities* states: "To know the best that has been thought and said in former times can make us wiser than we otherwise might be, and in this respect the humanities are . . . the world's best hope." And Robert Scholes's 2004 MLA Presidential Address maintains: "We need to show that our learning is worth something by . . . broadening the minds of our students and helping our fellow citizens to more thoughtful interpretations of the crucial texts that shape our culture. . . . We have nothing to offer but the sweetness of reason and the light of learning."[42] This language in both quotations, separated by forty years, is, of course, derived from Matthew Arnold's *Culture and Anarchy*, published in 1869. *Culture and Anarchy* has, in the words of Gerald Graff, "established the categories and the grammar through which we think about cultural crises." Graff adds that "the book has virtually been rewritten every decade" since it originally appeared.

These rewritings all posit the modern university as the preeminent place where discussions of culture and cultural crisis are conducted. Yet the rewriters Graff lists follow Arnold's lead in obscuring the interests of the parties engaged in this debate. Arnold was mercilessly acerbic about the makeup of these parties, but he held out hope that the "best selves" among the disparate classes could resolve the cultural crisis impartially.

This makes the recipe of *Culture and Anarchy*, adopted by so many later cultural critics, impossible to apply to real institutions of higher learning. The vagueness of Arnold's solution is only exacerbated by his notoriously evasive prose style, rich in tautology and commonplace. The university, as Sinclair insists, rigidifies and perpetuates social stratification; thus it actually prevents the "best selves" in each class from emerging or talking to one another. So long as the question of *who* gets to debate cultural crisis is left confused and unresolved, the focus of that debate will remain only on curricular content; the debaters will obscure even the content so long as they reuse Arnoldian mottoes such as "sweetness and light" and "the best that has been thought and said."

The second corporate objection that humanists have failed to address has been less carefully studied. The figures I have discussed in this chapter choose to focus as much, if not more, on university personnel as on university curriculum. In doing so, they offer a valuable discursive path that the rest of this book will follow. The early twentieth-century corporate critiques of higher education make clear not only that the university should train young people in business-related subjects but also that the university itself should function like a business. Birdseye, Taylor, and Cooke's writings all either state directly or clearly imply that university professors are no different from other workers and should be managed accordingly. Both Veblen and Sinclair are quick to point out the circumstances by which faculty work had already come to be managed in their time and also offer insightful explanations of why professors failed to resist the management of their work.

Neither academics nor their critics have sufficiently taken Veblen and Sinclair's reflections into account. They have instead focused on the content of their disciplines—philosophy, literature, history—a preoccupation that intensified during the 1980s and 1990s as the "Culture Wars" rose to prominence in the popular press.[43] Far more attention was paid during this debate, however, to *what* was being taught and *how*, rather than who was doing the teaching. When conservative critics and the mostly liberal defenders of the humanities did turn their attention to issues of personnel, both spoke as though universities were composed *only* of professors and students. Those on the right argue that professors have hijacked Arnold's precious Western cultural heritage. They identify the professor as "the real villain" and are thus led to make outrageously inaccurate assessments, such as Charles Sykes's claim that "professors, after all, control everything that matters in the university."[44] Those on the left, subscribers to Arnold's belief in the transformative power of culture, advocate "oppositional" or "critical" pedagogies. Both sides, in other words, place the job of directing the university wholly in the hands of professors, thus wildly overrating the influence of professors on students, either for good or evil. Both fail to see that the evolution of academic labor now fundamentally supersedes the choice that Arnold long ago posed between culture and anarchy.

Many professors would, I suspect, prefer to contest their critics solely on the ideological terrain that Arnold demarcated more than a century ago. That is, they believe that their prominence in the university and their legitimacy in society at large will be vindicated if they secure the right to define culture and preside unchallenged over the study of literature, history, and philosophy. By extension, many would prefer to think of their intellectual labor as something that stands outside ordinary definitions of work. This is a dangerous assumption. Sinclair predicted in 1923 that professors' obliviousness to the material conditions of their employment would make them "fat rabbits to the plutocracy" (455). Professors are even more vulnerable today to having their jobs redefined, as universities more completely adopt the management philosophies that industrialists urged on them a century ago.[45] Many professors are slow to sense the impending danger, reluctant perhaps to imagine changes that could radically curtail their autonomy and standardize and measure their productivity. Yet, as I hope to show, the mechanisms for imposing just these changes are already in place.

Furthermore, if professors assume, with little warrant, that they will retain their autonomy in the academic workplace, they are even more un-realistic about their position in the extracurricular society. Specifically, professors often romanticize their jobs by clinging to the empty fantasy that they are public intellectuals. Stanley Fish's definition of the public intellectual powerfully illustrates what is wrong with this dream:

> A public intellectual is not someone who takes as his or her subject matters of public concern—every law professor does that; a public intellectual is someone who takes as his or her subject matters of public concern, and *has the public's attention*. Since one cannot gain that attention from the stage of the academy (except by some happy contingency) academics, by definition, are not candidates for the role of public intellectual. Whatever the answer to the question "How does one get to be a public intellectual?", we know the answer *won't* be "by joining the academy."[46]

What is missing from any of the abstract scenarios by which academics describe their yearning to become public intellectuals is, Fish continues, "any awareness of the routes and networks that would have to be in place before academic views, however packaged and however translated (and they would have to be), could even have a chance of being heard in extra-academic precincts" (123).[47] As I have suggested, this lack of awareness is part of a more basic lack of professional self-consciousness. Professors who figure themselves as public intellectuals are not only unaware of the communication and translation problems that Fish describes, but they have also, I believe, lost their awareness of what it means to be an intellectual *within* the academy. Reviewing the earliest chapters in the long dialectic between business and higher education is a first step in this process of professional self-definition, one in which professors of humanities urgently need to engage.

CHAPTER 2

Competing in Academia

The most prominent discussions of professional life in the humanities share three characteristics: they date from the 1980s forward, they are narrowly focused, and they are intensely polemical. The focus has been the job "crisis," as almost everyone in this branch of academia calls it. The origins of that "crisis," however, can be traced back to the early 1970s, when universities began hiring adjunct teachers as a money-saving policy. As that practice became standard across the country, the proportion of tenure-track jobs steadily declined. This development took place largely under radar or at least went unnoticed by those in a position to make official pronouncements about higher-education demographics and employment data. Observing a large increase in the number of students entering college during that period and projecting the retirements of current instructional staff, university presidents and spokesmen for the Carnegie Institute and MLA confidently predicted, well into the 1980s, a strong future demand for professors, particularly in the years 1989–2012. Some even called for the expansion of Ph.D. programs to accommodate the anticipated demand, and at some institutions the size of such programs duly increased.

Others, clearly more prescient, but vested with less authority, were far more skeptical and spoke their minds long before the MLA gave up its stubborn optimism. In a report for *The New Yorker* on the 1977 MLA Convention in New York City and the state of English studies, Calvin Trillin observed that although "the shrinking job market has been widely discussed since at least the 1969 MLA meeting in Denver, graduate departments of English are turning our more Ph.D.s now than they did then." When Trillin asked "why English departments did not make a more serious effort to adjust the supply to fit the demand," Neal Wood-ruff, an English professor at Coe College, told him, "Don't underestimate autism as a cause."[1] Ben Morreale, in his memoir, *Down and Out in Academia*, recalls a fellow young historian informing him, "My advisor told me to be sure to be settled at some school before 1970," implying that the job market in history would collapse shortly thereafter.[2] David W. Breneman, currently Dean of the Curry School of Education at the University of Virginia, predicted a glut of Ph.D.s in his 1970 Ph.D. dissertation, "The Doctor of Philosophy Production Process: A Study of Department Behavior," an econometric analysis of the inefficiencies in Ph.D. supply and demand. Even Clark Kerr, President of the University of California system, spoke of this looming glut in 1966.[3]

The officially predicted job boom, of course, never did happen. It is simply inconceivable that we will again hear recommendations like those made by John H. Raleigh. Writing as Placement Officer for the English department at Berkeley in 1964, he assumes without reservation that all his department's Ph.D. students will have several tenure-track jobs from which to choose. His main task is figuring out whether a given student and a given institution "would seem to go well together." His one firm piece of advice for job seekers: "Our students are told not to take jobs until after the MLA meeting because they may cut themselves off" from better possibilities that may arise later. English Ph.D.s since the early 1970s do not need advice on how to sift through a plethora of job offers.[4] Though no university administrators talk about it candidly, casual teaching labor proved cheaper and more practical than the old practice of staffing all courses with professors. Adjunct labor thus became a permanent feature of the academic landscape, and full-time, tenure-track job prospects for Ph.D.s in the humanities have been wretched ever since. This problem, then, is not a crisis because no one who started graduate school after 1970 has experienced anything else. The academic culture of the humanities has been forged since then in conditions of extreme hardship, defined by the constant prospect of unemployment or underemployment and suffused with an atmosphere of brutal competition. That culture starts not with the search for work in the straitened job market, but with the experience of graduate school itself, lived out in the face of very bleak employment prospects. That competition ends not when one gets a tenure-track job, but only when one gets to *keep* that job, that is, when one finally gets tenure, at the very least six or seven years after one's initial appointment. That is yet another withering stretch of time, for, since the

1970s as well, increasing pressure to publish in order to earn tenure pits new scholars—this time Assistant Professors rather than graduate students—against one another in a competition that many do not survive.

What comes of all this? In short, a collective behavior that ironically duplicates the very corporate values from which we humanists wish to distance ourselves. Since the 1970s, we in the humanities have adapted to the conditions of our profession by developing a culture as steeped in the ethos of productivity and salesmanship as any one might encounter in the business world. This chapter isolates the most critical points on the timeline from graduate school to tenure to expose the ways that we have internalized corporate culture. My chief topics—attrition from Ph.D. programs, the job market in the humanities, and the poor health of scholarly publishing—have all been insightfully studied as separate phenomena. I argue that they need to be linked as part of a single continuum because only then do we see how competitions of one kind or another govern our professional lives. I conclude by suggesting that institutional changes, even if we had the power to make them, would not by themselves solve our problems. We would also need to renounce the values that we think of as alien to the humanities, but that have nevertheless insinuated themselves into our profession and now control how we do our jobs.

I

We know less about graduate school than about any of the subsequent stages of competition in academia that I will try to describe. The popular novelist Tom Wolfe has noted that even fictional accounts of it are quite scarce and has theorized simply that "graduate school is painful to recollect and difficult to represent."[5] We need at least to start solving this painful and difficult mystery. A bird's-eye view of graduate school populations exposes a steadily intensifying and not always rational competitive environment. Nearly 80 percent of the total Ph.D.s in the country are awarded by just 133 universities.[6] This is a staggering imbalance, as those one hundred-odd universities make up a tiny fraction—less than two percent—of the 3,500 traditional institutions of higher learning in the country and only one-fifth of all the institutions that grant Ph.D.s. Given a subset this small, we should hardly be surprised to find that their graduate programs are very selective. Even the large public research universities, which are (often by state mandate) not selective at all in undergraduate admissions, are very choosy when it comes to admitting Ph.D. students. In 2004, for example, the average English Ph.D. program received 65 applications and accepted just 14.[7] Ph.D. students are obviously the high achievers among the baccalaureate population and they come to graduate school exuding confidence born of their many academic victories as undergraduates. Forty-seven percent of students beginning graduate study in the humanities rate themselves in the top 10 percent of the student population; clearly not all beginning graduate students take into account the selectivity of their own cohort.[8]

What happens to this elite corps of students has proven very difficult to explain. Attrition rates from medical schools and law schools average between 5 and 10 percent; the attrition rate from Ph.D. programs is much higher. Michael T. Nettles and Catherine M. Millett, in their important survey, *Three Magic Letters: Getting to Ph.D.* (2006), summarize research that covers the last half century, citing estimates as high as 45 to 50 percent overall attrition, with the highest percentages in the humanities. In 2006, the Modern Language Association made its first attempt to document attrition rates in doctoral programs, but their survey produced a huge information gap. They asked departments of English for a three-year average of the annual percentage of students who had dropped out before completing three years of study. The authors of the survey admit, then, that "the attrition rates reported thus focused on the early years of graduate study and do not address attrition, for instance, at the dissertation stage." They found an average annual rate of 6.5 percent of students withdrew from programs before completing three years of doctoral study, a figure roughly in line with those of law schools and medical schools.[9] The same report counts a total of 6,457 students in doctoral programs in their first through fourth years who are supported by various teaching assignments: composition instructor, literature instructor, discussion leader, paper grader. The companion "Report on the Survey of Earned Doctorates, 2004," however, notes that 933 Ph.D.s were awarded in 2004, a number slightly lower, but consistent with that recorded in previous recent surveys (1,070 in 2000, 1,079 in 1995).[10] The obvious question, of course, is what happened to the roughly 5,500 Ph.D. students who were reported as holding teaching assignments during their first four years, but who are absent from the tally of Ph.D.s awarded? The MLA's attempt to track attrition, in other words, fails to capture the 85 percent of students who were enrolled and receiving teaching stipends as late as their fourth year, but who never completed their Ph.D.s.

Conceding that "defining a doctoral-level dropout is not at all simple," Nettles and Millett note that while the attrition estimates have changed little since Bernard Berelson's first study in 1960, "failure to complete the doctorate has more severe career consequences" now.[11] Clearly a serious systemic problem, Ph.D. attrition has nevertheless been largely ignored by education scholars and university administrators alike. Administrators, as well as many professors, naively rationalize attrition as the result of a kind of academic natural selection: the smarter students complete their Ph.D.s, the weaker ones drop out. The obvious and widespread emotional damage done to the students (each with an outstanding undergraduate record) who are thus written off as "dropouts" is perhaps inestimable. Specialists in higher education have been slow to investigate the problem as well.

The researchers' findings only complicate the problem. On paper at least, those who leave Ph.D. programs are actually better students than their counterparts who stay and earn the degree. The dropouts have, on average, higher undergraduate GPAs and higher GRE scores.[12] This unexplored anomaly has far-reaching consequences. While writing samples are obviously crucial components of applications in the humanities, Ph.D. admissions committees across the country also rely heavily on applicants' grades and GREs in making their decisions about whom to admit. In spite of the evidence, they seem not to question the value of these criteria in predicting a successful transition from undergraduate to graduate school. Graduate students with strong undergraduate records and high GREs are themselves likely to overrate the predictive value of these factors and thus be unprepared for the difficulty of the transition and fragile in the face of criticism. If we are to understand the reasons that people succeed or fail in graduate school, then, we must look beyond traditional measures of academic success and examine the complex nature of graduate education itself.

The most valuable investigations of this subject have focused on environmental factors, the cultures of various disciplines and departments as they either support or discourage graduate students from progressing. Most significantly, a clear divide falls between the hard sciences and the humanities, with the social sciences falling perhaps somewhere in the middle. As Chris Golde, Senior Scholar at the Carnegie Foundation for the Advancement of Teaching, describes it, "the organizational unit of the 'lab' is critical" to understanding life in science departments. "Each faculty member sits at the center of a small solar system" orbited by "graduate students at various stages and postdoctoral research fellows." This organizational structure, in turn, "defines a number of key features of graduate life: these features include the lab as a site in which research is carried out; an emphasis on knowledge acquisition in the lab . . . an expectation that the dissertation research topic relates to, stems from, and feeds back into the advisor's research; the interconnected nature of the research projects of lab mates."[13] The contrast between this picture and life in an English department partly explains the higher rate of attrition in the humanities. In the humanities, there is no equivalent to the lab, in which a community of students bonds in pursuit of a common research mission. Instead, the research and scholarship is solitary: students typically cap each course they take with an individually authored seminar paper and spend years on their own, researching and writing a dissertation. Even interaction with one's teachers can often seem disembodied, as one receives written feedback on papers or dissertation chapters well after the moment of composition. Nettles and Millett continually return to the importance of mentoring to the success of Ph.D. students.[14] In the humanities, without shared experience of a lab and its straightforward hierarchy, mentoring relationships can be very difficult to cultivate.

The one experience that all humanities graduate students do share is that of undergraduate teaching, yet this likely confuses rather than clarifies their situation. The humanities is teaching-intensive; Ph.D. students in English departments, for example, typically support themselves largely by teaching expository writing or introductory literature courses. These subjects are usually quite far afield from the students' own research interests, which means that the work of teaching and the work of research is disconnected right from the beginning of graduate school, leaving students uncertain how to balance the two. Summarizing the results of their collaborative project on the graduate student experience, Jody Nyquist and her fellow authors confirm the centrality of this confusion. Participants in their study "report that there seems to be a 'secret model' of graduate education with implicit norms and rules that may differ from the explicit messages they receive. . . . The most apparent contradictory or ambiguous messages concern the relative value of the teaching and research dimensions of academic life."[15] They go on to state that this contradiction is most acute at the very research universities that grant the vast majority of Ph.D.s.

Nyquist's data, collected at a multitude of universities, is corroborated by Golde's more detailed case studies. Golde screens out any factors in attrition that might be characterized, albeit hardheartedly, as idiosyncratic (serious health problems, failed marriages, etc.) and concentrates on issues that are institutionally integral to the graduate student experience. The disconnection between research and teaching comes up again and again. A few samples from her interviews with people who decided to leave their Ph.D. programs illustrate their difficulty integrating the facets of academic life:

> [My advisor] is brilliant and a wonderful writer and a great thinker. And he's also someone who seems to get intense joy out of being alone in his office reading and writing. . . . I looked at him and I thought "I admire this man. . . . But I'm nothing like him in terms of basic character."

> I think what attracted many of us into that field in the first place [was that]many of our English professors were the most charismatic [classroom teachers] we had as undergraduates. It was exciting stuff . . . it looked like fun. I want to be up there. I want to be doing that.

> I discovered after I got into the graduate program that I really didn't know very much about what it's like to be a professor. . . . I saw a side of academia I hadn't considered before . . . the competition for grants, the "publish or perish," and also the devaluation of the teaching experience.[16]

Not only does the dominant place of research come as a surprise and discouragement to many graduate students, but so too does the personal commitment that a life in research demands. Indeed, the shock comes both from the discovery that research is central to the "secret model" for success in graduate school and the realization that the research obligation shapes professors' lives. Golde's subjects discovered that when it comes to research, as one student was unofficially told by a more advanced colleague, "it doesn't matter when you work as long as it's all the time." Another student concludes that being a successful researcher is "an all consuming process. They live their jobs." This spills over into a general perception that faculty life is "unbalanced." One female student "confided that she never saw women faculty whose lives she wanted to emulate. 'In fact,' she said, 'it was the opposite. I thought "God, I hope I never end up like that." ' "[17] Louise Mowder, in an essay on graduate experience, concludes a discussion of the difficulties of balancing personal life and the demands of solitary research by touching on a largely unexamined graduate school phenomenon: "the close relationship between graduate study and therapy." She wonders "how much Prozac aids dissertation completion." Prozac, though, is only new to this torment as a brand name. In a tour-de-force 1955 essay, "Toward a Modus Vivendi," R. P. Blackmur predicted not only the exact date when the academic job shortage in the humanities would begin—1970—but that, as a result, "psychiatrists and the inventors of sedative and stimulating drugs" would enjoy success of "geometric progression."[18]

Some reformers have sought to change the normally toxic environment of graduate school and the confusing messages that it sends to students. Efforts to make academic departments homier, though, run the risk of misrepresenting the inevitable difficulty of doctoral study, especially the lonely process of writing a dissertation. As a solution to runaway Ph.D. attrition, Barbara Lovitts and Cary Nelson propose to supply students with a steady stream of information about the models, both secret and open, for success in graduate school, to assimilate students so completely into their chosen discipline and department that dropping out can never be a matter of private, isolated disillusionment. They present a series of diagnostic questions:

> Does the department display photographs of current students and faculty? Are the names of those who receive Ph.D.s and their dissertation titles given public recognition? Is there a detailed orientation not only for teaching or research assistants but also for all others entering the program? . . . Does the department have a collective intellectual life in the form of brown-bag lunches and colloquia? . . . Are graduate students invited to serve on committees? . . . Does the department have a collective social life, from parties to sports teams, and are new students integrated into these activities rapidly?[19]

Lovitts and Nelson sum up their list with one either-or question: "Does the department culture seem to say 'join our family' as opposed to 'do your work and leave'?"

Lovitts and Nelson's assumption that there are only "bad programs," but not "bad students" is commendably humane, as are their recommendations to enhance communication among the various ranks and members of academic departments. Unfortunately, the thrust of those recommendations is directly at odds with the findings of Nyquist and Golde. The paradox is this: "join our family" is a great message to send to students whom you wish retain in your Ph.D. program, but "do your work and leave" is the best message to send to students if you wish them to succeed in the profession beyond. Even though Golde does not draw the conclusion that anti-collegiality is the recipe for success as a professor, her interview subjects all but make that point for her. One even confides that her department used to have the sports teams and parties that Lovitts and Nelson recommend, but that "these activities had died out as the department culture had become more competitive and individualistic."[20]

In fact, many graduate students have figured out that the secret model for success is "do your work and leave." They follow that dictum and proceed accordingly toward the Ph.D. Even Golde's subjects recognize that the path to success entails an all-consuming devotion to research to the point that one's job becomes indistinguishable from one's life. Both that path to professional success as well as the intense pressure to get on it and stay on it are driven by the conditions of employment in the humanities that have been in place since the 1970s. John Guillory explores the consequences of this pressure. In an important essay, "Preprofessionalism: What Graduate Students Want," he elaborates on the simple answer to his opening question: they want a job. The "uncertainty and arbitrary brutality" of the job market all but determine academic job seekers' behavior right from the moment they enter graduate school. He labels that behavior "preprofessionalism," the "penetration of graduate education by professional practices formerly confined to later phases of the career." The practices to which he refers—publication and the delivery of conference papers—used to mark *professors* as successful. Guillory laments, though, that now "what the market demands, incredibly, is a graduate student who is already in some sense a successful professional before that student can be considered for a position as a professor." This, he concludes, "conflates graduate education with self-marketing, as though getting a job were somehow the culmination of a successful career."[21]

For the (ultimately) successful graduate student, the transformation of the Ph.D. into a self-marketing marathon consumes an enormous amount of time and money. Telescoping an entire professional career into the time frame of graduate schooling inevitably means prolonging that schooling to allow for the papers to be delivered; the articles to be published; and the dissertation not only to be completed, but also brought as near as possible to a finished book manuscript. Time-to-degree has been a favorite administrative worry for some years, as the median time to complete a Ph.D. in the humanities increased from 9.6 years in 1975 to 12 years in 1987, where it has since remained as a reflection of the collapsed job market of the last thirty years. It simply takes more time to complete the pre-career that Guillory describes.

The cost in financial terms to the students involved is both less well known and far more alarming. Only Indiana University has done a comprehensive survey of the debt burden carried by its graduate students. The results, summarized in Cary Nelson and Stephen Watt's *Office Hours*, tell a story that will not have a happy ending. Since the survey, done in 1999, was university-wide, some of the debt levels it uncovered were not out of line with the likely future earnings of the students borrowing money. Thirty-seven of 252 optometry students, for example, were over $100,000 in debt. More troubling, though, were the records of students in far less remunerative fields where there is, in addition, no certainty of getting a job at all. One hundred and twenty-seven of 216 graduate students in English borrowed money; 22 of them had accumulated debt of over $50,000. When we couple this information with other key statistics, the problem seems even worse. The surveys tell us that at least 40 to 50 percent of these borrowers will not finish their Ph.D.s. Those who do finish will have spent an average of twelve of their peak earning years *borrowing* money to supplement meager graduate stipends and assistantships.[22] Finally, at the average age of 35, they will try to find full-time, tenure-track jobs in a market where there are far more Ph.D.s than there are available positions. Those who fail to become professors will spend an indefinite length of time, perhaps their entire "careers," as adjuncts whose positions offer no long-term security, no health insurance, no retirement benefits and, most urgently, no realistic way of getting out of debt.[23]

A grim scenario, and this is only the beginning. Even before they start looking for an academic job, Ph.D. students have already made not one but two all-or-nothing commitments: one to the research that they hope will continue to elevate them to professional success and another to a monumental financial investment in their Ph.D. training that will be recouped only if they meet with professional success in the form of a tenure-track job and eventually tenure itself. Taking stock of the graduate school experience in this way lends depth to the stark problem of Ph.D. attrition. The dropout rate is not simply a function of a learning environment that is unstructured compared to law school or medical school. Graduate school is a unique kind of competition in which the stakes are extremely high and the rules are never fully explained.

2

Students who do make it through graduate school face the far more daunting prospect of finding an academic job. Of the 1,106 students who received their Ph.D.s in English literature in 1996–97, 372, or 33.6 percent, found tenure-track academic jobs within one year of receiving their degree. In 2001–2, 410 of 976 Ph.D.s, or 42 percent, found tenure-track jobs within one year of graduating. These percentages, dismal as they are, greatly minimize the problem because they fail to explain what happens to those Ph.D.s who have been searching for a job for more than a year. Another way of putting it: brand-new Ph.D.s compete for tenure-track jobs not only with each other, but also with all the less recent Ph.D.s who have not yet given up looking for a tenure-track position. This means (assuming that the numbers held steady between the two surveys) that there were closer to 3,000 competitors for the 431 tenure-track jobs in 2001–2, meaning that the strictly arithmetical chances of getting such a job were about one in seven.[24]

The job market in the humanities, then, is not a market at all. As Marc Bousquet has convincingly explained, the laws of supply and demand do not determine (or even influence) the hiring of Ph.D.s because for the last thirty years the most cost-efficient higher-education teachers have been adjuncts without Ph.D.s. Universities do not prefer to hire the best or most experienced teachers, but rather the cheapest teachers, thus the "market" demand for Ph.D.s is permanently and artificially suppressed.[25] This holds true no matter how diligently departments regulate the supply of new Ph.D.s by downsizing their programs, "mentoring" their job seekers, and so on.

Yet the idea of a genuine "job market" in the humanities remains resiliently popular. Bousquet traces much of this belief's popularity to a study, *Prospects for Faculty: A Study of Factors Affecting Demand and Supply, 1987–2012*, authored by the unlikely duo of William G. Bowen (president of Princeton University) and Julie Ann Sosa (an undergraduate, then editor of Princeton's student newspaper). *Prospects for Faculty*, published in 1989, makes the unfortunate prediction that there would be "a *substantial* excess of demand for faculty in the arts and sciences" during the coming decades."[26] Though the book rests its credibility on extensive empirical data, the accounting logic of its forecast is fundamentally flawed. As Bousquet notes, Bowen and Sosa take into account "only the ladder ranks [assistant, associate, and full professor] and full-time instructors, virtually excluding part-timers and faculty without the doctoral degree." This blunder has far-reaching ramifications, since it leads the authors to attempt "to understand the employment system *as* a system while excluding the largest categories of its working parts [that is, adjuncts]." In an interview in 1994, Bowen tried to explain why his prediction showed no signs of coming true.

He said that he couldn't have predicted what he called "massive . . . cut-backs of the 1990s." Bousquet observes, though, that this excuse only displays more of the obliviousness that informed the original forecast five years earlier. Bowen speaks "as if retrenchment and casualization were a phenomenon of that decade and not well-established twenty years earlier. . . . [T]here was already by 1989 a well-developed understanding of the exploitation of part-timers and graduate students," with enough supporting quantitative data to rival Bowen's own.[27]

In 1996, seven years after the appearance of *Prospects for Faculty*, the Modern Language Association published its official *Guide to the Job Search*, which included an essay by Jack Schuster, who had during the 1980s shared Bowen and Sosa's confidence in a bright future for job seekers in the humanities. The essay is rich in the language of financial analysis, surveying an assortment of "emerging factors" that will affect the "market," some for better, others for worse. These include economic and political constraints; early retirement; and a reemphasis on teaching, technology, and "staffing flexibility." To count this last as an "emerging" factor is, of course, to miss both the point that (1) adjunct hiring was by 1996 an even more firmly established practice than in 1989 and (2) the growing adjunct workforce far outweighs all of the other factors on the list. Schuster's lack of understanding on this point leads him to make a series of misguided conjectures. He too persists in predicting that "the market *will* improve," even after opening his essay with an apology for having made that same prediction—inaccurately—in the mid-1980s. His faith in his reiterated forecast rests on his belief that the job system is a market and that markets have cycles of high and low demand, the very self-authenticating rhetoric that Bousquet exposes as flawed. Accordingly, Schuster encourages excellent undergraduates to pursue academic careers because "by the time they have completed doctoral programs, there will likely by openings for them." His advice for advanced graduate students is equally dubious and more impractical: "Wholesale change will not occur within the next several years—but it will occur . . . while there is considerable cause for optimism, the ability to tread water for another five years or so would help." Though Schuster seems unaware of it, in the context of his essay, "tread water" can only mean accepting an indefinite series of adjunct appointments, thus helping the system of casualization to perpetuate itself. Schuster saves his most ludicrous advice for humanists who already have doctorates, but don't have permanent jobs. They are to tread water along with all the advanced graduate students, working as adjuncts and awaiting a brighter future. He explains that "the relatively few institutions that can afford to be choosy in hiring new faculty members after the market turn-around will have little interest in the cohort of nonregular" teachers [i.e., adjuncts without Ph.D.s]![28]

The following year, 1997, witnessed the publication of the *Final Report of the MLA Committee on Professional Employment*. Cary Nelson correctly notes that this document, collaboratively authored by seventeen humanit-ies professors from an assortment of institutions and circulated to the en-tire membership of the organization, effectively removes the MLA's "imprimatur from its official posture of denial" about bleak job pros-pects.[29] While this is true in the sense that the MLA finally admits that there *is* a serious problem, the report nevertheless clings to the belief that the employment situation is the consequence of a market downturn rather than a permanent and nationwide transformation of hiring practices. The *Final Report*'s general conclusion cites Schuster's essay uncritically and maintains that the present situation is "a crisis in the truest sense of the word: not just an 'unstable condition' but a 'turning point,' which we hope will evoke significant transformations of the academic settings we in-habit."[30] Brave rhetoric, but naively belated. There was no "crisis," cer-tainly not in 1997, for by then the transformation of the academic workplace had been underway for nearly three decades. The authors of the report seem only occasionally to recognize the permanence of this transformation; they present, for example, recommendations for the equi-table treatment of adjunct instructors, including the bold but unenforce-able suggestion that "departmental and campus administrators make every effort to convert an optimal number of part-time positions to full-time—preferably tenure-track—positions."[31] However, they also recommend that departments downsize their Ph.D. programs and offer Ph.D.s direc-tion on nonacademic careers. Both of these measures imply—against all evidence—that the current poor job "market" is a down cycle caused by an oversupply of Ph.D.s and not by the pervasive casualization of the teaching workforce.

Only when we turn to the "market" rhetoric's effect on graduate stu-dents do we see its most pernicious ramifications. According to that rheto-ric, markets determine fair value, so if searching for an academic job means that one enters a market, then the market itself will sort out the more valuable candidates from the less valuable. The most valuable will get the few available tenure-track jobs, with the best positions—at research uni-versities and elite colleges that reward research—going to those who most clearly distinguish themselves in the supposedly open competition. This logic assigns the responsibility of being valued to the job seekers themselves, a cruel injustice given the way that the hiring system actually works. A couple of examples will suffice to illustrate how these connections unfairly shift the focus of the problem. Karen Sowers-Hoag and Dianne F. Harrison base the authority of their book *Finding an Academic Job* (1998) on their "combined 35 years of experience in higher education institutions." They make the obligatory reference to Bowen and Sosa's *Prospects for Faculty*, citing it like a scriptural promise of the Rapture, and then use its predictions to justify publishing their book: "Given these anticipated faculty shortages, why would anyone need a book on how to get a faculty job? Our reason is that many faculty candidates enter the job market severely underprepared for the process—naïve at best."[32]

This take-charge, self-help approach is perfectly pitched to an audience of job seekers who have survived graduate school and earned the Ph.D., and who cannot bring themselves to admit that the academic labor system is rigged against them. Instead, they deny it, or, more accurately, they don't believe that the system will personally victimize *them*. If they fail, it is because they were "underprepared." Ideally, they believe that their personal merit and thorough preparation will override the workings of the "market." In the end, "with a little bit of luck and a whole lot of forethought" (as Linda Haverty puts it in her contribution to a collection of essays breezily billed as *A Practical Guide for the Beginning Professor*) they will succeed.[33] If you believe that success or failure is largely up to you, the job search itself becomes an intense personal drama about individual distinction and merit.

Drawing on their graduate experience in research culture, their "pre-professionalism," job seekers reasonably conclude that the key element in their preparation is scholarly publication. Emily Toth's guide, *Ms. Mentor's Impeccable Advice for Women in Academia*, makes the typical connection between the heroic job seeker and her publication record. Answering the question, "Do I need to publish to get a first job? Should I be sending my seminar papers to academic journals . . . ?" Ms. Mentor answers unequivocally:

> You cannot wait to be brilliant. You need to make yourself known as soon as possible. . . . You must be ambitious; you must aim to publish early and often. That is the only way you'll distinguish yourself from the hordes of people who apply for every tenure-track job.[34]

Virtually every job seeker accedes to Ms. Mentor's generalization and takes her advice. That advice, coupled with the fact that only a fraction of new Ph.D.s will get the few available tenure-track jobs, creates a desperate environment for all job seekers. It creates an ever-escalating standard of expectations for those doing the hiring as well.[35]

This environment was perfectly illustrated in the fall of 1995 by a parody letter of application sent to English departments across the country that were seeking to hire an assistant professor specializing in eighteenth-century British literature. The letter details a frenzy of research and publication activity, all undertaken in the hope that the applicant, "Manfred Mickleson," would get a job. The manuscript of his dissertation, Manfred writes, is under contract to be published by Routledge. He has "given over forty papers at various conferences on literature and cultural studies in the last three years" and has "articles under consideration at twelve scholarly journals." His dossier of recommenders is a Who's Who of senior scholars in the field—Michael McKeon, Terry Castle, F. V. Bogel, Jonathan Culler, Laura Brown, Felicity Nussbaum, and Peter deBolla—proof that Manfred's many conference appearances have yielded him an impressive network of professional supporters. "To write a letter of application," Terry Caesar observes, "is always to be found wanting on some basis,"[36] Mickleson's letter exemplifies every applicant's fantasy, for Manfred simply cannot be found wanting on any basis.

The Mickleson story would likely have faded after its initial circulation had not an amended version of his letter of application been posted online, on the Eighteenth-century Listserve in April, 1996, under the subject, "One of the Year's Best Job Candidates," where it provoked a firestorm of debate. The most significant alteration to the original was the introduction of a frame narrative, identifying the letter as a hoax, but claiming that Mickleson had "received over forty dossier requests, and six invitations to be interviewed at the MLA convention. We still have not learned," the posting continues, "whether or not, despite being unable to show up in person for his MLA interviews, Manfred received any actual offers" (posted April 22, 1996). While senior professors—those with job security—found a lot to laugh about, the many graduate students and still unemployed and untenured found a focus for their exasperation and resentment in the frame narrative. They were offended not so much by the parody itself, and Manfred's frenetic productivity, but by the "fact" that his efforts were so handsomely rewarded with interviews, possibly with job offers. That revealed a disturbing shared understanding among job seekers and hiring committees alike about the professional profile of a "year's best job candidate." As real job seeker Nathaniel Paradiso explains, the message is infuriating no matter how one interprets it:

> The possibility that Mickleson did indeed get interview requests when I have been informed that at several institutions my name was one of the very last cut from the interview list—meaning that fictional Mickleson could have gotten "my" interview—is too painful to contemplate. It makes me want to throw my computer out the window and begin a new career. On the other hand, if the frame [the tale of Mickleson's success] is part of the fiction, the fact that so many people are willing to believe that the Mickleson letter garnered invitations to interview is incredibly unnerving, and makes me want to throw my computer out the window and begin a new career. (posted April 29, 1996)

The issues highlighted by the Manfred Mickleson hoax continue, unaltered, to shape the professional behavior of assistant professors. At the next point on my timeline, those Ph.D.s fortunate enough to get tenure-track jobs seek distinction—and ultimately tenure—exclusively through their scholarship, since that is the only means by which they can compete with one another. One need only to look at a couple of the profession's more pragmatic shibboleths to understand why university presses are overburdened: "It takes a book to get a job." "If you're unhappy at your current university job you need to publish your way out of it." Publication is the profession's *only* universally recognized marker of distinction. The glut of publications and planned publications renders the actual content of books and articles almost insignificant. First and foremost, publication is a demonstration of productivity. As Guillory has observed, the products have no value in any actual market where products are bought and sold. Thus, even though there is a perceived hierarchy of first- and second-rate university presses and journals, presumably with audiences of consuming readers, administrators set consumption aside and trust only productivity itself as the measure of success. "Active" scholars are rewarded while those who publish infrequently are not; at most, the influence of scholarship is estimated by counting numbers of citations. It has been obvious for many years that the scholarly publishing industry cannot sustain the ever-growing responsibilities thrust upon it by the imperative to publish. However, recognizing that scholarly publishing is a broken prestige model has proven far easier than finding a solution. The forces that keep pushing university presses far past their limit originate in everyone's Ph.D. education, and those lessons would be very difficult to unlearn.

The job search is a cruel reward for those who manage to remain in graduate school through the Ph.D. level. After surviving the forty to fifty percent attrition rate, they find themselves in a competition where the casualty rates are even higher. Moreover, the logic of this new competition, the job search, has been mystified and misrepresented for a long time now. If graduate school contained a secret model for success, the job system in the humanities offers erroneous models. Ph.D.s are led to believe that tenure-track hiring does indeed function as a market like any other, with periodic troughs and peaks, and that there will be phases of that market when conditions will be favorable to all job seekers. Yet Ph.D.s are at the same time taught to take that market personally, to view success or failure not in terms of uncontrollable fluctuations, but in terms of individual preparation and qualification. The myths governing the job search are, in other words, perfectly suited to a group of people, the job seekers, whose personal optimism and confidence have successfully carried them through graduate school. At the heart of this myth is a curious absence of agency, as if an invisible hand—the original and still profound metaphor of market operations—guided everything. Agents are not only missing from endorsements of the academic job market, but also from critiques of it as well. Guillory's "preprofessionalism" stands as an impersonal phenomenon to which all graduate students are subject; Bousquet's "job system," while it is a far more accurate description of academic hiring practices, is no less abstract than the usual "job market." The terminology makes it impossible for anyone either to assign or to accept responsibility for this stage of competition.

3

Those few humanities Ph.D.s who do get tenure-track jobs cannot afford time to celebrate, for they must immediately embark on a new competition that ends only with tenure. Particularly in the disciplines of literature and history, succeeding in this new competition entails publishing a book. Everyone who has studied the problems currently facing scholarly publishing notes their complexity. I wish to focus on the ways that professors and would-be professors participate in the problems. University presses are being squeezed from several directions at once. Nationwide, universities are cutting the budgets for their presses and requiring them to be financially self-sufficient. This directive puts the presses at odds with their own historical mission. In 1890, the president of Columbia University described university presses, then in their infancy, as havens for the publication of books that are important for scholars, but that are "destitute of commercial value."[37] Cathy Davidson elaborates: "The bottom line is that scholarly publishing isn't financially feasible as a business model—never was, never was intended to be, and should not be. If scholarship paid, we wouldn't need university presses."[38] The more and more common demand that university presses pay their own way forces them to behave like trade presses, a job for which they are unprepared, and one in which they and the books they publish perform poorly.

At the same time that universities are requiring their presses to function as stand-alone, financially self-sufficient units, they are also reducing their library budgets. This cost-cutting measure takes away the university presses' best customers, for libraries have traditionally purchased by far the largest number of copies of academic books. Several university press directors recall that not long ago during their own careers, they could count on selling 1,000 or more copies of any title they published to the libraries of colleges and universities across the country. Now they can count on only 200 or so purchases from these straitened institutions. This means that the sales of a typical academic book, which could once have been relied on at least to pay for the cost of its own production, now does not stand a chance of doing so. Columbia University Press's editorial director, Jennifer Crewe, attaches dollar amounts to this losing proposition. After first determining that the average cost to produce a monograph is $30,000, she

> assessed six first books—revised dissertations—in the field of literary studies published by Columbia University Press two and three years ago. Our income from sales of each of these books (all of which have received very favorable reviews) averaged $12,500. More than half what we spent on each book has not been earned back.[39]

Another feature of this particular problem is that a generation ago, books made up 80 percent of the typical university library's acquisition budget, with journals making up the remaining 20 percent. Now, largely because of the escalating cost of scientific journals and expensive electronic journal storage services such as J-STOR, that 80:20 percent proportion has been reversed, and libraries have a harder and harder time protecting their book-purchasing budgets.

The final source of pressure on the scholarly publishing industry derives from the obligation that scholars have to publish, and this crucially connects the industry to the inculcation of the research model that I discussed earlier. The academic monograph is widely and only half-jokingly referred to as the holy grail or the gold standard of the tenure process. Most tenure-track assistant professors have to publish one in order to gain promotion and job security. The competition to publish a book is thus just as intense as the competition to get a tenure-track job. Indeed, the two competitions increasingly bleed into one another, as many take to heart the rule of thumb that it takes a book just to get a job. William Germano, publishing director at Routledge, reports in a 2001 interview that "We've been seeing a lot of [book] proposals from graduate students, and some of them quite good."[40] These proposals come from scholars who have yet to complete their dissertations, yet who, following the dictum to "publish early and often," are already marketing the books that will evolve from those dissertations. (It is perhaps amusing to recall that the fictional Manfred Mickleson claimed that his as-yet-unfinished dissertation was forthcoming from Germano's press, Routledge.)

I will have more to say about the imperative of scholarly publication shortly. For now, though, I wish only to link it with the direct and indirect economic issues that I have just considered. Tying tenure to the scholarly monograph transfers considerable power from academic departments to university presses, a point widely noted by publishers and academics alike. For better or worse, this practice turns the presses into the ultimate gate-keepers at just the point when the work of an assistant professor comes under closest scrutiny from his or her senior colleagues. At that crucial point, the decision to tenure or not to tenure often depends on whether the candidate has a book contract from a university press or has already published a book. Since the requirement of a book for tenure is often inflexible, a university press serves as the de facto arbiter of the candidate's fate. Many see this transfer of power as an act of cowardice on the part of the academic departments that support it; they are sidestepping an important responsibility by outsourcing the job of quality control to a press, most commonly a press not even affiliated with their own university.[41] In light of the financial constraints newly thrust upon university presses, this transfer of power seems especially dubious now. Presses can no longer afford to evaluate a manuscript solely on the basis of its intellectual and scholarly content, but now must take into account marketing factors such as the breadth of the book's likely reading audience and its chances of earning back production costs. Universities willing to abide by the standard that an assistant professor in the humanities must publish a book in order to get tenure rarely bear these factors in mind.

Viewed from any angle, then, the situation of scholarly publishing is a grim prospect, and the fate of the academic monograph looks especially precarious. The problems have evoked a host of practical recommendations. Not surprisingly, given the complexity of the situation, they all fall well short of a solution. Among the more widely circulated ideas are new financial plans, quick fixes, and, most important to my inquiry here, basic changes in the way that we value publication.

The two leading proposed financial reforms are publication subsidies for assistant professors and a more aggressive adoption of electronic publishing. Plans organized around the first of these ideas ask "If we all admit that scholarly publishing has lost a large portion of its traditional subsidies from well-funded university presses and university libraries, why not reintroduce that money directly into the salary and compensation packages offered to assistant professors in the form of publication subvention funds?' Scholars would, in effect, pay for book production costs themselves. The drawback to this plan is that, except for a utopian scenario, in which equal subsidies are paid to all assistant professors out of, for example, increased MLA dues, the money would simply not be distributed equally. Since the subsidy plan would represent an added cost, some universities might support it and others might not. Imagine two assistant professors with comparable book projects, one at an Ivy League university with a generous subsidy for publication subvention, the other at a state university with a much smaller subsidy program or none at all. Crewe concludes that in such situations, which would surely occur frequently, the difference would risk prejudicing a press's decision about which book to publish.[42]

Electronic publication is also usually advanced as a financial cure, but rarely with a complete awareness of how the costs of book production are actually distributed. Crewe again explains:

> The lion's share of the money [to produce a book] pays for all the press staff time that goes into really publishing the book, as opposed to just getting the copies printed—the time it takes to evaluate the field and get to know the author; assess the value of the book and its potential market; solicit peer review; judge the book's suitability for a press's particular list and its contribution to the field; publicize it, by sending review copies to journals, preparing press

releases, pitching it to book-review editors, perhaps booking the author on radio shows or book tours and entering the book in prize competitions; announce the book in catalogs and flyers; exhibit it at conventions; advertise it and pitch it to buyers at wholesalers and chains and the independent stores.

The switch to wide-scale electronic publication would also entail new costs: "the cost of coding the book in XML, of paying for a Web developer's time, and of selling subscriptions to libraries."[43] Advocates of e-publishing typically focus on the problem of whether the various hiring and tenure committees at universities would accept this new format as legitimate. Even if that were to happen, the problem of costs would remain.

Cathy Davidson enumerates a few quick fixes in her article, "Understanding the Burden of Scholarly Publishing," but unfortunately they prove either impractical or too insubstantial to influence the overall situation. For example, she recommends that academics redirect the money that comes to them from university presses in the form of royalties and readers' fees back to the presses as charitable gifts to supplement the costs of future publications. Yet even Davidson admits that making such meager gifts the customary practice would only amount to "a small token in a larger project of cultural change." She also recommends that we "stamp out course packs! Professors should be aware that every course pack assigned is a university-press book unsold. University-press books are often cheaper for students than course packs, and certainly less hassle than taking on all the copyright issues these days."[44] As Judith Ryan points out, though, replacing course packs with books would rarely save students money and would also be unlikely to register significant sales of any given book. She wonders, hypothetically, "if I devote two weeks of a course to Rilke's poetry, does that justify assigning a single book by you know whom [Ryan is a prominent Rilke scholar], at sixty-five dollars a pop? Even one of the 'companion' volumes that presses have already created to help balance their financial losses in the literary fields would surely seem excessive to assign unless the course were a seminar devoted to a single author."[45]

The financial recommendations and everyday fixes advanced by editors and academics alike seem to share a uniform understanding of the problems that face scholarly publishing. Clearly, though, their suggestions will not solve the problems. Short of the "larger project of cultural change" to which Davidson alludes, the condition of university presses will continue to deteriorate. Yet the possibility of this fundamental revaluation of the way that scholars conceive of publication evokes wildly and confusingly disparate views from everyone concerned.

There seems to be widespread agreement that the current state of scholarly publishing, driven by the imperative to publish monographs (which in turn serve as the key to tenure for their authors), has become a disaster. Robert Markley, ingeniously paraphrasing Oscar Wilde, calls scholarly publishing "the production of the unreadable by the unprofitable."[46] The general observations of editors confirm his dismissive tone. Germano sums it up:

> I think we're . . . faced with the fact that we all publish too many books, there isn't enough space to house them in libraries nor do libraries have the budgets to buy them, people don't have the time to read them, and there is the suspicion that a great many books get published merely because scholars are told they have to publish books in order to be tenured and promoted. I think those are the open secrets.[47]

Willis Regier of University of Illinois Press reports the candid but depressing comment from a Barnes and Noble buyer that "university press books are furniture for the coffee shop."[48]

The hopelessness of academic publishing, and the fact that its predicament is an open secret, translates into shrieks of panic among scholars for whom monographs are the only means to promotion. In 1997, the Association of American University Presses convened a group of professors and university administrators to talk about *The Specialized Scholarly Monograph in Crisis*. The subtitle, not of an individual paper, but of the entire conference, was "How Can I Get Tenure If You Won't Publish My Book?" This note of alarm is also captured, as we have seen, in the Manfred Mickleson job application parody and in the real anxiety of thousands of Ph.D. students and new Ph.D.s. The research culture in which they have been immersed has correctly confirmed that professional success depends on publication, and that the first crucial task is to turn one's dissertation into a monograph. They understandably see the troubled university presses as an assortment of rapidly closing windows of opportunity.

Markley observes that "there is not a great deal that can be done to change the nature of scholarly publishing without also radically changing the institutions that support it."[49] Editors share a sense of how this could be done. In a much cited 2000 article, Harvard University Press's executive editor for the humanities, Lindsay Waters, says, "I propose that essays should be the prime publication for winning tenure. . . . [M]y suggestion that tenure be decoupled from book publication is meant to free university presses of the pressure to publish books that have little justification other than to build up a tenure case." The notion that the book is a superior genre to the article, he observes, has been shaped by little other than evolving customs and traditions that are peculiar to departments of literature and history. In his experience as an editor, he discovered that in other fields—philosophy and economics, for example—the article reigns supreme and the book represents primarily "a failure to be concise."[50] Crewe elaborates on the process by which articles are puffed up into books: "In many monographs the core argument containing the original idea is about fifty to seventy pages long, and the rest of the book could be described as filler to fit the form—the review of the literature, the arguments with other colleagues, the taking on of related issues, the reworking of the idea in yet another iteration. These monographs could simply be articles."[51]

So why does this change not simply happen? The commitment of the humanities to the monograph as the scholar's ultimate triumph in research culture remains defiantly intransigent. Despite the financial quagmire that I have described, and in the face of the considered opinions of prominent and experienced university press editors, one still finds extraordinary defenses of the monograph. In the course of rehearsing these very problems, Davidson, vice provost and also an English professor at Duke, states flatly, "I am not in favor of uncoupling book publishing from tenure." Philip Lewis, Professor of Romance Studies at Cornell, vows "the publishability of serious, high-quality work [in monograph form] should somehow be sustained." A report from an ad hoc committee of the MLA acknowledges that the sales of a typical monograph in the humanities numbers about 250 copies, yet still maintains that "the scholarly book is well worth preserving. Neither its convenience nor its *cultural impact* has been supplanted" (emphasis mine). Moreover, R. Stephen Humphreys, the King Abdul Aziz Al Saud Professor of Islamic Studies at the University of California, Santa Barbara, in an essay entitled, "Why do We Write Stuff That Even Our Colleagues Don't Want to Read?" presents a long diatribe on the theme that "there are just too many books." Yet he too concludes that "when all is said and done, however, it is hard to think of anything that really replaces the scholarly monograph. For a scholar, there is really nothing physically, professionally, and intellectually so satisfying as a well-produced monograph in the palm of your hand, especially when it has your name on the cover."[52]

Though these statements offer little hint of motive (unless one counts the desire for tactility), the mighty struggle of the humanists to forestall the death of the monograph is more than a case of sheer stubbornness tinged with narcissism. Stubbornness and narcissism do not account for the unaffected fascination with books that unites most humanists. Furthermore, we should not forget that the current generation of university press editors shares the educational background of their authors. Germano, Regier, and Waters, for example, all have Ph.D.s in English literature and considered careers as professors. The next generation seems no different; Regier says of all his junior colleagues at University of Illinois Press, "they love books, they love scholarship."[53]

There are at least two salient explanations for the support enjoyed by the monograph that go beyond personal considerations. First, it is no coincidence that the individual defenses of the monograph that I have just cited come from two professors at elite private universities and one who holds an endowed chair in the University of California system. The hierarchy that structures American colleges and universities also sorts out participants in the arena of scholarly publishing. Davidson, Lewis, and Humphreys's loyalty to the monograph is echoed by Oxford University Press's academic editor, Niko Pfund, who makes the sweeping claim that "university presses are not endangered."[54] Certainly, Oxford University Press is not endangered and may never be, nor are the faculty members at Duke and Cornell likely to be the first to be shut out of book publishing opportunities altogether. As Zelda Gamson notes, research culture is in no peril at the universities where it originated.[55] Loyalty to the monograph is integrally related to the hierarchical nature of American colleges and universities. Professors and institutions at the top are very reluctant to give up on the monograph altogether because its declining viability affects them least. They can still count on it as the chief means of advancement and marker of prestige.

A second explanation, related to the first, is that the ideals of research culture are already built into academic labor to varying degrees at various kinds of universities. They are defined not only by professors, but also, more importantly, by administrators. At the end of his self-described screed about the excess of scholarly publication, Markley openly acknowledges that his work is managed. "I have certainly no intention of stopping writing," he says; "if I did, I would have to go back to teaching four courses a semester and give up my travel money [and] grants."[56] Very few academics are so alert to and honest about the conditions of their labor.

As I will argue in my next chapter, most professors grossly underestimate the scope and power of management as it affects their work. For example, while he was president of the MLA, Stephen Greenblatt, professor of English at Harvard, circulated an open letter to the organization, urging members to reconsider using the monograph as the prime criteria for deciding tenure cases. "After all," he wrote, "these expectations [about the monograph] are, for the most part, set by us and not by administrators."[57] "We" professors certainly had a role in endowing the monograph with the institutional cachet it now possesses, but we no longer have the power to strip it of its allure and perceived value. For, as the monograph rose to prominence in the 1960s and 1970s, higher education continued to mirror corporate models of operation more and more closely. This pattern of imitation puts a greater and greater premium on productivity, and administrators measure productivity in monographs.

The 2006 *MLA Task Force on Evaluating Scholarship for Tenure and Promotion* ties the rise of the monograph to the collapse of the job market in the early 1970s and the resulting surplus of Ph.D.s. The consequence, the authors say, was a buyer's market that "made it possible for hiring departments to demand more of candidates seeking entry-level jobs, particularly evidence of scholarly potential. . . . Such increased demands on graduate students exerted pressure on programs to adjust their curricula; as they did, the dissertation was reconceived as the first draft of a publishable book. The appearance of the tenure monograph was thus linked to a reconceptualization of the dissertation. In turn, the expectation that the dissertation would be published after revision made it easier for departments to demand a monograph of tenure candidates."[58] Still, the apotheosis of the monograph in literary studies seems a random choice. Articles are far less expensive to produce, are valued more highly than books in other disciplines, and are less likely to be prolix. Administrators clearly assume that publication of any kind is somehow a more public achievement than, say, teaching, but that is flatly contradicted by the facts. As Deborah C. Rohde notes, "the vast majority of scholarship vanishes without apparent influence"; ninety-eight percent of all publications (articles or monographs) in the arts and humanities are never cited.[59]

It is no surprise that many would agree with Greenblatt that such an irrational system should be easily reformed. Such optimism, though, greatly underestimates the power of the managerial culture in which professors work. Phillip Lewis describes the scenario that would likely play out if professors in the humanities tried to de-privilege the monograph:

The message [university] trustees insist on hearing from their presidents and provosts is that individual faculty members in every discipline are producing more, drawing students at all levels into engagement with state-of-the-art research. . . . Any move to relax standards or to make the young faculty members' initiation into this big, vitally important business more reasonable and humane will meet strenuous objections if the rationale for it is the shrinking market for scholarly books in all but a few niches. The retort will be that markets and producers adapt to changes and that the top scholars whom the successful research universities want to recruit and retain will be clever academic entrepreneurs, capable of developing means of conveying their wares to audiences they will either find or create.[60]

Lewis notes that it is futile to "attack the vacuity, insensitivity, or irrealism of the established managerial view," but he does offer a shrewd if unlikely recommendation for bringing about the project of cultural change that Davidson and others claim to desire. Lewis maintains that only a counterargument based on competition would persuade administrators to accept a redesigned tenure process for the humanities. That is, underfunded public universities would have to be able to point to major research institutions and say "*they* have de-emphasized the monograph. We must do so as well if we hope to keep up with them."

4

Are such elite institutions likely to lead the way? In 1991, Stanford's president, Donald Kennedy, called for a revision of the tenure process, specifically for basing tenure on something other than the *quantity* of a scholar's publications, and in particular for uncoupling tenure from the scholarly monograph.[61] His successor, Gerhard Casper, reaffirmed that recommendation. Myles Brand, while he was president of Indiana University, called for reform along similar lines. While these ideas, not to mention the institutions from which they originate, are encouraging, we need to consider both how universities change and how slowly they change to recognize that a policy revolution on this scale is highly unlikely.

Administrators and professors can lay the foundation for a transformation of values, I believe, only if they look harder at the connection between research culture and faculty reward systems, and in turn at the way those reward systems stratify America's universities and isolate the professors who work there. This self-examination means questioning some of the most dearly held truisms about academia as a professional culture. Here are just a few.

Professors are authors. That sad story of scholarly publishing clearly reveals that we are not, and that fact makes this assumption the simplest to refute. The typical academic monograph sells 250 copies and goes largely unread, except in institutional venues of evaluation. The *MLA Task Force Report* notes that "scholars tend to read monographs in very restricted contexts: in relation to their own research, requests for reviews, teaching, and the evaluation of tenure and promotion cases."[62] Beyond that, almost all of the copies end up in university libraries; we rarely buy each other's books, and librarians complain that we rarely even check them out. If the "author" is among the fortunate two percent whose work is cited, his or her monograph is mined for information that is then put to use in *other scholars'* monographs. Ordinarily, what a scholar produces is the textual equivalent of the tree that falls in the forest with no one to hear it. Yet professors cloak themselves in the mystique of authorship. Invariably, we define ourselves by the books we publish without ever stopping to wonder if they really ought to be counted as books.

Our scholarship determines our relative prestige. This idea appears especially dubious to those outside academia. Russell Jacoby insightfully observes that, in academic parlance, a "famous" sociologist or art historian means someone whose name is recognized by *other* sociologists and art historians. Martin Anderson goes further. He argues that "the research ethos that now dominates the academic world has been tragic for many professors. They delude themselves when they claim their research is important . . . most of them probably know what they write is not important. And when they act as if it were, when they allow others to assume it is . . . they are engaging in a subtle form of intellectual corruption."[63]

Scholarship is integrally related to teaching. This is both the most utilitarian and the most inconclusive argument for the research model. It has been eloquently advanced by Ernest Boyer and Robert Scholes, among others, and is practiced most diligently by Stanley Fish, whose scholarly books and articles contain extensive transcriptions from his classroom lectures. Boyer argues for a "scholarship of integration," a "recognition that knowledge is acquired through research, through synthesis, through practice, and through teaching." He recommends that universities redesign their faculty reward systems to reflect this holistic definition instead of focusing exclusively on research. Scholes defines scholarship in the humanities as "a pedagogy enhanced by the best knowledge available. Scholarship is learning in the service of teaching."[64] Yet, except for graduate seminars and other highly specialized courses, humanities professors rarely get to teach the exact material on which they do their research. Beyond that, the idealistic harmony that Scholes and Boyer describe is not borne out in practice. Rohde reviews thirty studies on the relationship between research and teaching done over the last three decades: "about a third found a small positive correlation between professors' research and teaching; only one found a negative relationship, and close to two-thirds found no relationship."[65] Yet in countless tenure cases, a strong record of research and publication is used to excuse a poor teaching record on the grounds that the candidate's industry as a scholar *must* somehow make him or her a good teacher. The connection between the two is never explained (indeed, perhaps it could not be), but rather accepted as a self-evident truth.

Though much soul-searching needs to be done about assertions such as these, the problems are not entirely personal, and we must also take historical and institutional considerations into account as we contemplate revolutionary changes. The idea that research is the preeminent marker of academic prestige, for example, has a clearly identifiable beginning in American higher education. In the post–Civil War period, when America's colleges still existed primarily to train young men for the clergy, American students wishing to embark on an intensive graduate research program culminating in a dissertation typically enrolled in German universities. More than 2,000 did so during the 1880s; 500 did so in 1895–96 alone. The founding of The Johns Hopkins University on the Germanic model in 1876, however, inaugurated a sweeping and rapid change in the way that the nation perceived the Ph.D. as an academic credential. In 1884, for example, only 19 of the 189 faculty members at Harvard had Ph.D.s, but by 1905, even some public universities, such as CCNY and the University of Illinois, required that all professors have them.[66]

The American universities' initial indifference to research also determined the kind of work that professors were expected to do. In 1857, the Columbia College board of trustees attributed the poor quality of the college to the fact that three of its professors "wrote books."[67] Upon assuming the presidency of Harvard in 1869, Charles W. Eliot declared that "the prime business of American professors . . . must be regular and assiduous class teaching."[68] As late as 1910, the president of the University of

Minnesota took the position that a professor's research was "his own private business, much like playing the piano or colleting etchings."[69] The Hopkins model quickly took root at elite universities; in 1901, Yale "advocated 'productive work' [i.e., research and publication] for its staff in order to help establish 'a national reputation.'" Yet the notion that professors must publish their research for the sake of their professional reputations and that of their universities spread very slowly at first. In a study sponsored by the American Council on Education and the Carnegie Foundation in 1970, a full 30 percent of university faculty reported that they had not published a single professional article.[70] Their sense of what was expected of them, though, changed drastically during the next two decades. Two surveys, one taken in 1969 and the next in 1989, mark a definite trend that continues today. The percentage of faculty who "strongly agreed" that tenure is difficult to achieve without publishing rose from 21 to 42 percent at colleges, from 44 to 83 percent at research universities, and from 6 to 43 percent at comprehensive universities.[71] As we shall see in a later chapter, the proprietors of the rapidly expanding for-profit universities actually resume the practice of defining research as a professor's "private business." As those institutions come to dominate the higher-education landscape of the twenty-first century, research culture and the prestige it now generates may also have a clearly definable *conclusion* at some point in the future, after a life of perhaps 150 years.

The relationship between research culture and the system by which professors are rewarded presents a different challenge, as it requires us to look outside the institutional framework in which we operate every day. Those who have studied this relationship most extensively speak as one, warning universities to change the standard faculty reward system or face the certainty that it will be changed for them. Robert Diamond, one of the first to issue this warning, describes the alternatives most clearly:

> A chorus of voices from the public and private sectors is calling for a shift in priorities, and our most important clients—our students—are demanding it. The question is how significant a role we, as faculty and administrators, want to play. We can sit back and mildly protest the status quo until frustrated government officials or external accreditation agencies define for us what we shall do and how we shall do it, or we can take a proactive role in shaping our future.[72]

Another problem compounds the inclination of faculty and administrators to sit back and mildly protest: the way that universities change. They do so not by distinguishing themselves, but by emulating other universities that they perceive to be more elite. This tendency toward emulation is homogenizing the requirements for tenure across the country, standardizing the expectation that assistant professors focus their energy on research and publication.[73] Surveying higher education in the twentieth century, Ernest Boyer observes that over the course of a few decades, "the research mission, which was appropriate to *some* institutions, created a shadow over the entire learning enterprise—and the model of a 'Berkeley' or an 'Amherst' became the yardstick by which all institutions would be measured." This may be an immutable function of how institutions operate; Magali S. Larson has argued that "a profession is always defined by its elites."[74] Even so, the workings of this process of emulation deserve closer scrutiny because they are irrational and intangible. As I will argue later, the pattern of advance by emulation rests on ideas of prestige that have become central to higher education and to the values that guide our work and fix our rewards.

Without dealing explicitly with prestige, Zelda Gamson offers an intriguing start toward reforming these values. She describes just how specific the yardstick of emulation has become, noting that "the preeminence of research culture is underscored by almost a century's worth of institutional ranking schemes." These ranking schemes operate as a "kind of invisible hand" that has guided the competition for faculty reputation, power, and prestige and, by extension, institutional prestige."[75] Indeed, prestige gained by productivity in research is the currency in which universities trade and is a concept that allows higher education and the corporate world to make sense of each other. Fittingly, the ranking schemes all owe a great deal to Andrew Carnegie's legacy, the Carnegie Foundation for the Advancement of Research and Teaching. The Foundation's classification system, devised in 1973, sorts colleges and universities into ranked categories (Research I universities, Research II universities, Master's Colleges, and Universities I and II, and so on). These original categories still serve as everyone's standard of prestige, even though the Foundation has since drastically revised them.[76] The Carnegie system, which the NRC, the *Princeton Review*, and *US News and World Report* largely adopt, determines how universities win or lose their competitions with each other—indeed, dictates *that* they compete with each other in the first place. Serving as gladiators for their universities, graduate students and professors steeped in research culture wage this competition through their publications. Books and articles are the signs of prestige that universities have come to reify. They are also, though, our best efforts to display the industriousness and tangible labor that the corporate world values most. The ambitions of individual professors, then, have a broader, institutional basis.

The research model, though, is clearly broken. Boyer's survey suggests that many academics have lost faith in research and the way it is assessed and they see teaching as the most fulfilling aspect of their job. The extra-academic public, it is safe to say, has always been deeply skeptical of scholarly research and has always perceived professors as teachers (and, accordingly, as teachers whose time in the classroom is diminished by the demands of dubious research). This chapter records a series of disasters: Ph.D. attrition, the collapsed job market, and a scholarly publishing industry on life support; these indicate that research culture is in very poor shape. Whether professors, as we know them, survive its likely demise remains for now uncertain.

CHAPTER 3

The Erosion of Tenure

Any meaningful debate about tenure has to start with the fact that it is slowly but surely disappearing, and the current workforce in higher education is unwittingly hastening its extinction. These may seem counterintuitive, even bizarre assertions, but both the numbers and the prevailing attitudes of the academic workers involved bear them out. I'll make the case for the disappearance of tenure first, since it can be done fairly straightforwardly. Then, equipped with an accurate map, one that shows tenure to be a receding feature in the landscape of academic labor, I will plunge into the chaos of current debate about it. The extreme polemics of this debate are striking: tenure is alternately heralded as the lynchpin of the entire academic endeavor or lambasted as a unique sinecure in American society, offering lifetime job protection for slothful incompetents. Both characterizations, though, are almost wholly irrelevant to the demographic realities and the firsthand accounts of the changing nature of work in higher education. Thus I will conclude by considering the question of why everyone concerned feels compelled to preserve the *idea* of tenure, even as the practice itself, as well as its beneficiaries, becomes more and more rare.

I

Confusion about tenure hinges on the popular misconception that courses in American colleges and universities are taught by professors, plain and simple. This common assumption is occasionally jolted by exposés about unqualified graduate teaching assistants. The non-English-speaking Math TA is a favorite illustration of the problem in such pieces. Rarely if ever is it noted though, that in addition to professors and graduate teaching assistants, adjunct instructors make up a large portion of the teaching workforce. Even professors familiar with these categories would likely be surprised to learn that tenured and tenure-track professors currently constitute only 35 percent of college teaching personnel and that this number is steadily falling. They would also likely be shocked by the working conditions of the adjuncts who make up the remaining 65 percent, not to mention the teaching assistants, who are technically counted as students.[1] Professors know that adjuncts are not eligible for tenure and have heard them euphemistically described as "freeway fliers" or "scholar gypsies," but know little else.

Not only are adjuncts ineligible for tenure, but 85 percent of them are hired on contracts of a year or less in duration. They are usually employed on a part-time basis, which means that they are also ineligible for benefits such as health insurance and 403b retirement plans. They are typically paid by the course and earn as little as $1,000 per class taught. Their part-time status often forces them to work simultaneously at more than one university and to commute between jobs. Twelve percent of them work at least three jobs.[2] They rarely have a voice in departmental meetings, especially the important deliberations about hiring, tenure, and salaries. In fact, they rarely have adequate office space, if they have any at all. Taking into account the job-to-job commute, one adjunct calculated her salary in 2001 as an hourly wage of $2.12, without benefits.[3]

How did this happen? Why are the details of adjunct working conditions so widely unacknowledged, familiar only to those who specifically study the subject of academic labor? There are several key explanations. First, the abundant use of part-time, adjunct labor is a fairly recent phenomenon. In 1975, 43 percent of college faculty were ineligible for tenure. That is, colleges actually *were* mainly populated by professors and students not too long ago, so it's not surprising that so many assume that they still are today. Only relatively recent college graduates have experienced a university environment in which a steadily growing percentage of the teachers are adjuncts.[4]

Second, greatly increasing the number of adjuncts (from 43 to 65 percent) in the last thirty years was never part of a grand plan. While it may be true that from an administrative perspective, the ideal college or university is one without permanent faculty,[5] drastic attempts to eliminate tenure and fundamentally alter the makeup of the teaching workforce all at once have usually backfired or been notoriously controversial. In 1996, the University of Minnesota tried to eliminate tenure. A lawyer for the university justified the move with rare candor: "We are in a downward spiral on funding for our university from the taxpayers . . . and we're in the midst of selecting a new president here. We think that down the line, our president might need some tools [i.e., a cheaper, more flexible teaching staff] to react to those funding problems."[6] However, when a faculty vote to unionize very nearly passed, the university backed off. When Bennington College, citing financial exigency, eliminated tenure in 1994, the ensuing lawsuits, sharp decline in alumni donations, and negative publicity—including a front-page story in the *New York Times Sunday Magazine*—made the decision a Pyrrhic victory, not worth the money that it saved in the short term.

The most alarming instance of a drastic change that has so far gone largely unrectified was precipitated by Hurricane Katrina. In the wake of the extensive damage done by the storm, several of New Orleans's universities laid off faculty with no due process, means of appeal, or independent oversight. Dillard University laid off two-thirds of its faculty; Xavier University of Louisiana released 73 of its 246 faculty members; Southern University of New Orleans placed 45 of its 163 full-time faculty members on furlough; and Loyola University of New Orleans laid off 28 professors. Most disturbingly, New Orleans's richest university, Tulane, laid off 230 faculty members and eliminated fourteen doctoral programs and several departments altogether. This dramatic restructuring plan reduced the university's annual budget by $60 million, but left its endowment of nearly $1 billion untapped. Tulane's president, Scott Corwin, sounded almost proud of these changes, describing the cuts as "strategically" implemented and declaring that they constituted "the most significant reinvention of a university in the United States in over a century." The abruptness of the cuts combined with their characterization strongly resemble the corporate downsizings that have become routine in the extra-academic world, with the hurricane serving as a convenient pretext.[7] Although the AAUP recommends guidelines that universities should follow if they terminate faculty appointments because of financial exigency (none of which were followed by New Orleans's universities), Katrina threatens to set a dangerous precedent. It created immediate financial exigencies that seemed to transcend the normal rules and in so doing freed university administrators from blame, or even agency, in the decisions that they subsequently made. The *St. Petersburg Herald*'s headline neatly sums up this exoneration: "Battered by Katrina, Tulane University forced into layoffs, cutbacks."[8]

Except for extreme cases such as these, however, one cannot point to a systematic, gradualist administrative strategy to replace tenured faculty with adjuncts. Hiring adjuncts in times of budget shortfalls simply became a widespread practice, and adjuncts, introduced as stop-gap personnel, became a permanent underclass. The logic is easy to understand. As Judith Gappa and David Leslie summarize it: "Once part-timers are employed to absorb new enrollment without commensurate budget increments it becomes difficult in future budget cycles to recoup the lost funding."[9] As a result, an adjunct workforce, however imperceptible its origins and insidious its expansion, has now mushroomed into a significant fact of academic life and it continues to gather momentum.

Third, adjunct instructors are distributed very unevenly across America's universities in a way that defies easy generalization, as peer institutions have widely disparate ratios. For example, at Stanford, 6.4 percent of full-time faculty members are off the tenure track, while at Harvard the figure is 45.4 percent.[10] One pattern, though, is indisputable: those sectors of higher education that are currently expanding at the fastest pace—community colleges and for-profit institutions—are most resistant to the idea of a tenured faculty. Nationwide, 65 percent of the faculty at two-year institutions are part-timers, and 80 percent are not on the tenure track.[11] At some two-year colleges, the entire faculty may consist of instructors paid by the course. This distribution becomes more firmly entrenched over time because students are increasingly likely to enter the postsecondary hierarchy at the bottom rather than at the top. In 1970, community colleges enrolled 27 percent of all students; by 1994, they enrolled 42 percent of the total.[12] Moreover, the community college boom has been accompanied by the rapid growth of for-profit universities, where none of the faculty has tenure and 90 percent of instructors work part time. Time and time again, nostalgic memories combine with an idealized sense of the uniformity of American colleges and universities to obscure the real profile of the people who teach there today.

Many attribute the personnel shift in the higher-education workforce to "late capitalism," or our "post-Fordist" production economy. Stefano Harney and Frederick Moten, for example, state matter-of-factly that higher-education teachers, including professors, are "part of the service sector proletariat." More creatively, Marc Bousquet argues that Ph.D.s are actually the *waste* product of graduate education—if they fail to find tenure-track jobs, they find themselves overqualified to work as adjuncts and thus fall into an employment limbo. The real product of graduate education, according to Bousquet, is the vast contingent of ABDs who make up higher education's on-demand labor force.[13] Unquestionably, this is how the system functions and it seems to do so without anyone's explicit approval.

Adjuncts, along with graduate students, are currently organizing more aggressively than any other sector of the teaching workforce. Yet the aims of adjunct activism are deeply ambivalent, leading each of the major higher-education union organizations, the AAUP, the AFT, and the NEA, to approach the subject differently. The philosophical divide is as follows: the AAUP and the AFT seek to convert as much of the higher-education teaching workforce as possible to tenured and tenure-track status, virtually eliminating the category of "adjunct" altogether. Younger Ph.D.s currently working as adjuncts view these positions as way stations on the path to tenure-track jobs. They look favorably on the AAUP and the AFT plan because it would ideally lead to the creation of more tenure-track jobs. Older adjuncts, those who have been teaching for a decade or more and have thus been unable to keep up a scholarly profile, worry that they would never be considered for these newly created tenure-track positions, but would simply be terminated as universities phase out adjunct labor. The NEA's plan seeks instead to improve the working conditions of adjuncts, guaranteeing them improvements in pay, benefits, and job security. This plan, were it to gain widespread backing, would offer immediate relief to the vast majority of the adjunct workforce, but would institutionalize it as well. For some, this is too high a price to pay for improved working conditions, for it would grant official status to what they consider an academic underclass and thus promote the further erosion of tenured and tenure-track positions. Neither of these plans, nor the assumptions that underlie them, has slowed the steady progress toward more and more adjunct hiring. From the fall of 2003 to the fall of 2005, universities across the country saw an increase of 2.3 percent in tenured and tenure-track faculty and an increase of 7.2 percent in faculty ineligible for tenure.[14]

To get a vivid sense of the academic labor hierarchy, we need to move beyond numbers and look at the expectations and professional fantasies that animate people both at the top (tenured professors at research universities) and at the bottom (the growing corps of adjuncts). In no other workforce is there such a wide disparity, both in income and in day-to-day life, between groups of people whose jobs are, in part at least, so similar. Tenured professors did not make an appearance in my last chapter because the rewards of academic work change significantly once the tenure hurdle has been scaled. The demand for published research required to get tenure and the attendant ambitions and anxieties that turn all Ph.D. students and tenure-track assistant professors into salespeople suddenly disappear. Stanley Aronowitz, a tenured full professor in the CUNY system, admits that "for all practical purposes my career is over, so none of [my] work is motivated by the ambition or necessity of academic advancement." Freed from the external impositions and judgments that the professor awaiting tenure must constantly face, Aronowitz has a very different kind of job; as he puts it in his title, he has "the last good job in America."

He elaborates on the nature of his work, asking and answering the question, "What is included in this form of academic labor?":

> I read a fair amount of detective and science fiction, but sometimes I write and teach what begins as entertainment. The same goes for reading philosophy and social and cultural theory. I really enjoy a lot of it and experience it as *recreation* but often integrate what I have learned into my teaching and writing repertoire. . . . And even though I *must* appear for some four hours a week in a seminar or two, I don't experience this as institutional robbery of my own time.

While he is not affluent, Aronowitz places his standard of living slightly above that of an auto-worker, but definitely below that of a beginning associate in a New York corporate law firm or a physician in an HMO. The key difference is that he does not "work under the gun of a manager." Practically confirming Henry Rosovsky's suspicion that public antagonism toward academic tenure springs from the combination of freedom and security that tenured professors enjoy, Aronowitz confesses, "What I enjoy most is the ability to procrastinate and control my own worktime, especially its pace: taking a walk in the middle of the day, reading between writing, listening to a CD or tape anytime I want, calling up a friend for a chat."[15] Any smugness one might impute to Aronowitz's remarks and the title of his essay must be tempered by recognition of the author's long history as a labor activist and his keen awareness of the discrepancies among various kinds of academic work lives. Indeed, he is writing to make the case that his good job *should not* be the last one in America.

It's possible to find examples that are far less self-conscious and others that are far more privileged. Terry Caesar, whose essay "On Teaching at a Second-Rate University" launched his career as one of the most cynical critics of academic life and institutional behavior, is a connoisseur of instances in which the privileges of professorial labor are both taken for granted and taken to excess. He quotes the following passage from a memoir by the eminent scholar of American literature, Cathy Davidson, in which she and her husband decide where they will work: "Sitting in a Japanese tea room off the rue du Faubourg St. Honoré, we found ourselves thinking about the various jobs we'd been offered and suddenly knew that we wanted to take the positions at Duke University, situated in the lush, overly green Carolina countryside that reminded us of rural Japan."[16] If Aronowitz claims the last good job in America, is Davidson's the last good job in the world, one so liberated from the ordinary constraints of labor that she can "work" in Durham while dining in Paris, all the while thinking fondly of rural Japan? I'm assuming, of course, that the reverie was so powerful that Davidson and her husband faxed their acceptances directly from the restaurant, discreetly omitting the fact that they chose to teach at Duke not because of its prestige, but because it reminded them of someplace else.

In an essay called "Writing Resignation," Caeser composes a hilarious fantasy of an even cushier job. On a Fulbright fellowship in Saudi Arabia in 1982, he writes a parody letter of resignation to his department chair back home at second-rate Clarion University in Pennsylvania. He says that he is resigning because he has been hired as a tutor by a member of the Saudi royal family. He will, in this new position, have only two students—the prince's sons—an exorbitant salary, a small villa in which to live, a Mercedes, three months' vacation a year, and no expectations that he continue his scholarly research. What better academic job could there be than one where the professor is lifted out of academia altogether, not required to publish, and barely required to teach?

Contrast these descriptions of good, great, and fantastic jobs with Martin Scott's account of his experiences teaching in some of Houston's community colleges. His workload is representative of adjuncts everywhere—"five classes a semester . . . at widely spaced campuses"—but his description of his day-to-day experiences reveals the role of management to be far more forceful than tenured professors might ever suspect. Barraged by regular warnings about such matters as "not turning in some form on time or not giving out our home numbers to students," Scott concludes that "judging by the faculty meetings, one would think that education had no place in a community college." His eeriest image is of a learning space literally transformed into a factory. He recalls teaching in a building where the back walls of all the classrooms were made of glass.

An administrator would circulate through the building "making sure none of us released our class five minutes early."[17]

In the world of part-time academic labor, we constantly find teachers overpowered by the hard realities of their wage labor and the micromanagement of working conditions. Adjuncts cannot help being preoccupied with the huge financial strain caused by the low pay of the intellectual piecework they do. They note the irony that they cannot afford to participate in the very education system that they themselves help run: they are unable to repay student loans and cannot foresee being able to send their children to college. Inasmuch as they are often employed simultaneously by more than one university in an often random series of term appointments, they struggle to see themselves as part of a profession that they can rationally hope to negotiate. The material privation extends to their workspaces, if they are lucky enough to have any. The Department of Education's survey of part-time, higher-education faculty revealed that 37 percent did not have a PC in their office and 33 percent had no office space at all on campus.[18] These financial hardships and insults to professional self-esteem are accompanied by wide-ranging and heartbreaking emotional damage.

The vignettes provided by Aronowitz, Davidson, Caesar, and Scott alone make clear that it is impossible to describe a *typical* academic teaching job. How, then, do the holders of the various types of jobs perceive one another? How does each come to conclusions about whether his or her own situation is tolerable or about what might be possible? At one extreme, Ed Meek is alone among the many adjunct contributors to Michael Dubson's collection of autobiographical essays, *Ghosts in the Classroom*, to state defiantly that "we must refuse to work for $1000 or $2000 per class," even though all are clearly demoralized. At the other extreme is the astonishing punch line to Caesar's prank letter of resignation: his department chair at Clarion University took it seriously, going so far as to follow Caesar's instructions and leave his office door open so that his colleagues could help themselves to Caesar's books. As the new royal tutor, he would presumably have a generous book-buying budget.[19] We need to figure out what holds adjuncts in their places for $2.12 an hour. We need to wonder as well what allows a department chair at an obscure state university to think that fantastic working conditions like those that Caesar describes are out there to be had.

A step toward an answer, I believe, is to question whether the laws of supply and demand affect professionals differently than other working people because professions do not prepare their members to deal with layoffs, chronic unemployment, or underemployment. Such phenomena, long routine in the world of manual production, crept into the professional domain, including academia in the 1970s, and have become increasingly common ever since. Exploitative working conditions are equally painful for everyone, but professionals—and adjuncts get the same professional training as those who end up with tenure—are socialized to view success or failure in personal terms. By contrast, Ben Hamper, in *Rivethead: Tales from the Assembly Line*, describes the experience of being laid off from the General Motors plant in Flint, Michigan, as one of initial shock, followed by the realization that the severance check of $2,700 would give him leisure time that he could never before have imagined and would liberate him, at least for a while, from the drudgery of his job on the line. He says, "I felt like a kid on Christmas morning."[20] I doubt that any professional would characterize a layoff in the same terms. When professionals get fired, they cry. Moreover, no profession more fervently believes in the myth of meritocracy than academics. The conviction that somehow one's talent alone ultimately determines one's place in the hierarchy of academic labor gives rise to a constellation of fantasies: my charisma as a teacher will be properly valued; my completed dissertation or published book will confirm my rare intelligence. In short, someone will discover me and celebrate my intellectual powers. Since these epiphanies almost never happen, meritocracies have the effect of making everyone feel insufficiently appreciated. For adjuncts, the academic meritocracy creates a state of mind in which giving up hope signifies something far worse psychologically than a sensible change of careers, and finding a foothold on the first rung of the ladder seems impossible as well.

In response to this intense pressure, adjuncts have evolved success narratives that give purpose to their professional lives. They need to retrieve a measure of dignity from low-paying, overmanaged jobs made all the more difficult because adjuncts often perform those jobs side by side with far more generously compensated professors. Adjuncts cast themselves as self-sacrificing artists, and they seek to benefit from the aura of prestige that universities strenuously try to project. These myths connect adjuncts in complex ways to the icon of the professor. The first hint of this link is that amid all their material complaints, adjuncts also say a lot of things that one might expect to hear from a tenured professor, things that one *does*, in fact, hear from Stanley Aronowitz as he describes the last good job in America; among the sentiments expressed in Dubson's collection: "I love the work. I love my field. I love the students." "For as long as I can remember I have loved all aspects of English." "It's the most rewarding job I've ever had or will ever have."[21] Many specifically state that a few magic moments in the classroom are rewarding enough to offset the constant material deprivation. Their accounts are remarkably similar to one another, and every tenured professor can certainly relate to them:

> I love the energy of the classroom and those special moments when I can do something good, when I see their eyes glowing and their faces shining, knowing that I am teaching them, I am doing something worthwhile.

> The rewards of teaching may be intermittent and transparent, but they are there lurking in the ether of the classroom. . . . It takes only one serious inquiry, one student who genuinely wants to know why a certain painting looks the way it does . . . a single pair of shining eyes in your dim classroom that cancels out all the dulled ones . . . those brief flames in your teaching week are a kind of fuel. They are enough to sustain you from class to class. There are moments when . . . you feel that you're not speaking into the void the way you thought, that you are having an effect on how people think about life and reading.[22]

In each of these cases, job satisfaction is something that one gets *instead of* rather than in addition to a decent salary. In relation to headliners such as Davidson and Aronowitz, these adjuncts are like the workers employed to clean up the dung of circus elephants, rationalizing as they do that "at least it's show business."

Andrew Ross makes sense of this sad artifice by explaining that academics of all ranks, along with artists, are uniquely willing to tolerate exploitation in the workplace. Ross claims that scholars' readiness "to accept a discounted wage out of 'love for their subject' has helped not only to sustain the cheap labor supply but also to magnify its strength and volume. Like artists and performers, academics are inclined by training to sacrifice earnings for the opportunity to exercise their craft."[23] The adjuncts' willingness to accept this tradeoff illustrates in extreme form "the mental labor problem" that Ross describes, since the sacrifices that they make differ so much in degree than any that professors might have to consider.

Universities themselves compound the problem by adding the lure of prestige to the craftsman's ethic on which adjuncts already lean so heavily. Micki McGee argues that "prestige has played an important factor in the deprofessionalization of college teaching." From the perspective of the general public, all college teachers, from tenured professors to part-timers, benefit equally from their association with their institution. "What adjunct faculty member earning minimum wage or scarcely more," McGee asks, "has not had the experience of being asked what they do and then seeing the eyes of their interlocutor light up after they've revealed that they teach at such-and-such prestigious university?" The university eagerly reinforces this reaction, as it has "a vested interest in maintaining that its faculty, whether full- or part-time, are the experts, the bearers of excellence, the best that money can buy (even if paid at a bargain basement rate)"[24]

While the traffic in prestige is not a factor in the lives of adjuncts at two-year colleges, it is crucial to the workings of research universities. These are the very places where professors and adjuncts teach in parallel situations, but are compensated at vastly different rates; thus they are also the places where the dynamics of prestige are most important and potentially most divisive.

Indeed, in McGee's experience, adjunct faculty are actually instructed by administrators "not to share the conditions of their employment with their students, the consumers, or others," but instead to 'be upbeat.'"[25] Institutions of higher learning are, in other words, unwilling to admit how they are changing. Under financial pressure since the 1970s, universities across the country have regularly cut corners by phasing in a cheaper, less credentialed instructional force, but they have not shared the extent of that personnel shift with the public or even with their own students. Their silence serves a public relations interest by presenting the education they deliver as undiminished and undiluted. Left ignorant about the status of the people who are teaching them, students are usually able to identify graduate teaching assistants by their relative youth, but discern little else. They have no way of distinguishing tenured professors from adjuncts and have no sense of the very different working conditions that those two positions entail.

Students, moreover, are not the only ones who are ignorant. Gary Rhoades concludes that most tenured and tenure-track professors are "oblivious" to "the scope and significance of the restructuring that is ongoing in higher education."[26] Others claim that professors rationalize these ongoing changes in ways that are worse than obliviousness. Professors tend to naturalize the role of management, accepting the erosion of their working conditions as an unpleasant fact of life. As such, they deal with hardships such as "responsibility based" budgeting and administratively determined decisions to hire more and more adjuncts by assuming that such concessions themselves are inevitable.[27] Rhoades describes what is at stake for professors who underestimate this seemingly inexorable drift toward casualization by noting that professors, like any professional group, "establish 'closure' by controlling entry into, and the definition and practice of, a domain of work. The growing number of part-time faculty is a challenge to the academic profession's closure. It is a challenge most plainly to the professor's definition of faculty positions as full-time, as careers with a secure future. It is a challenge to tenure as the professional structure defining faculty's terms of employment; for part-time faculty have no chance to gain tenure."[28]

Instead, almost everyone contributes to an illusion born of incomplete awareness or outright denial of the situation of academic labor. Adjuncts stay on the job because they are transfixed by the ideal of the starving artist whose sacrifices are part of a dedication to craft. Soon to make up the majority of college-level teachers, they have neither the time, the resources, nor the means of access that would allow them to present the realities of their worklives even to an audience of academics. They are invisible.[29] The university recognizes that its public image depends on a uniform faculty profile, on the impression that everyone who teaches has undergone the same rigorous screening and is compensated on the same salary scale. Accordingly, it produces advertising copy showcasing this message to attract students. Students are uninformed because, either through edict or by custom, their teachers do not divulge the details of their working conditions. Tenured and tenure-track professors are largely unaware of the accelerating rate at which their teaching tasks are being outsourced. As we have seen, they are rewarded for published scholarship and socialized to recognize only that less time spent teaching means more time for research; they are not accustomed to worry about who will teach in their places.

As with the actual distribution of adjuncts, these problems too are magnified as one moves downward from the top of the country's higher-education hierarchy. The rhetoric deployed to preserve the appearance of prestige becomes forced, almost desperate. Caesar writes incredulously about the language that Clarion University's administrators regularly use—its "strong academic reputation" and potential for a "great future"—to describe an institution that he bluntly calls second-rate.[30] Burton Clark explains how the widening differences between public relations and reality affect faculty. He concludes that "at the top of the institutional hierarchy, faculty influence is well and strong," but "as we descend the hierarchy . . . faculty authority weakens and managerialism increases."

Thus, only research universities and the leading private liberal-arts colleges "retain the capacity to appear as academic communities, not bureaucracies." As one descends the hierarchy and the number of adjuncts typically increases, the hand of management becomes more apparent, and the whole educational environment changes for the worse. At the top, according to Clark, "academic work is a calling" that is "inseparable" from the rest of the professor's life. Toward the middle and the bottom, "academic work becomes just a job," and "material rewards such as salary [however meager] are placed front and center." In a setting such as this, students are processed in a routine way by the contingent workers who teach them.[31]

The silent but steady casualization of the college and university teaching workforce is, unfortunately, a familiar drama everywhere on the American labor scene. Contingent workers do more and more of the clinical labor once performed by professionals alone. Dental assistants, medical assistants, and paralegals routinely prepare fillings, take medical histories and x-rays, and draft legal briefs. All these tasks would have been unthinkable, not to mention illegal, thirty years ago were they not performed by dentists, doctors, and lawyers themselves. Elliott Krause explains the economic foundations of this broad shift in work roles by arguing that, since the end of the Great Depression, both government and capitalism have become more centralized, but the traditional professions have not. In practice, this means that professional organizations, almost all of them formed in the late nineteenth century, have right up to the present functioned as informal associations rather than as governing bodies to which all members and affiliates are answerable. Thus, they have never consolidated their control over memberships and have been especially unsuccessful at limiting the training and production of new professionals.

As a result, doctors, lawyers, and academics "have massively overexpanded their ranks since 1970 . . . compared with population ratios of the previous era." The oversupply has weakened what Krause calls the "professional group guild power," the social strength that professions gain by acting as a close-knit cohort.[32] As I mentioned earlier, the MLA formalized its position against the expansion of Ph.D. programs (in the face of chronically poor job markets) in its 1997 *Report on Professional Employment*. Since the MLA has no authority, though, reducing the size of Ph.D. programs has been left to the discretion of individual departments of language and literature. With no means of enforcing its recommended policy, the MLA can only record the continued overproduction of Ph.Ds.

In addition to the failure of professional organizations to limit the training and production of new members, the very idea of professionalism has shifted during the past half century in a way that hurts the humanities in particular. Steven Brint describes the displacement of the "social-trustee professional" by the "expert professional," a trend that has accelerated rapidly since the 1960s. While social-trustee professionalism embraces ideals cherished in universities—collegial organization, learning, the spirit of public service—expert professionalism values specialized knowledge that is independent of any social ideals. British economic historian and social critic R. H. Tawney elaborated on the older, traditional conception of professionalism when he wrote in 1920 that professionals "may, as in the case of the successful doctor, grow rich; but the meaning of their profession, both for themselves and for the public, is not that they make money, but that they make health, or safety, or knowledge, or good government, or good law."[33] In the generations since then, expert professionals, liberated from any vocational obligation to sustain social ideals, *do* define their work primarily in terms of the money that they make. The transformation has been so complete that we now live, according to Brint, in an "age of experts."

How then are professors of humanities supposed to justify the significance of the work that they do? In an earlier era, they thrived more directly than doctors or lawyers on their roles as trustees of the socially important knowledge and cultural ideals embodied in literature, history, and philosophy. They still have nothing else on which to stake their authority and are thus inextricably wedded to an obsolete model of professional life. Expert professionalism foregrounds aspects of work—technical and engineering know-how and the capacity to make money—for which humanities professors are distinctly ill-suited. Brint's framework allows us to view the late twentieth-century development of literary studies in a very different way than is usually done, namely, as a prolonged and largely fruitless effort to conform to the new expectations of professional work. Literature scholars have tended in recent decades to mine other disciplines—philosophy of language, psychoanalysis, and most recently, cognitive psychology—for vocabularies that suggest a systematic method and scientific rigor. Also, over the same period, literary studies has become vastly more specialized, with each specialty appearing more and more esoteric to anyone outside that particular field of study. These are all, according to many, positive signs of the evolution of a body of scholarly learning.

They are also, though, proof that the expectations of expert professionalism now strongly influence the way that humanities professors do their jobs.[34]

Even if one might deem these efforts at conformity successful, one cannot escape the humanities' absolute lack of profitability. No professor in the humanities could seriously assert that his or her primary objective is to make money. James Engell and Anthony Dangerfield have argued that this relegates humanists to Cinderella status in the contemporary version of the market-model university. They concisely define "The Three Criteria" that qualify some departments for power in that model:

> A Promise of Money. The field is popularly linked (even if erroneously) to improved chances of securing an occupation or profession that promises above average lifetime earnings.
>
> A Knowledge of Money. The field itself studies money, whether practically or more theoretically, i.e., fiscal business, financial, or economic matters and markets.
>
> A Source of Money. The field receives significant external money, i.e., research contracts, federal grants or funding support, or corporate underwriting.[35]

Disciplines that hold out the promise of money and cultivate a knowledge of money both attract and produce expert professionals who stand at the farthest remove from the humanities. This shifting balance of disciplinary power has not been lost on undergraduates. Engell and Dangerfield report that in 1971, 78 percent more degrees were granted in business than in English; by 1994, the differential had soared to 400 percent.

The forces conspiring to alter the role of humanities professors for the worse cannot realistically be stemmed. Cary Nelson, Richard Ohmann, and others have been heartened by a new wave of labor activism among adjuncts and graduate teaching assistants. This development may secure short-term victories for both groups in the form of fairer wages and benefits. It will not, though, stop the eventual disappearance of professors. For, as soon as we draw back from the immediate and tangible disputes in which adjuncts rightfully engage, we encounter problems that will ensure that the vast pool of cheap academic labor remains in place. The longer that pool stays unchanged, the more quickly professors will come to be seen by everyone (not just those outside the academy) as unaffordable anomalies. The "mental labor problem" that Ross outlines—the willingness of academics to think of their work as its own reward and thus not to concern themselves with money or think of themselves as a class—will always work against the impulse to unionize. The prestige of university affiliation that McGee describes will also always be taken by many as a kind of compensation for the low wages that most higher-education teachers actually make. More broadly still, the weakening and changing nature of professions in general, factors far beyond our control, threaten to diminish the social role of humanities professors irreversibly.

All of this is often quite cruelly laid at our feet, not only in the inflammatory conservative attacks on higher education from the early 1990s, but also more recently in Derek Bok's *Universities in the Marketplace* (2003). Bok writes that complaints about the modern university's lack of purpose "invariably come from philosophers, literary scholars, and other humanists. Since these are the fields of study most widely accused of having lost their intellectual moorings, it is not surprising that their professors see a similar aimlessness as the cause of other ills that have overtaken the academy."[36] As a former and now acting president of Harvard University, Bok should know better than to consider any university problem as a purely intellectual matter. Indeed, as his title suggests, he has much to say about the corporate underpinnings of modern-day higher education, from intellectual property to intercollegiate athletics. However, he attributes the disaffection of humanists to their own aimlessness, implying that no other factors are involved. As we have seen, though, much of that disaffection deserves to be analyzed as a labor problem, specifically as a question of how the evolving nature of professional labor acutely affects higher-education workers at all levels in the humanities.

2

Viewed in the context of the general conditions of employment in the humanities, the story of tenure is, not surprisingly, one of steady erosion. If the current trends continue, tenure is likely to disappear almost altogether in the foreseeable future. The broad weakening of traditional professions will converge with the peculiar tolerance that academics have for miserable working conditions to bring about its demise. Yet the popular debate about the subject yields a very different picture, one that is almost unrecognizable in light of the points that I have raised in the previous section. One might conclude from that debate that tenure is not only alive and well, but the rightful focal point in any discussion of higher education.

Moreover, the popular debate enjoys a much higher profile than the ethnography of academics' daily lives. To get a sense of the latter, one has to piece together statistics from the Department of Education Web site and hunt for personal narratives and anecdotes. The subject of tenure, by contrast, evokes attacks funded by conservative think tanks and defenses sponsored by the National Education Association. The two sides also exchange their positions in trade publications, even, in one notorious instance, on *60 Minutes*.[37] My purposes in this section are twofold: first, to make the case that the disproportionate focus on the issue of tenure renders the popular debate largely irrelevant to the realities of academic labor, and second, to speculate about why that irrelevant debate has itself commanded such acute attention.

Hyperboles abound in the language of tenure's supporters and detractors alike. Supporters invariably link tenure to the revered ideal of academic freedom, even though *academic* freedom rarely comes up when professors talk about their day-to-day work. Aronowitz is typical of professors in that he cherishes the freedom of his schedule or his freedom from direct supervision, but he does not view his leisure to listen to a CD of his own choosing during working hours as the provision of some academic First Amendment. Adjuncts do not seem to have time for freedom of any kind. Yet prominent spokesmen for academia defend tenure in the most grandiose ideological terms. Here are just a few examples: Louis Menand defends tenure by characterizing it as the guarantor of academic freedom, which he claims is the key "legitimating concept of the entire enterprise" of higher education. Fritz Machlup says the "only justification for the system of academic tenure . . . lies in the social products of academic freedom, a freedom which . . . can only be guaranteed by the instrument of tenure." Walter Metzger, too, says that academic freedom "is not only relevant to the modern university, but essential to it—the one grace the institution may not lose without losing everything."[38]

The links in the chain that connect tenure to academic freedom to the very essence of the university were forged through complicated negotiations during the first half of the twentieth century and finally codified in the AAUP's *Statement of Principles* in 1940. I will explore the history of that document shortly, but I need to make two important points about it. First, assumptions about academic freedom and its relation to tenure are now badly outdated, reflecting a university very different from the one that professors inhabit today. Second, because university personnel are as slow to recognize changes as they are reluctant to make them, the 1940

Statement is still treated as a sacred text whose central claims are echoed uncritically, but have not been carefully reassessed over time. A representative example of these problems can be found in a joint National Education Association–American Federation of Teachers brochure on the subject, "The Truth about Tenure in Higher Education," that is still prominently displayed on the Web sites of both unions.[39] The pamphlet presents four different instances of "myth" and "reality" about tenure, one of which deals with academic freedom. The "myth" discredits professors who "say they need to have 'academic freedom.'" The "reality"—the NEA–AFT's official position—is that "academic freedom is important because society must have 'safe havens,' places where students and scholars can challenge the conventional wisdom of any field—art, science, politics for whatever." Once the NEA's position moves beyond abstractions, however, its categories fall apart. The pamphlet offers two examples designed to illustrate the necessary connection between tenure and academic freedom.

(1) "An untenured professor was fired by the University of Georgia when she blew the whistle on the administration's practice of changing grades and waiving academic standards for athletes." Here, the professor in question is not challenging the conventional wisdom of anything; she is exposing the fraudulent practices of the university. In fact, she is not acting in her capacity as a professor at all: a secretary or a clerk in the university registrar's office could conceivably have unearthed the same scandalous information. The professor, as the pamphlet admits, is untenured, a fact that begs a couple of important questions: How does the protection of tenure help the untenured? What does one have to do to earn that protection; that is, how does one move from the ranks of the untenured to the tenured?

(2) "In Oklahoma, a number of state legislators attempted to have Anita Hill fired from her university position because of her testimony before the U.S. Senate." Again, Anita Hill did not testify against Clarence Thomas in her capacity as a professor at the University of Oklahoma, but as his subordinate in the office of the Equal Employment Opportunity Commission. She was in fact not hired by Oklahoma until *after* her stint at the EEOC, the chapter of her professional past that was revisited in Thomas's confirmation hearing. Her allegations of sexual harassment, like the accusations of the professor at Georgia, involved no challenge to conventional wisdom, since they sprang not from her academic training, but rather

from her experience working with Thomas. Finally, when those Oklahoma legislators tried to remove Professor Hill in the immediate aftermath of her testimony, she was also untenured.

My point in reviewing these examples is not to cast doubt on the good intentions of the two unions or to trivialize the situations of the two professors, but to point out how weak the examples themselves are. Could the NEA not have found at least two cases in which a *tenured* professor challenged the conventional wisdom of his or her discipline and was spared punishment thanks to the protection of tenure?

They could not, in my opinion, for two reasons that reveal the vagueness and obsolescence of the 1940 *Statement of Principles* and the entire defense of tenure on the basis of academic freedom. First, the concept of a discipline, an academic field of study, already evolving in 1940 in the direction of greater and greater specialization, has continued to do so at a very rapid pace. This means that challenges to conventional wisdom are likely to be so specific to already delimited academic fields—a materialist interpretation of Alexander Pope's pastoral poetry or the discovery of a new fragment of a late medieval chronicle—that they will raise the eyebrows of very few people, none of them outside academia. Hence, the NEA must reach outside of scholarship altogether to find examples that convey a sense of urgency about the concepts at stake—tenure and academic freedom—that a general audience will appreciate.[40] A well-informed and mean-spirited observer might even argue that the NEA's examples, by virtue of their obvious magnitude, inadvertently offer proof that typical academic controversies are inconsequential. I only wish to make the point that "academic freedom" no longer packs the rhetorical punch that it was meant to.

A more glaring problem than that of the NEA's examples of Anita Hill and the unnamed Georgia professor, who were both untenured at the time of their ordeals, also stems from the confused logic of the academic freedom defense of tenure. For the AAUP's 1940 *Statement of Principles*, at the same time that it elaborates on the working definition of academic freedom, actually *instructs* universities how to go about tenuring professors. So ambiguous were the contractual terms of most higher-education teaching jobs in 1940 that the *Statement*'s guidelines were a fundamental innovation. There, set out for the first time, are the seven-year probationary period and regular reviews of untenured faculty that have since become the norm in most American universities. Only because these two very different concepts are treated in the same landmark document, I believe, are tenure and academic freedom inextricably linked in the minds of defenders of higher education and its professors.

The vagueness of the connection, though, raises a question that is almost never seriously addressed by the academic defenders of the conventions of tenure and the ideal of academic freedom, namely, why do only the tenured enjoy the full protection of their academic freedom? What about the legion of adjuncts and the graduate teaching assistants, not to mention professors on the tenure track, but not yet tenured? To find answers, one must look to the origin of the debate on tenure in the early twentieth century and the pressures that shaped the 1940 *Statement*. That *Statement*, it must be understood, reflects a fundamental compromise between administrators and professors, management and employees. Only by recognizing it as such do the inconsistencies that I have described make sense.

The story begins several decades earlier. The American Association of University Professors was founded in 1915 by a group of prominent professors at elite universities who were concerned about recent instances in which higher-education teachers were fired under suspicious circumstances. The most infamous of these was Stanford University's dismissal in 1900 of social scientist Edward A. Ross, who repeatedly spoke out against both privately owned railroads and Chinese immigration. These positions were obviously contrary to those of the university founder's lifework as a railroad tycoon who had employed thousands of coolies, and to the opinion of his widow. Mrs. Leland Stanford eventually enjoined President David Starr Jordan to terminate Ross's appointment. Provoked by the Ross affair, the AAUP set about investigating similar cases and published the results of five of them.

These early reports offer far better examples of the infringement of academic freedom than does the current NEA brochure, for in each case, the professors or instructors in question were acting in an academic or scholarly capacity (as was Ross in 1900). At a commencement address in 1914 at the University of Utah, for example, graduating senior Milton Sevy argued that the state was too influenced by "ultraconservatism" (his term) and called for reforms: a fairer system of taxation and a public utilities commission. On the order of the state's governor, two instructors and two professors suspected of inspiring Sevy's speech through their teachings were dismissed. In 1915 at the University of Colorado, distinguished law professor James H. Brewster was dismissed after he represented the state's miners' union, which had struck in 1913. In the same year, Scott

Nearing, a professor at the Wharton School of Business at the University of Pennsylvania for nine years, was given written notice of his customary one-year reappointment by his dean. That promise was overturned by the Board of Regents, acting on the wishes of an "influential group of alumni," who felt that Nearing, among others, was engaged in "radical" and "unsound" teaching on economic and social questions.[41]

To a modern academic reader, the most striking common thread in these cases is the uncertain employment status of the victims. Yet this was not the primary point of emphasis for the AAUP's investigators, for in 1915, the now familiar norms of academic ranks and tenure had not yet been imagined. Indeed, as late as the mid-1930s, half of 125 colleges and universities surveyed by the AAUP appointed all faculty members on an annual basis. At the other half (mostly private universities in the East and flagship state universities in the Midwest and West), the contracts of more senior professors typically bore no date of expiration, but tenure "as a set of due process rights" simply did not exist.[42] Instead, the norm throughout the country was presumptive tenure—the annual contracts at most universities were automatically renewed by custom, not by rule.

In this climate, the fourteen founding members of the AAUP formulated their first important policy paper, the *General Declaration of Principles*, published in December, 1915.[43] Using language consistent with the conventions of academic employment at the time, the *Declaration* never uses the word "tenure," and uses the word "professor" only in quotations from outside sources, preferring the more inclusive term "university teacher." It is solely concerned with explaining and defending "academic freedom," a term that it derives not from the First Amendment to the Constitution, but from the German tradition of higher learning, specifically its notions of *Lehrfreiheit*, the freedom of the teacher.

The 1915 *Declaration* elaborates on "academic freedom" largely by way of legal analogies that grant college teachers considerable power and autonomy. Specifically, it compares the appointment of teachers by boards of trustees to the appointment of federal court justices by the president, emphasizing the distinction between an appointee and an employee. If trustees hold an "essential and highly honorable place" in the university, "the faculties hold an independent place, with quite equal responsibilities—and in relation to purely scientific and educational questions," the latter hold "the primary responsibility" (4). Accordingly, the *Declaration* states that, like judicial deliberations, "discussions in the classroom ought not to be supposed to be utterances for the public at large"; similar also to attorney–client conversations, "they are privileged, and may not be published" without the teacher's authorization. The *Declaration* sets only what it considers to be commonsense limits on this autonomy, enjoining teachers in their "extramural utterances" to avoid "hasty or unverified or exaggerated statements, and to refrain from intemperate or sensational modes of expression." It concludes by stating clearly that scholars should not "be debarred from giving expression to their judgments upon controversial questions." Nor should "their freedom of speech outside the university . . . be limited to questions falling within their specialties" (9).

Much to their surprise, the founders of the Association, philosopher A. O. Lovejoy of Johns Hopkins and progressive economist E. R. A. Seligman of Columbia, were "inundated by calls for help from members of far-flung campuses who alleged they were about to be dismissed because of their spoken or written views."[44] The breadth of the problem prompted the professors of the Association to enter into uneasy collaboration with college and university presidents and regents, since it was clear that academic freedom could not realistically be protected without their cooperation. As a result of twenty-five years of sporadic and at times acrimonious negotiations, the AAUP's *Statement of Principles on Academic Freedom and Tenure*, issued in 1940, was actually "co-authored by representatives of the AAUP and representatives of the Association of American Colleges (AAC), an organization composed of undergraduate academic institutions and run by their administrators."[45]

The 1940 *Statement* significantly retrenches the position taken by the AAUP in its 1915 *Declaration*. It qualifies the *Declaration*'s broad defense of academic free speech by emphasizing the professor's ties to his or her university. While professors speak or write freely, as do all citizens, according to the 1940 *Statement*, "their special position in the community imposes special obligations. As scholars and educational officers, they should remember that the public may judge their profession and their institution by their utterances" (1–2). More strikingly, the 1940 *Statement* limits the professor's classroom freedom to his or her specialty, an outright reversal of the AAUP's earlier position. The *Statement* asserts that "Teachers are entitled to freedom in the classroom in discussing their subject, but they should be careful not to introduce into their teaching matter which has no relation to their subject" (1). Both of these restrictions suffer from a curious lack of agency; they come not from an employer, but rather from obligations derived from the professor's "special position" or from some unspecified but nevertheless universally acknowledged understanding of what is or is not relevant to the subject of a classroom discussion. In both areas, the professor's behavior is silently but consequentially managed.

The most basic retrenchment of the autonomy in the 1915 *Declaration*, though, is the very mechanism of tenure itself. The *Declaration*'s analogy between professors and federal judges makes it clear that professors are autonomous from the day of their initial appointment. The 1940 *Statement* introduces a crucial division between "teachers or investigators" with "permanent or continuous tenure" and those without it (2). It then spells out both the probationary period—"not to exceed seven years," during which a teacher comes to be tenured—as well as the specific procedures by which a teacher may be terminated "for adequate cause." The latter is a due process arrangement in which the teacher's case would be considered "by both a faculty committee and the governing board of the institution." The *Statement* then adds the baffling principle that "During the probationary period a teacher should have the academic freedom that all other members of the faculty have" (2). If, indeed, probationary faculty have that freedom from recrimination, then what additional freedom do they gain by being tenured? What is the purpose of tenure? These questions go unaddressed, but lead us to view the compromises between the AAUP and the AAC between 1915 and 1940 in a skeptical light, for the conventions of tenure that we all know actually take away academic freedom from those with less than seven years' service at an institution.

Very few professors would ever consider that tenure weakens academic freedom. Instead, the traditional connection between the two concepts exudes an almost revolutionary aura, as captured by the figure of the "tenured radical," the candid maverick who speaks truth to power, as the cliché goes.[46] So it is that we romanticize our jobs and fail to recognize how the tenure process works to deaden the possibility of radical freedom of expression. The standard seven-year probationary period is, as John C. Livingston puts it, "a hostage given to the forces attacking tenure—an assurance that the professoriate does after all still share a commitment to the assumption underlying the great American game of corporate rivalry for place and power. It permits academicians to present themselves as winning their spurs through competition."[47] Like all corporate rivalries for place, the academic spur-winning competition is a contest in which conformity is privileged at every turn—in scholarship, in teaching, and in university citizenship. John Huer elaborates on the devaluation of tenure:

> By making it primarily a sign of career success, the professor has made tenure *irrelevant* in the real sense. As tenure is taken wholly as a career and economic

measure in a professor's life, the academic freedom it is supposed to produce has become meaningless.[48]

The tacit corporatization of tenure in fact turns the ideal of academic freedom on its head. "The trouble is that professors get their tenure by *suppressing* the expression of unpopular expression, not *in order to express* unpopular opinion. . . . The modern university, by its conservative inertia, has become the most hostile place for pursuing the truth. And tenure, once deemed precious, has become the most wasted, irrelevant principle."[49]

Academics should not, of course, turn against tenure. They should, though, stop defending it on the grounds of academic freedom, since that defense, born of compromise, is fraught with logical inconsistencies. These exacerbate the divide between the dwindling number of tenured professors and the growing rank of adjuncts. Given the seemingly inexorable trend in higher-education employment practices, professors need to recognize that divide and work toward closing it. We can start doing so, as Jeffrey Williams puts it, by recognizing that "our sometimes vehement defense of tenure stems not from the threat to academic freedom but from the threat to our class distinction," to the separation of the tenured from the tenure-ineligible.[50]

Significantly, opponents of tenure also seem oblivious to the current makeup of the higher-education teaching workforce. In a book ominously titled *The Moral Collapse of the University*, Bruce Wiltshire presents the following portrait of the typical professor:

> Alone and unmonitored in his or her classroom, the professor is unchallenged; perhaps the earlier drive to excel was shallowly based in the personality; growth ceases and something dies within. Too flaccid and insecure to look for other employment, the Professor hangs on as "dead wood."[51]

Though Wiltshire's suffusion of impotence imagery puts his characterization over the top, the rest of it—the burnout, the ineffectiveness, the complete lack of accountability or supervision—are all representative components of the current conservative attack on tenure. Richard Chait, himself a critic of tenure speaking from within the academy, notes the relative newness of this line of attack. The "impetus to revamp tenure codes" during the 1970s was, according to Chait, "essentially political," a response to social unrest on campuses during the late 1960s and early 1970s. By the late 1970s, once the campuses themselves had calmed down, "all was relatively quiet on the tenure front."[52] That silence was broken in the early and mid-1990s by Wiltshire (1992), Charles Sykes's *Profscam* (1990), Page Smith's *Killing the Spirit* (1990), and Martin Anderson's *Imposters in the Temple* (1996), among others.

The new wave of hostility toward tenure is motivated far more by straightforwardly economic rather than by political concerns. Beginning in the early 1990s, large-scale layoffs became commonplace, even in the white-collar sector. These practices fueled the popular complaint that professors were "insulated from the economic vicissitudes that routinely place lay citizens at [risk]." At the same time, Chait notes, university administrators, themselves in a tightening financial bind because of diminished funding, began to cast themselves in explicitly corporate roles: "Presidents have become CEOs, the administration has become management, and long-range plans have become strategic plans." Coincidentally, they too came to see tenure as a practice that "insulates professors from accountability and so limits management's capacity to replace marginal performers" and to carry out "central initiatives."[53] This convergence of sentiment has produced a dangerous two-front assault on tenure. Caricatures of the tenured professor abound in the popular media, and some university professors side with the caricaturists. Thus, when arch-conservative Martin Anderson says that "tenure is corrupting, it gives academic intellectuals almost unlimited license to do as they please with no fear of consequences. Its major effect is to encourage sloth," and former Stanford University President Donald Kennedy says that "the public perception that tenure protects 'deadwood' is, alas, correct," professors can hardly know where to turn for support.[54]

Indeed, Kennedy shifts into the very same corporate rhetoric that has informed public scrutiny of higher education since R. T. Crane and Clarence Birdseye at the turn of the twentieth century. Speaking of professors' lack of accountability, Kennedy says "there is no time clock and nobody checks up." "The public wants to know more about how the store is being minded and is less satisfied with reassuring statements about product quality." Martin Anderson draws the unfavorable comparison to a point: "tenure is what really separates the universities from business corporations."[55] The perceived lack of accountability and efficiency also underlies Richard Huber's cliché-ridden portrait of the typical professor:

> How many hours do faculty actually labor? A teaching "load" of 6 to 9 hours per week, plus 3 office hours for student advising, and several hours for committee work can be comfortably accomplished in $2\frac{1}{2}$ days. In addition to the

free time of the other 2 ½ days there are summer vacations and holiday breaks of four months which may be filled with golf, fooling around with a hobby, or just loafing. And the paycheck is guaranteed until age 65 when a dependable TIAA-CREF pension eases the transition into fulltime leisure.[56]

Nuanced responses to this line of attack have been advanced, among them eloquent defenses of universities as "safe havens" that *must* be insulated from standards of accountability as the business world defines them, as well as patient explanations of the personal and professional sacrifices that academics make in order to attain positions in which they are largely accountable only to themselves. The most powerful counterargument, though, is the plain fact that these attacks on tenure apply to a dwindling number of academic workers. All the information that we have about adjunct teachers confirms that they are held to exacting standards of accountability (by any definition), and one certainly finds no evidence of sloth. These, not tenured professors, are the typical higher-education teachers of the present and the future.

The arguments of attackers and defenders of tenure alike share an oddly similar flaw. Both focus, unwittingly it seems, on a shrinking segment of the higher-education teaching force. Defenders advocating the sacrality of academic freedom speak only for the already tenured; attackers decrying the lack of accountability and efficiency single out that same tenured subset for abuse. Significantly, both sides grant the figure of the professor a grossly exaggerated measure of power. The academic freedom defense assumes not only that professors, by virtue of their special position, have a right to speak freely, but also that their speech will be widely noteworthy, in short, that professors are public intellectuals. They are autonomous, independent thinkers and authors whose tenure permits them to say controversial things. That is simply not true; the topics that professors typically address and the venues in which they communicate in fact guarantee that they will have small audiences comprised of other professors. Their students' primary aim is more likely that of getting a good grade rather than being converted by a course's content.

Attackers, though, ironically grant professors similar exalted status. Although Martin Anderson begins *Imposters in the Temple* by disqualifying professors as public intellectuals, he nevertheless ascribes to them a tremendous amount of power in the sphere of higher learning. Throughout his book he implies that universities are made up exclusively of professors and students, with professors calling all the shots and answerable to no one. He claims, for example, that *professors* invented the position of the teaching assistant as a "clever solution" to their supposedly onerous teaching responsibilities.[57] The assumption that professors *make* rather than follow university policy is, like the professor as public intellectual, a wild mischaracterization. It completely omits the extensive fiscal constraints and administrative policies that fundamentally shape universities as institutions.

The curious disconnection between the debate over tenure and the current realities of academic labor highlights the problem posed by the figure of the professor. Only if that figure is nebulous and misunderstood to begin with can it be imbued with so much power for good or for bad. The relationship between the teaching and the scholarly dimensions of professorial work remains particularly inscrutable for both sides. The academic freedom defense of tenure assumes that research and scholarship, which it imagines to be public intellectual speech, must be preserved at all costs. Conservative attacks discount scholarship and thus define professors as too slothful to do their one real job—teaching—efficiently. The true nature of the job seems to be a moving target. In an amusing report on the 2003 MLA Convention for *The Believer*, Gideon Lewis-Kraus confesses that "for an almost embarrassing portion of my life, the word 'professor' had the resonance most eight-year-olds reserve for 'astronaut.'"[58] The actual day-to-day activities of professors, like that of astronauts, are a mystery to all outsiders, and academics tend to be either silent or (uncharacteristically) inarticulate about what they do.[59]

There seems no doubt, though, that the trend toward increased use of adjunct teachers will continue. It is, as Gary Rhoades, Sheila Slaughter, and others have pointed out, the cheapest way to run a university. The heavy use of adjunct labor accords with the bedrock corporate values of efficiency and accountability that are now embraced by growing numbers of university administrators. The tendency of so many, both inside and outside the academy, to reduce all academic labor issues to the one narrow subject of tenure only contributes to the problem. The truth, though, is that tenure, however useful it might be as a hook for conversations about higher education, is becoming a mirage.

What the disappearance of tenure will mean is a more abstract problem than how and where it will disappear. I have touched several times on the uneven way that academic labor problems ripple through the whole of the academic world. In 1974, Alaine Touraine observed that the higher-education system in America is changing in a way that is "not reducing, but actually reinforcing and extending the inequality of opportunities between students from different social backgrounds."[60] Richard Ohmann offers a more detailed prognosis:

> Community colleges . . . have always had a relatively direct and simple relationship to the market for education and training . . . community college is a place to take courses for career-related needs. . . . At the other end of a familiar spectrum, Princeton, Swarthmore, and the like will continue to experience accountability in only the most genteel and indirect terms. . . . Between these two locations, life will be strenuous. That is to say, most public and private universities will be scrambling to meet standards of accountability imposed either by hard-nosed trustees and legislators or by the market itself.[61]

The disappearance of tenure, if my prediction turns out to be correct, will not affect all students at the same time or in the same way. Tenure is, as Ohmann's overview implies, already irrelevant to the function of two-year colleges and their kindred, the vocationally oriented for-profit universities. The grandchildren of today's Princeton and Swarthmore students may still be taught by tenured professors. Those of us living and working strenuously in the middle need to recognize that tenure codes will most likely weaken at our institutions, and that the tenure-ineligible will continue to replace the tenured.

CHAPTER 4

Professors of the Future

Writing in 1842, Francis Wayland, president of Brown University, offered an astonishingly prescient speculation about the future of American higher education. If the colleges did not provide the training desired by the mercantile and industrial interests, he argued, businesses would set up their own competing schools.[1] At a time when America's colleges primarily trained future clergymen, schooling them in a uniform classical curriculum, Wayland managed to recognize that higher education ultimately answers to larger economic demands. Even more remarkably, he intuited that the mercantile and industrial interests, then in their infancy in the United States, drive that economic agenda, and that in the end they determine the educational qualifications and skills that workers must possess.[2] My predictions about higher education in the first half of the present century stem precisely from the concerns that Wayland voiced more than 160 years ago. I have described the century-old relationship between the mercantile and industrial interests and academia, and I have argued that corporate values and corporate thinking are inexorably replacing the values and logic that once defined the liberal arts. Over the next two generations, I believe, the process of corporate reorientation will be nearly completed.

Universities always eventually adapt to their societies. This means that they will bend to corporate expectations about what a university should teach and how it should operate; more directly, they will accommodate student demands about what would make a college education worth the time and money spent on it. The corporate influences, always present, will become increasingly explicit; fifty years from now it will be the rule, not the exception, to think of a university as a company rather than a social institution. This transformation of universities into businesses will be fueled by student impatience with the restrictions of the traditional college education, with its expensive four-year time commitment and its abstract liberal-arts curriculum. The B.A. and the B.S. will largely be replaced by a kind of educational passport that will document each student's various educational certifications from one or several schools, the credentials directly relevant to his or her future occupation.[3] Since this kind of on-demand schooling does not require a full-scale baccalaureate program, the two-year college, often run for profit, will become the new standard post-secondary-education vehicle.

This will not be the whole picture. Like American society as a whole, with its widening gap between haves and have-nots, America's universities will grow increasingly stratified. The elite, privileged universities and colleges (about 100 of them, according to *Barron's* and similar surveys) will continue to function much as they do today, championing the liberal arts and the humanities and educating the children of the elite and privileged for positions of leadership in law, politics, science, medicine, the corporate sector, and, of course, their own exclusive brand of higher education. Presidential campaigns will continue to be waged by graduates of Yale, Harvard, Swarthmore, and Georgetown, and the presidents of Harvard and Yale will continue to be selected from among the past graduates of Harvard and Yale. The gulf between these elite universities and the institutions that educate everyone else will widen in new ways that will complicate our efforts to define both the idea of higher education and the concept of access to higher education. This divergence and its consequences for humanities professors form the subject of this and the following chapter.

Wayland's prediction entails two related premises that I will examine in this chapter. First, students, not professors, will ultimately determine the future of higher education. When President Dwight D. Eisenhower addressed faculty at Columbia as "employees of the university," a professor corrected him by saying, "the faculty *are* the university."[4] This may not have been true even in the 1950s, let alone now. The student population is the most important and the most dynamic part of America's universities and thus the earliest harbinger of change. Except for those few students who *become* professors, college is a means to an end. Students attend college because they are convinced that it will best prepare them for a life of work after graduation. Should they lose that belief or qualify it in some basic way, college will have to change accordingly or suffer as a result. Second, higher education is job training, however much academics may like to think otherwise. The training may in many instances be general, theoretical, and abstract, but its very purpose places the academy in the service of its country's, and increasingly, the world's employers, the mercantile and industrial interests.[5]

If we wish to chart the future of higher education in America, then, we need to start by making basic inquiries about our students. To make any plausible predictions about the future, we need to figure out how the present generation of undergraduates differs from its predecessors, and whether there are patterns to its changing demographic makeup and ideological outlook. We also need to examine the means by which corporate interests seek to influence higher learning. As we shall see, comprehensive marketing initiatives have replaced vituperative attacks like those of R. T. Crane. Corporations now wage a far subtler battle against traditional higher education, seeking to reshape the hopes and expectations of future students and, by extension, to reshape the social function of universities and professors.

The answers to these inquiries are not comforting to the humanities. Indeed, if we wish to glimpse the likely fate of the entire liberal arts in the twenty-first century, we need look no further than the history of classics in the twentieth. Standing perhaps at the furthest extreme from businesslike practicality, classics was once central to the universal curriculum of America's colleges and universities. Shortly after the Civil War, however, larger social forces set its erosion in motion, and the peculiar course of that erosion is representative of the way that universities change. Here is a schematic account of the key events. First, the Morrill Act of 1862 paved the way for the postwar establishment of several large land-grant universities that emphasized the practical and mechanical arts, engineering, and architecture. This, in effect, permitted an abundance of college students to study something other than Greek and Latin. The decade of the 1880s then witnessed Harvard president Charles Eliot's tireless promotion of the free elective curriculum, which subsequently replaced the uniform classical standard at almost all institutions. His innovations opened an assortment of new academic disciplines to undergraduates, eventually allowing them to specialize in these subjects; Harvard invented the concept of the academic major in 1910.[6]

More than twenty years elapsed after the advent of the elective curriculum before the effects of these significant and, as it turned out, lasting curricular changes began to make their full impact on the preparation and interests of all American undergraduates. When the changes did occur, however, they came suddenly. At Yale in 1907, 98 percent of all entering students had a prior knowledge of Greek; by 1921, just fourteen years later, less than 50 percent of Yale's freshmen came to college with some knowledge of Greek and, once at Yale, only 8 percent chose to study it.[7] This abrupt shift occurred at colleges all over the country at about the same time.

Yet the undergraduate abdication of the classics in the early twentieth century had no immediate consequences on the shape of universities, especially on university teaching personnel; such is the nature of change in higher education. The depopulation of classics occurred side by side with the bureaucratic development of the modern university, as broad fields of study were coalescing into discrete academic departments, and the tenure system was taking shape. This meant that any debate conducted within universities about the fate of the classical curriculum would necessarily include turf-minded classics professors with lifetime appointments. Classicists were able to stand their ground and not fall victim to the changes in student preferences. They found ways to augment the instruction of Greek and Latin, such as Western Civilization programs, which allowed them to justify the continued hiring of classics professors. Thus, as the decades passed, the presence of classics in the university shrank very slowly, even though student interest had drifted from the subject long ago. Where did this standoff, with students and professors pulling in opposite directions, lead? In their book *Who Killed Homer?* Victor David Hanson and John Heath estimate that, as of 1994, there were six classics professors for every one undergraduate classics major in America.[8]

The imbalance may take another fifty years to sort itself out. Student demand will inexorably continue to influence budgeting decisions, which in turn will dictate that even fewer classicists be hired in the future or that classics programs be reduced or eliminated altogether. Hanson and Heath document such events from their own experiences.[9] For the most part, though, their reaction to the death of classics epitomizes the other monumental problem that the humanities now face. Not only are the humanities losing the battle over the curriculum to more practical and more business-friendly disciplines, but humanists are also losing the rhetorical battle to define the meaning of higher education. Hanson and Heath chastise America's universities for their intellectual waywardness and insist that classics be restored to its rightful place at the core of every college education. This kind of zealous nostalgia is the sure sign of a frustrated humanist, yet it is a typical attitude among those who have grown accustomed to academic life. Professors such as Hanson and Heath have been socialized in graduate school to the importance of classics and have spent their careers striving for and achieving tenure, promotion, and professional significance in the classics departments of universities. The peculiar insularity of universities explains why their defenses are both so tenacious and so unimaginative.

Drawing from both Wayland's prediction and the cautionary tale of classics, I build my speculations about the future of the humanities around a few salient features. First, for several decades now, the college student population has been changing in significant ways, both demographically and ideologically. Though one can debate the factors prompting this change, the result is a cadre of students who both approach college with more pragmatic aims and who are more willing to integrate the college experience into their work lives. We in the humanities have been losing students to other, occupation-oriented disciplines for a long time. We are doing a poor job of coping with these losses because we believe, without any justification, that the students will someday come back to us.

Second, the needs of this new type of undergraduate are being aggressively met by a new breed of college, the for-profit university. The astonishing rise to prominence of the for-profit universities is the single most important recent development in American higher education. Their innovations in curriculum and instruction are transforming the conception of college. They are also eliminating the figure of the professor from higher education, detaching research from the mission of the modern university and turning faculty into full-time, information-delivery personnel.

Third, the for-profits have developed an extremely persuasive marketing strategy for promoting their new idea of a university. So powerful is their message that not only have individual students adopted it by the hundreds of thousands, but also whole universities have. That is, many traditional colleges and universities, chronically strapped for cash, have embraced the business model of the for-profits in the hope of reversing their fortunes. The for-profit revolution, in other words, is spreading far beyond the confines of the companies at which it originated.

Fourth, those traditional universities that are not adopting the marketing strategies of their for-profit rivals are developing a new message themselves. After decades of stubbornly adhering to the humanist ideal of college as a means to self-improvement, America's elite institutions of higher learning are now embracing the notion that a college education (at the right school) is a means of acquiring prestige. College redefined as a

path to prestige explains the preoccupation, dating to the 1980s, with national rankings, such as those presented annually by *U.S. News & World
Report*. For-profit colleges don't participate in national rankings; many traditional colleges and universities seem to value nothing else. The phenomenon of prestige envy and the marketing of prestige are sufficiently new
and important to warrant a separate treatment in my next chapter.

Professors in the humanities cannot look backwards—whether to
Homeric Greece or to more recent times of stability—if they wish to have
a place in the university of the future. The imperative to be practical,
efficient, and profitable, which I have traced as a strong influence on past
and present versions of academia, will be an even stronger force in the
future. This means that all fields deemed impractical, such as philosophy,
art history, and literature, will henceforward face a constant danger of
being deemed unnecessary. In an effort to stem that tide, humanists have
tended to produce one manifesto after another in defense of the intrinsic
good of critical thinking.[10] Instead, I believe that humanists must first use
the tools of critical thinking to question the widespread assumption that
efficiency, productivity, and profitability are intrinsically good.

Here's an illustration. Stanley Aronowitz, in his humanist manifesto,
*The Knowledge Factory: Dismantling the Corporate University and Creating
True Higher Learning*, asks, "Can faculty and students disengage from the
orientation to jobs, jobs, jobs, and to corporate culture to found [a culture]
of their own?"[11] That's the wrong starting point. Faculty and students
first need to determine *whether* it is necessary to disengage from corporate
culture. At present, faculty in the humanities reply "yes," while students
resoundingly respond "no." Each camp offers only a narrow and defensive
rationale to justify its position. It is impossible for students not to think of
"jobs, jobs, jobs" as the price of a college education escalates and they plan
for a life of work after graduation. Faculty in the humanities cannot help
resenting a corporate culture that has permeated universities, marginaliz-
ing their disciplines and managing their work lives. For a new academic
culture to take shape, humanities professors and students would first have
to agree in their assessment of corporate culture. Currently, their views
are drifting apart, an ominous sign, since in the end, faculty can do little
more than react to the dynamic student population. Our only hope might
be to persuade students to look more skeptically upon the promises of
college as job training. This will be a tough sell. As we have seen, Veblen
argued nearly a century ago that the value of practicality and usefulness,
the cornerstone of occupational majors, is a self-evident principle in

America. Richard Hofstadter offers a general theory of the problem. Noting that it has been "the fate of American higher education to develop in a pre-eminently businesslike culture, with a shallow base of cultural traditions," he claims that "Americans have shown an intense, almost touching faith in both the personal and civic *uses* of education; but this faith has not been accompanied by an equally profound understanding of the cultural *content* of education."[12] To get a sense of the resistance that we will face, we need to look closely first at the current American university students, then at the specific elements of the businesslike version of postsecondary education that is recruiting them.

If the student population and its desires cause the genuinely irresistible changes in academia, we need to gather the answers to some basic questions about American college students. Over the last generation, their profile has changed dramatically, largely in response to the rapidly escalating cost of college. Since 1980, average college tuition costs have risen three times faster than the consumer price index, and that steep incline is transforming America's universities at every level, from the kind of students who attend them to the philosophies by which they operate.[13] Due to the fact that college gets so much more expensive by the year, students and their families are unable to pay for it in the way that was traditional in the 1960s and 1970s, as a four-year package that begins after high-school graduation. Students are starting college at a later age, going to college part-time to accommodate their work schedules, and thus taking longer than four years to finish their formal education. Far more students attend public universities than did two generations ago, since for many, the cost of private universities has become prohibitive. Once in college, students increasingly see their studies as an investment in their financial future. Perhaps no statistic is rehearsed more frequently for their benefit than the average difference between a high-school graduate's lifetime earnings and that of a college graduate: $1.2 million versus $2.1 million.[14] Today's students have taken that probable income gap to heart and, as we shall see, they choose their majors in light of it.[15]

The Department of Education's regular censuses corroborate this general picture. Perhaps moved by the premise that we all must adapt to a new, knowledge-based economy, a record 17.3 million students enrolled in college in 2004, up 28 percent since 1991. Enrollment is expected to increase another 11 percent by 2013. The image of an 18- to 22-year–old, full-time student in residence at a traditional college, however, is now a figment of the past; only 16 percent of all undergraduates now fit that profile.[16] Today, the majority of students are over the age of twenty-five, as compared to just 22 percent in 1970.[17] That figure is influenced most by the expansion of part-time higher-education options. In 1959, the first year that a breakdown of full-time versus part-time was made, one in three students attended college part-time; by 2001, the percentage of part-time students had doubled to one in two. A big reason for this difference is that 82 percent of all college students now work while attending school and 32 percent of them work full-time. By contrast, Michael Moffatt's study of student life at Rutgers (a typical large public university) during the late 1970s and early 1980s estimated that only 12 percent of undergraduates worked at all during the school year.[18] In 1947, college enrollments were equally divided between private and public colleges; in 2001, 81 percent of all undergraduates were enrolled in public institutions, including 44 percent at community colleges.

This last demographic shift can be traced to the uneven pace at which college costs have risen. Though tuition everywhere has increased, the gap in price between private institutions and public institutions, measured in dollars, has steadily widened over the past three decades. In 2006, the average annual tuition and fees stood at $5,491 for four-year public universities (up 54 percent since 1996) and $21,235 for four-year private universities (up 37 percent since 1996). Only two-year public universities have remained relatively affordable, with tuition and fees averaging $2,191, up only $500 since 1996.[19] The upward ranges are staggering: tuition and room and board at both Harvard and Princeton for 2005–6 is more than $40,000. Note, though, that state universities have witnessed sharper tuition hikes (in percentage terms) than their private counterparts during recent years, largely a function of decreases in state funding for higher education over the last two decades. Tuition from 2004 to 2006 is up 24 percent at the University of Arizona, 30 percent at the University of Kansas, and 32 percent at the University of Colorado.[20] Very few people pay the actual sticker price for a college education—financial aid is widely available to students at all institutions. However, the standard *types* of financial aid are shifting dramatically too, with more aid packages distributed on the basis of academic merit rather than financial need, and more loans issued than scholarships awarded across the board. From 1985 to 2000, student loan volume increased by 435 percent.[21] This means that college is a greater financial burden for all but the most gifted among impoverished students, and that a whole generation of students is graduating with enormous debt.

The expense of college is perhaps most clearly reflected by what students expect from their education and what they choose to study. Since 1966, the Higher Education Research Institute at UCLA's survey of incoming freshmen has asked its respondents to rank twenty goals that they hoped to achieve by going to college. In 1971, the top three answers were "to help others who are in difficulty" (68.5 percent), "to become an authority in my field" (66 percent), and "to keep up to date on politics" (57.8 percent). In 2001, the survey found that "being very well-off financially" (a distant fifth in 1971) topped the list at 73 percent. "Help others who are in difficulty" had slipped to 61.5 percent, while "keep up to date with political affairs" had dropped all the way to 28.1 percent.[22] It is fair to presume further that the change in the top responses is heavily influenced by rising tuitions, which have pushed students to define their life goals in terms of money. The steep drop in "keeping up to date on politics" exposes as ludicrous the humanist shibboleth that college prepares people for responsible citizenship. It may have that capability, but today's students have been forced to approach college as apolitical egoists. More than ever, they see college primarily as an investment in their personal financial future, the expense of which must ultimately be justified.

As a consequence, we have seen a seismic shift in what undergraduates want to learn in college. The last academic year in which 50 percent of students graduated with traditional liberal arts majors was 1969–70. Between 1970 and 2001, Bachelor's degrees in English have declined from 7.6 percent to 4 percent, as have degrees in foreign languages (2.4 percent to 1 percent), mathematics (3 percent to 1 percent), social science and history (18.4 percent to 10 percent). These are all drop-offs of around 50 percent or more. Bachelor's degrees in business, the subject that openly promises to launch students on the path to prosperity, are up sharply. Since 1970–71, business majors have risen from 13.6 percent of the graduating population to 21.7 percent, replacing education as the most popular major. During that time, education has suffered a liberal arts-like decline in majors from 21 percent to 8.2 percent.

The demographic profile of both the new college student and the new student's preferences will, I believe, produce an even more stratified version of higher education in America than the one that currently exists. The largest stratum will consist of those institutions that explicitly cater to the new breed of student, who is older, more pragmatic, and more earnings-conscious than ever before. For the past two generations, a great many students who fit that profile have attended community colleges, swelling the ranks of such schools significantly. Yet community colleges have during that time uneasily sought to fulfill two distinct missions: they offer training in a wide range of occupational skills, with the Associate's Degree serving as the credential for a job, and they also serve as feeder schools for four-year universities, thus also offering a full menu of prerequisite courses toward a liberal arts Bachelor's Degree.[23] For-profit universities are usurping much of the community college market and will continue to do so. The for-profits focus exclusively on the training and job placement of career-minded students. They aim to capitalize on the connection, now dominant in the minds of so many, between a college education and a high-paying job. They bolster a bare bones curriculum with an intensive marketing campaign, devoting enormous amounts of money to recruiting and advertising. Their quick responsiveness to the changing student population is paying off; the for-profit universities are the fastest-growing sector in higher education today. Perhaps most alarming for humanists, in 2000–1, the entire, for-profit, postsecondary education industry graduated 28,000 Business and Management A.A.s and B.A.s, 11,500 A.A.s and B.A.s in the health professions, and not a single English major.[24]

Meanwhile, the top stratum of higher education, the elite private colleges and universities, will change very little over the next two generations. They will continue to serve an exclusive cohort of students.[25] Moreover, because their entering classes remain stable and their admissions standards consistently stringent, they will determine who belongs to that exclusive cohort. Unhurried by market demands, their curricula will change very slowly as well and will largely continue to exclude occupational majors. Large percentages of students at the elite schools will declare traditional liberal arts majors, which means in turn that these institutions will continue to hire professors in the humanities in the same numbers that they always have. Imperturbable as they may be, however, the elite colleges and universities will become a smaller and smaller part of the steadily expanding higher-education universe. Over time—and it may take two or three generations—humanists will thus become an insignificant percentage of the country's university instructional workforce.

The middle stratum will be dominated by those institutions that used to, and perhaps still do, form the bulwark of American higher education: the large state universities and university systems. Their vulnerability as we advance into the future cannot be overstated. As James Duderstadt and Farris W. Womack put it in *The Future of Public Universities in America*, they now stand "beyond the crossroads." Simultaneously squeezed by community colleges (and now for-profits) to prepare their students for employment and anxious to compete for prestige with the elite institutions, America's state universities have lost their way. If they continue to operate without clarifying their mission, they will risk gradually becoming obsolete. The institutions at opposite ends of the higher education spectrum—the for-profits and the elite universities—will occupy the key positions in the future, for each will exert tremendous influence on all the colleges in between the extremes. Each of the schools in between will be pushed to define itself either as a proving ground for the business community or as a place where students can acquire a prestige marker, an index of their social status.[26]

Clearly, the changing student demographics guide us to look closely at for-profit universities. To get a sense of the for-profit revolution in higher education, one can hardly do better than to look at the sports pages. After leaving Louisiana State University for the NBA in 1992, Shaquille O'Neal continued to take courses and returned with great fanfare to receive his B.A. in 2001. He attended LSU's commencement ceremony, rechristening his *alma mater* Love Shaq University. Four years later, in July of 2005, ESPN and other sports and entertainment outlets reported that O'Neal had earned an M.B.A. What the reports (or at least their headlines) failed to note was that he earned the degree entirely online from the University of Phoenix, the nation's largest for-profit university. The omission of these two details (the virtual degree and its grantor), as I see it, accords the for-profit education sector unprecedented legitimacy. The University of Phoenix only added to its luster in 2006 when it bought the naming rights to a stadium which would be home to the NFL's Arizona Cardinals. ESPN.com's story announcing the move simply calls the University of Phoenix "the nation's largest private university." Though subsequent paragraphs mention that it is operated for profit and has been the subject of SEC investigations, for ESPN's vast audience such details pale in comparison to the revelation that the 2008 Super Bowl will be played at the "University of Phoenix Stadium."[27] David Noble, the for-profits' most vocal critic, has long compared them to the fly-by-night correspondence schools that flourished in the 1920s. That no one thought to suggest that Shaq's online M.B.A. was somehow spurious, or thought to object that the

University of Phoenix is neither a university nor in Phoenix, reveals those correspondence school comparisons to be wishful thinking on Noble's part. The for-profits are a serious and permanent phenomenon.

The for-profits themselves insist on both the clarity of their mission and their right to a place in the world of higher education. Ronald Taylor, the chief operator and co-founder of DeVry, the second-largest, for-profit, higher-education provider, says, "The colossally simple notion that drives DeVry's business is that if you ask employers what they want and then provide what they want, the people you supply to them will be hired."[28] John Sperling, founder of Apollo Group (the University of Phoenix's parent company), casts his competition with traditional higher education in explicitly warlike terms. Chronicling his company's long struggle for legitimacy, he says that his various efforts to expand Apollo's accreditation status "were largely proxies for cultural battles between defenders of 800 years of educational (and largely religious) traditions, and innovation that was based on the ideas of the marketplace—transparency, efficiency, productivity, and accountability."[29] Taylor and Sperling speak to the twin ruling principles of the for-profit revolution in higher education: that the only mission of for-profit universities is job training, and that the universities themselves operate according to the conventions and values of the business universe that they supply with employees. One would be hard-pressed to find such uniformity or certainty in the world of traditional, non-profit education. Recognizing the single-mindedness of the for-profit education industry allows us to understand both its rise to prominence as well as its organizational makeup, its way of doing business.

That industry is a vast topic, the subject of two recent book-length treatments, by Richard S. Ruch, *Higher Ed. Inc., The Rise of the For-Profit University* (2001) and David W. Breneman, Brian Pusser, and Sarah E. Turner, eds., *Earnings from Learning: The Rise of For-Profit Universities* (2006), as well as a considerable section of David L. Kirp's *Shakespeare, Einstein, and the Bottom Line: The Marketing of Higher Education* (2004). I will focus specifically on the impact that the for-profit revolution is already having on the work lives of humanities professors. Its footprints will ultimately extend beyond the institutions such as the University of Phoenix for two reasons. First, the for-profit universities bear a message rooted in the "ideas of the marketplace" that is certain to appeal to the emerging student population that I have just described. It appeals, moreover, not just to students actually enrolled in for-profits, but to all students who are inclined to see college education as an investment in their future profes-sional success. The values of the message "transparency, efficiency, pro-ductivity, and accountability," are, as Veblen pointed out long ago, foreign to the humanities and to its professors. That the for-profit universities are themselves businesses only reinforces their message. Second, the for-profit universities have been the pioneers and leading proponents of online learning. At the very least, they have proven that online instruction is a cost-effective pedagogical model. The *quality* of online education is, of course, the subject of a highly charged, ongoing debate. Yet a great many traditional colleges and universities, in the face of shrinking resources and rising tuition, have adopted many of the for-profits' innovations in the application of information technology to higher-education instruction. As we shall see, this trend toward increased reliance on IT in teaching funda-mentally alters the professor's relationship with his or her students and thus changes the role of the professor in the university as well.

It is worth pausing, before I explore the effect of the for-profit revolu-tion on professors, to outline the revolution itself. The phenomenon of for-profit higher education is extremely recent: the industry hardly existed in 1990, but grew exponentially in the last decade of the twentieth century and is currently in a period of consolidation. In the early 1960s, there were only a handful of for-profit, postsecondary institutions, all of them privately owned and functioning much like trade schools. By 2003, there were 2,383 accredited, for-profit colleges and universities, making up one-third of the total number of two- and four-year institutions in the coun-try.[30] The vast majority of them offer only training certificates or Associate degrees; some for-profits, though, now offer not only Bachelor's degrees, but also M.B.A.s (as we have seen) and doctoral degrees in law, education, and psychology. When the Department of Education first started keeping track of them in 1976, for-profit universities enrolled a barely measurable 44,352 students. Now, Apollo's flagship institution, the University of Phoenix, alone enrolls 300,000, making it, as ESPN reminds us, the largest university in the country. Since 1990, the number of for-profit university campuses has exploded, while during that same period, at least 200 non-profit colleges closed because of financial difficulty.

The growth of these institutions can be measured in dollars as well as in campuses and students. In 1991, only one for-profit, DeVry, was a publicly traded corporation; Apollo Group, the parent company of the University of Phoenix, followed in 1994. By 2000, forty-five colleges and universities were listed on either the NYSE or the NASDAQ. The higher education

companies benefited enormously from the 2000–2 recession, since economic downturns typically generate higher college enrollments. During
the 15-month period from January 1, 2000 to March 31, 2001, the Dow
Jones average declined by 13 percent and the NASDAQ composite lost 55
percent of its value, but the top eleven higher-education corporation
stocks enjoyed an average return of 108 percent.[31]

After a few failures and a flurry of merger and acquisition activity in the
period 2000–6, there are six major players in the industry: Apollo Group
(ticker symbol: APOL), with a current market cap of $8.1 billion and
300,000 students; ITT Educational Services (ESI), with a market cap of
$4.1 billion and 48,000 students; Career Education Corp. (CECO), with
a market cap of $3.3 billion and 83,000 students; Laureate Education
(LAUR), with a market cap of $3 billion and 83,000 students; DeVry
(DV), the oldest of the group, with a market cap of $2.4 billion and
240,000 students; and Strayer Education, with a market cap of $1.9 billion
and 32,000 students. A seventh industry giant, Education Management
Corporation, with an enrollment of 80,000, was purchased by a group
of private investors in June 2006 for $3.4 billion. In January 2007, the
independent equities research group Columbine Capital Services reported
that Laureate was entertaining a buyout offer from a private group as
well.[32] *Inside Higher Education* reporter Doug Lederman plausibly speculates that transactions such as the Education Management buyout symbol-
ize that the "era of 'hypergrowth' in for-profit higher education is over."[33]
Even if this is true, the biggest companies alone are currently worth more
than $22 billion and enroll nearly 700,000 students.

Over and over on the Web sites of these universities one finds a version
of the same mission statement: they focus on the tight relationship between curriculum and job preparation and they appeal primarily to the
older, working adults who are steadily becoming the typical American college student. ITT Educational Services bills itself as a "leading provider of
technology-oriented postsecondary degree programs." Strayer Education
boasts that it offers undergraduate and graduate degrees in business administration, accounting, and related subjects to "working adults." It reports that its average student is thirty-four years old, with "annual incomes
ranging from $20,000 to $80,000 plus," which a degree from Strayer will
presumably increase. DeVry states its purposes as follows: "To offer appli-
cations-oriented undergraduate education. . . . To offer practitioner-
oriented graduate education. . . . To serve student and employer needs by
offering effective career entry and career development services." Apollo

Group sums up the formula in three phrases on the opening page of its 2005 *Annual Report* to shareholders: "Academic theory and business practices. Working students and practitioner faculty. One-on-one human interaction and leading-edge technologies."[34] The symbiosis between these institutions and the business world is perhaps better illustrated not by the slogans, but by financial bonds. Fifty-nine percent of all students at for-profit universities receive tuition subsidies from their current employer.[35] As David Collis observes, the for-profits' most important customers are Fortune 1000 companies, not individual student-consumers.[36]

The fate of the humanities and of humanities faculty in the burgeoning world of for-profit higher education is easy to predict, but painful to contemplate. Universities that, by virtue of their very mission, validate economic efficiency and productivity above all else also sanction apathy toward the humanities. Sperling, speaking of his University of Phoenix, puts it gruffly: "This is a corporation. . . . Coming here is not a rite of passage. We are not trying to develop [students'] value systems or go in for that 'expand their minds' bullshit."[37] David Kirp illustrates this sentiment through the contrast between a humanities course and an electrical engineering course, both taught at the same campus of DeVry. In a class called "Culture and Society," Kirp reports, "baseball caps [are] pulled over furrowed brows" and "no one is taking notes." Even the instructor readily acknowledges, "the students are here for the technical stuff." The engineering class is a world apart. The students are "much more engaged." When the instructor "gives them a circuitry problem, almost all of them take out their notebooks to perform the calculations." The reason for the difference, Kirp concludes, is obvious: the engineering instructor is no better a teacher than his humanities counterpart, "but he is talking about things the students must learn if they're going to get hired, and they know it."[38] The mission of the entire university, moreover, is squarely behind the efforts of the engineering instructor and largely indifferent to those of the man teaching "Culture and Society."

Because for-profit universities are not only bonded to the business world, but also actually operate as businesses themselves, they radically redefine the role of their teaching personnel. Most important for my purposes, faculty are *not* professors in any traditional sense of the word: "practitioner-faculty," coined by Apollo, is the universally preferred term. Faculty salaries represent the single biggest recurring expense for any kind of educational institution. In the new world of for-profit higher education, those salaries and the kinds of work they reward are thus most vulnerable to change. Richard Ruch, who, after a career at traditional universities, crossed over to become a dean at DeVry's Newark, New Jersey campus, explains exactly how for-profit universities reduce costs through their organizational structure. He establishes key contrasts in the treatment of faculty between non-profits and for-profits. While at traditional universities, faculty are released from one-third to one-half of their teaching time to pursue research or administrative work, at for-profits, all faculty are "fully deployed to teach."[39] He justifies this policy, standard in the industry, by insisting that faculty at a for-profit university are corporate employees, not traditional professors. The security of their salary and employment benefits comes in exchange for "the obligation to surrender control of their time for the pursuit of a corporate goal," which is occupational education.[40]

Corporate policy reaches instructors as a fait accompli. As Patrick Meyers, DeVry's vice president of student affairs, explains, "Decisions are made by the management, by the central office, not by faculty deliberation. . . . The expectation is that [the faculty] will do it, like it or not." When the North Central States Association accredited DeVry in 1992, it told the school to do a better job of "integrating the academic perspective into the organizational structure."[41] However, nine years later, Ruch reports that "the academic voice at the top of these companies is silent, or at best a whisper, and that the minimal attempts to include faculty in management deliberations are token gestures made only to appease accreditation organizations.[42]

The day-to-day work lives of faculty are thus left very much at the disposal of the central office, an arrangement that sometimes frustrates even for-profit deans. One describes the typical management attitude toward the start-up of new campuses: "They [the home-office executives] have the idea . . . that once the building is ready, all we need to do is drive up with a truck load of laborers (faculty), hand them textbooks and curriculum guides, and bingo, let them teach." In practice, faculty teaching schedules are subject to last-minute changes. Ruch justifies this: the "inconvenience is outweighed by the need to serve the customer and manage the business," both of which are higher priorities than the convenience of the faculty, who are, after all, "delivery people."[43] Since the students are openly considered to be customers, their evaluation of instructors carries far more weight than at traditional universities. The following comes from a memo about student evaluations circulated by Elaine S. Lerner, Academic Chair of the School of Paralegal Studies at for-profit Kaplan

University, to the instructors under her supervision: "The scale is 5.0—5.0 being the highest mark. The statistics in my department—where you teach—are overall VERY good! Most of you do an excellent job. . . . If you score below 4.0—I will be talking with you directly. We cannot retain instructors with scores in the 3.0 range. Have a good day!"[44] The brutal clarity of the assessment and its uncritical reliance on statistical evaluations from students are, for now at least, unique to the for-profit education environment.

More than any other factor, the for-profit universities' commitment to information technology accentuates the status of faculty as delivery people and threatens to hasten the reconceptualization of the job of professor. Indeed, IT as for-profits implement it could circumvent not only the need for traditional professors, but also for traditional brick-and-mortar universities as well. For the cost-efficient endpoint of an IT-centered learning environment is an entirely online college education and a digital diploma. Arthur Levine of Columbia University's Teachers College explains that logic as follows: "It is possible right now for a professor to give a lecture in Cairo, for me to attend that lecture at Teachers College, and for another student to attend it in Tokyo. . . . If we can do all that, and the demographics of higher education are changing so greatly, why do we need the physical plant called the college?"[45]

Apollo Group, the first postsecondary institution to commit whole-heartedly to the educational use of information technology, began offering accredited Bachelor's degrees entirely online in 1989. It is still the largest vendor of such programs, and its successes spurred Apollo toward further initiatives that, according to its 2000 annual report, "will enable us to granularize our course materials by creating a database of learning objects that can be mixed, matched, and continuously updated."[46] Other companies quickly followed Apollo's lead. In 1995, Walden University, a subsidiary of Sylvan Learning Centers (now Laureate Education, Inc.), became the first in the country to offer an M.A. in education entirely online, and in 1997, began offering an online Ph.D. in Professional Psychology. This trend spans the industry. While overall growth has slowed in recent years, every for-profit institution continues to report strong growth in its online divisions. The consulting company Eduventures, Inc. projects that online education revenues nationwide (at both traditional colleges and for-profits) will increase at a rate of 33 percent a year for the next several years. For-profit universities are well positioned to take the lion's share of this expansion; currently, 5 percent of the total higher-education student population are enrolled online, but 35 percent of them attend for-profit colleges.[47]

Any significant shift to online education reduces the number of faculty needed to staff an institution and thus alters the very nature of professorial work. Education scholars Robert Zemsky and William Massy, enthusiastic advocates of information technology-based teaching and learning strategies, offer two general propositions in its favor. (1) IT offers "access to very large amounts of information . . . at low incremental costs" and (2) "IT offers mass customization: Technology allows faculty to accommodate individual differences in student goals, learning styles, and abilities, while providing improved convenience for both students and faculty on an 'any time, any place' basis."[48] Massy and Zemsky's propositions raise as many questions about actual instruction as they answer. Who will guide students through this greatly expanded universe of information? How will faculty benefit from the "mass customization" of learning, which seems designed for the unique needs and convenience of countless students? Carol Twigg, formerly vice president of the academic-corporate consortium, Educause, and currently executive director of the Center for Academic Transformation at Rensselaer Polytechnic Institute, offers definitive positions. In an IT-centered learning environment, she suggests, "not all tasks associated with a course require highly trained, expert faculty: . . . expensive labor (faculty and graduate students)" could be replaced with "inexpensive labor (undergraduate peer mentors and course assistants) *where appropriate*" (emphasis mine). In Twigg's opinion, too, mass customization is indeed a one-way street:

> Currently in higher education, both on campus and online, we individualize faculty practice (that is, we allow individual faculty members great latitude in course development and delivery) and standardize the student learning experience (that is, we treat all students in a course as if their learning needs, interests, and abilities were the same). Instead, we need to do just the opposite: individualize student learning and standardize faculty practice.[49]

Here, Twigg largely sidesteps the implications for professors in this cost-cutting agenda, saying vaguely that the highly trained, expert faculty who would be replaced with inexpensive labor would then be free to "concentrate on academic rather than logistical tasks."[50] In an earlier essay on the same subject, though, she specifies what those tasks might be, and they are, in fact, far more logistical than academic. Twigg says that in a largely online university, the work now performed by professors would be "disaggregated," and that faculty "would move from being content experts to being a combination of content expert, learning-process design expert, and process-implementation manager; as presenters of that material; as expert assessors of learning and competencies; as advisors; or as specialists in other evolving roles."[51] Massy and Zemsky are more blunt: "Faculty might take over duties now performed by staff, or regular faculty might displace auxiliary faculty, or the regular faculty may decrease in number." After all:

> Workstations don't get tenure, and delegations are less likely to wait on the provost when particular equipment items are "laid off." The "retraining" of IT equipment (for example, reprogramming), while not inexpensive, is easier and more predictable than training a tenured professor.[52]

Noble, in his book *Digital Diploma Mills*, broadly spells out the shift in power that a full-scale IT model would bring about: "Once faculty and courses go online, administrators gain much greater direct control over faculty performance and course content than ever before and the potential for administrative scrutiny, supervision, regimentation, discipline and even censorship increases dramatically." Even without the extensive use of peer mentors, prepackaged courseware and self-guided courses would make it easier for less experienced, cheaper instructors to do the teaching.[53]

Besides this hostile takeover of the professor's traditional job, an additional problem for the humanities arises from the for-profits' comprehensive commitment to information technology-centered teaching and online education. Massy, Zemsky, and Twigg all conclude that the humanities is not an area of "codified knowledge and algorithmic skills;"[54] to use Apollo Group's word, the humanities cannot be "granularized." It thus makes a generally poor candidate for IT-enhanced online delivery. Their sterile methodological terminology masks a compelling ideological problem. What, after all, does one do with a subject that so poorly fits the preferred model of education delivery? The most likely answer, especially when the subject also fits poorly with the university's mission, is to dispense with it altogether.[55] By so clearly championing one range of disciplines and one notion of teaching, the for-profits push humanities professors to the periphery of their operations almost as a matter of policy.

At the institutional level, there are clear and sometimes shocking instances of for-profit encroachment on traditional higher education. With growing frequency, financially straitened traditional schools do not simply declare bankruptcy and close their doors; rather, their facilities and often their names are acquired by for-profit education companies. The scope of these acquisitions is surprisingly extensive, as a couple of examples will attest. Quest Education, an Atlanta-based company that expanded almost exclusively through acquisitions, bought out thirty private colleges between 1988 and 2000 before *it* was bought by the Washington Post Company.[56] *Investor's Business Daily* illustrates the standard methods of Career Education Corp., which, from its inception in 1994 through 2000, bought twenty-eight colleges in fifteen states and Canada, in these terms: "In 1997 . . . it bought the seven-campus Katherine Gibbs chain in New England. The company then went to work, morphing the 90-year old secretarial schools into high-tech training centers. It then cranked up its marketing machine, advertising the schools' changes to the community." Such takeovers are hard work, says Career Education's chief financial officer, Pat Pesch: "Every time we move a curriculum, it requires new faculty, new space requirements, new capital investment for computer labs and a new academic chair. . . . Then you have to get accreditation, start a new marketing program and get a whole new set of students in to the school."[57] However, it is worth it, boasts the company's founder and CEO, John M. Larson: "A lot of our [recently acquired] schools have histories of 50, 60, 70, 90, 120 years. They're great brand names."[58] Traditionalists will find the application of merger and acquisition language to higher education disconcerting, but it is a way of life for the industry, as is the brisk pace at which it all occurs. Indeed, Larson stepped down in September 2006 in the wake of an acrimonious proxy fight, prompted by Department of Education investigations of the company's recruiting practices. The new management promptly deemed the chain of Gibbs schools unprofitable and sold them all in November of that year.[59] As so often happens in America's corporate shake-ups, Pesch, the man who could readily tick off all the logistical steps required to start up a new campus, remains Career Education's CFO.

The consequences of such takeovers will also strike traditional academics as alien. Grand Canyon University, a small Christian college in Arizona, faced closure in 2004 when it was bought for $38 million by a group of investors who turned it into a for-profit institution. The following spring, in an episode replete with the clichés of corporate downsizing, seventeen professors (five of them tenured) found one day that their e-mail accounts were invalid and the locks on their office doors changed. When they complained, a spokeswoman for the university characterized them as "disgruntled employees" and announced a "redirection and reduction" at

Grand Canyon.[60] While it is easy to condemn such a high-handed managerial style, the college's new CEO, Brent Richardson, defended his decision by pointing out that were it not for the takeover, Grand Canyon
University would have closed, costing *all* of its professors their jobs.[61]
Moreover, the public of potential students is unlikely to miss the older
versions of Grand Canyon University or the Katherine Gibbs School once
they have been transformed into businesses. Professors are the only
casualties.

Recent bad publicity suggests that the for-profit higher education industry may not be able to carry out the devolution of the role of professors
all by itself. The current news may, I fear, create a false sense of security
among academics and the journalists who cover them, for it concentrates
on the companies themselves rather than the already widespread and powerful influence of their values and practices. The recent troubles of the
for-profits are generated by the same forces that led to their great success:
the pressure to show consistent growth in profits. In an increasingly competitive market, which the companies themselves created, the for-profits
have, according to education scholars, Department of Education investigators, and students/customers alike, succumbed to that pressure. A back-
lash has come in the form of increased scrutiny of the quality of both their
curricular content and their students.

An article by *New York Times* reporter Sam Dillon elaborates on the
specific compromises that Apollo Group (the University of Phoenix) has
made. Their granularized curriculum, with courses written at university
headquarters, has given rise to a culture of "come-and-go" faculty. By its
own admission, only 26 percent of instructors have been with the University of Phoenix for four or more years.[62] This has led to accreditation
problems, particularly at its business school. The University of Phoenix
never applied for accreditation from the most prestigious agency for business schools, the Association to Advance Collegiate Schools of Business.
John J. Fernandez, the association's president, estimates that their chances
of approval would have been low. The need for uniform course materials
across a host of campuses, virtual and real, has led, in the opinion of higher
education scholar Henry M. Levin, to a degree that he characterizes as
"an MBA lite." Even students speculate that the University of Phoenix's
academic program has deteriorated as a result of its breakneck expansion.
Dillon notes that "a cursory Internet search will turn up criticism on sites
like ripoffreport.com and uopexperience.com."

The breakneck expansion and the need to populate all the campuses with students has, perhaps inevitably, led to questionable recruiting practices by several of the for-profits. A Department of Education investigative report of the University of Phoenix's California and Arizona campuses concluded that the university had provided incentives to recruit unqualified students and "systematically operates in a duplicitous manner." Apollo settled the matter out of court for $9.8 million, admitting no wrongdoing.[63]

Stephen Burd, writing for the *Chronicle of Higher Education*, paints a shocking picture of for-profit recruiting practices. A former recruiter (called "admissions counselors") at Career Education Corp. admitted that "pressure . . . from the top" to recruit students made her job extremely stressful: "people know that they have to enroll a certain number of students or they will lose their job." The *Chronicle*'s investigation revealed that this pressure caused Career Education to "regularly" admit "students who had not graduated from high school or earned a General Education Development certificate," and that recruiters also "Improperly counted as 'starts' students who never showed up for class or dropped out before they had completed their first week of courses. Encouraged admissions officers to sign up themselves, as well as family members and friends, and counted them as 'starts' even if they never actually attended. Routinely misled prospective students about the college's classes and programs, as well as about the nature of the institution itself."[64] These recruiting schemes to pump up enrollments by counting all "starts" as students, lead, not surprisingly, to staggering dropout rates, since many of the dropouts were never real students in the first place. The University of Phoenix, for example, has a graduation rate of only 16 percent, one of the lowest in the country.

All this bad publicity, including a *60 Minutes* exposé of Career Education (the indisputable sign that things have gone horribly wrong), has indeed weakened the for-profit higher-education industry financially. Its detractors though, should not be too quick to triumph over the for-profits' decline. The real legacy of this industry, I believe, is its lasting and widespread influence on traditional universities. Whatever the fate of specific campuses of the University of Phoenix, Career Education, or DeVry, these companies have demonstrated that it is possible to operate a university as a business. As I will argue in my next chapter, the business model for higher education devised by the for-profits has tremendous appeal to administrators and lawmakers in an era of steadily declining public funding and tuition increases that are quickly becoming prohibitive. Many underfunded traditional public and private institutions are dealing with their financial problems by adopting the business methods and aspects of the for-profits' mission that I have outlined here. The embrace of the business model by these colleges and universities will significantly change the way that professors are treated; indeed, it could reshape their professional identities. As university presidents behave more and more like CEOs (already a cliché), provosts and deans become primarily managers and supervisors, and professors become the managed service workers, interacting on the front lines with the students/customers (also already a cliché). Universities' chief financial officers will become more powerful, conducting rigorous audits and influencing policies to control overhead and cut costs, just as they do in corporations. The typical CFO's outlook and influence will only increase the appeal of online instruction, since the for-profit higher-education industry has proven it to be much less expensive than the traditional classroom.

The most imminent technological threat, though, is aimed not at professors directly, but at *courses*. The business of course management has met with a far less hostile reception in traditional academia than have standalone for-profit universities. Yet the technologies that make online learning feasible on a large scale have themselves become disaggregated and now function independently of the for-profit institutions that pioneered them. As a result, speculates Princeton's technology outreach coordinator Howard Strauss, "The whole concept of the course might break down altogether, with individual students doing coursework in bits and pieces over a long period of time."[65] The drivers of this radical transformation of the concept of the course and of the move toward what the industry calls "asynchronous," or on-demand instruction, are a handful of companies that are, year by year, making themselves indispensable to America's universities.

Professors at traditional colleges and universities know about institutions like DeVry and the University of Phoenix from reading the *Chronicle* or *Inside Higher Education*. If they know about Blackboard or WebCT, it is because their universities already subscribe to the course-management software packages that these companies sell. Instructors at an increasing number of non-profit schools use the software to facilitate all the essential day-to-day elements of the courses that they teach. That is, the comprehensive suite of software products offered by companies like Blackboard simplifies the management of a course by providing a single "shell" in which the instructor can communicate with students, post syllabi and reading assignments, create discussion boards, administer quizzes and exams, and keep track of and circulate student grades and from which administrators can even gather and tabulate student evaluations. This convenience and ease of use, though, could come at a tremendous cost; the course-management industry poses, in my opinion, a more immediate threat to the autonomy and security of professors than do for-profit universities and their business practices. Traditional colleges can only go so far in adopting the practices of their for-profit counterparts. For example, as we have seen, except in rare cases, they cannot summarily abolish tenure. Online course-management companies, though, are migrating into the country's colleges at a very rapid pace, and administrators and faculty alike tend to welcome them. I'll conclude by explaining the potential dangers of this collaboration.

First, the course-management industry is far easier to describe and understand than the multifaceted for-profit university business. Indeed, at this writing, the business is simpler than ever, since, early in 2006, Blackboard, which controlled 40 percent of the online course-management market, bought its biggest competitor, WebCT, which at the time controlled 46 percent of the market. The merger, which gave Blackboard access to nearly 3,500 clients, most of them universities and community colleges, absolutely polarized the two different camps of journalists who covered it. Yahoo Finance's M&A researcher marveled, "it is almost difficult to believe that WebCT/Blackboard was allowed to proceed . . . under HSR (the Hart-Scott-Rodino Anti-Trust Improvements Act of 1976)." The popular investment site, *The Motley Fool*, raved, "Blackboard Gets High Marks," and enumerated the lessons that the now giant Blackboard offered in the benefits of being a monopoly: "Lesson No. 1. You don't have to spend as much on R&D to stay ahead of the other guy . . . when there *is no other guy*. . . . Lesson No. 2. You also don't have to advertise as much. When you're the only game in town, your name becomes synonymous with the services you provide. . . . Lesson No. 3. There's no need to coddle your customers when they've got little choice but to pay you if they want the service."[66]

The academic reaction to Blackboard's buyout of WebCT is perhaps best summed up by Scott Leslie, author of the blog *EdTechPost*: "Holy $#@!—Blackboard and WebCT to merge."[67] At first, the biggest worry was the prospect that Blackboard could increase prices without repercussions. However, as the expanded Blackboard, nicknamed BlackCT by university IT experts, began behaving like a monopoly—suing one of its competitors, Desire2Learn, over patent infringement—fear and anger in the academic community mounted. The Sakai Foundation, which helps colleges and universities run open-source, course-management systems, had this to say:

> The recent announcement by Blackboard that it is attempting to assert patent rights over simple and longstanding online technologies as applied to the area of course-management systems and e-learning technologies, and its subsequent litigation against a smaller commercial competitor [Desire2Learn] constitutes a threat to the effective and open development of software for higher education and the values underlying such open activities.[68]

Even the usually business-friendly association Educause wrote Blackboard a stern letter in October, 2006, urging the company to drop its lawsuit against Desire2Learn because such actions "go beyond competition to challenging the core values and interests of higher education."[69]

Both the Sakai Foundation and Educause feared that Blackboard might extend its proprietary claims to *any* entity (a non-profit organization providing free open-source software, an individual university) that dared to set up its own course-management system. When Blackboard pledged in February 2007 not to sue open-source, course-management software providers, academics were understandably skeptical. Lee Gonick, vice president and chief information officer at Case Western Reserve University, a Blackboard client, described the pledge as "a short term 'fix' on an unfortunate journey that starts with the anti-intellectual position of seeking a 'patent' on a 21st century version of . . . 'blackboard and chalk.' "[70]

Blackboard's reign as the Standard Oil of the online course-management industry came to a crashing end in May 2007 when one of its only other publicly traded competitors, eCollege, was purchased by Pearson, a multinational publishing giant (owner of *The Financial Times* and Penguin Books) three times the size of Blackboard. Neither Wall Street nor academia has yet to process this most recent transaction, but it is safe to predict that it will not be the last such move. From a business standpoint, the marriage of a publishing company (which owns the rights to vast amounts of content used in schools) and a course-management company (which can distribute that content far more efficiently than bookstores selling textbooks) is a supremely harmonious monopolistic match.

The prospect of more mergers like Pearson-eCollege flies in the face of the truism that "the faculty *are* the university," for the faculty would not be part of the arrangement between a combination publisher–online course-management company. This may not seem significant, since faculty are now out of the loop when universities contract with companies such as Blackboard. They are not offended, and in fact, many welcome course-management software as a helpful and convenient teaching add-on. Using or not using the course-management "shell" is the professor's choice to make, and, in the case of literature courses, for example, the professor alone decides what books will be required, which editions students will use, and what other readings will supplement the assignments. This balance of authority could quickly change, though, if the course-management company also owned the publishing rights to those required books, as well as to academic research databases. Then faculty would have little choice but to use the course-management software, as it would be the only means of getting access to the books that one wanted to teach. This scenario may seem far-fetched, but Twigg mapped it all out at an Educause (then Educom) roundtable in 1996:

> In today's academic culture, responsibility for content rests with the faculty. But a shift is occurring in higher education where increasingly the institution is, in a sense, buying content which it can control. We are seeing tremendous growth in the number of courses taught by untenured, part-time, adjunct, or temporary instructors. In addition, the decision-making structure of many community colleges, continuing education and distance learning programs is institution-based rather than faculty based. Those environments may provide more fertile ground for the adoption of instructional software.[71]

Remember that in his 1910 Carnegie Foundation report on academic and industrial inefficiency, Morris Llewellyn Cooke maintained that it made business sense for course materials and lectures to belong to universities rather than to professors. At the time, that policy would have been impossible to enforce. The online course-management industry, though, working in collaboration both with major publishing houses and university administrations, could provide the means by which such a transfer of control finally takes place.

Indeed, a look at specific trends in enrollments at community colleges, Twigg's "fertile ground," suggests that the transfer could be unstoppable. In 2007, the Instructional Technology Council surveyed 320 community colleges, a representative sample from across the country, and found that "online enrollments had increased by 15 percent on average over the last year, during a period when community colleges' total enrollment was up by 2 percent. In addition, 70 percent of responding institutions reported that there was more student demand for distance learning than they could meet."[72] This level of demand creates almost unlimited opportunities for companies like Blackboard and Pearson's new eCollege division.

The course-management industry and its potential for extensive partnerships with the publishing industry represent the latest phase of the for-profit higher education revolution and it poses three related problems for professors of the future. First, the industry capitalizes on the changing teaching workforce. The erosion of tenure and the consequent reliance on disempowered adjunct instructors gives university administrators the upper hand in determining both what their institution's curriculum will look like and how the courses will be taught. Specifically, administrators and corporations, not faculty, will decide which courses or portions of courses will be taught or managed online. This shift will affect not only community colleges, as Twigg noted in 1996, but also the whole spectrum of institutions, since faculty everywhere seem at best indifferent to the migration of course-management software into their daily lives as teachers.

Second, because online instruction, facilitated by course-management software packages, is cheaper and more convenient than its traditional "bricks and mortar" counterpart, the demand for this mode of instruction will only increase, expanding well beyond for-profit universities and community colleges. Even now, Blackboard and its peers have an impressive list of research universities among their clients. Blackboard has contracts with Temple University, the University of Illinois-Champaign, and the University of Southern California among many others; Desire2Learn serves the University of Arizona, the University of Iowa, Marquette University, the University of Wisconsin system, Ohio State University, and others. Moreover, once a deal is struck between an online course-management company and a college, it is virtually permanent, as changing vendors and thus switching to a new system would create logistical nightmares for students and faculty alike. Blackboard's contracts with its clients are renewed at a rate of 91 percent. More online learning means more disaggregation, and as a consequence, the coherence and distinctness of the job of professor will continue to unravel.

Finally, there is a fundamental question of intellectual property: if a university contracts with a company that owns both the textbook or the novels on your syllabus, *and* the means of distributing that content, *and* software that manages day-to-day classroom activities (reserve reading assignments, tests, grading, even student evaluations), then who owns the course that you teach? If the university owns the course, what is to prevent it from hiring someone other than a professor to manage it? These last questions could plausibly be resolved in a way that leads to the disintegration of the role that professors currently play in America's universities.

CHAPTER 5

Prestige and Prestige Envy

As one moves outside the realm of for-profit universities and the community colleges that increasingly resemble them, the key term in the marketing of higher education ceases to be "jobs, jobs, jobs," as Stanley Aronowitz decried, but instead becomes prestige. Prestige is both fascinating and frustrating to write about because it is so ghostly. Yet I believe that the concept of prestige is so crucial to understanding the current and future trends of many American universities, and of the humanities, that I will use it in this chapter to map both institutions and academic disciplines. My analysis will be guided by the assumption that the American version of prestige is distinctive: it is not perceived as a natural quality or necessarily as an aspect of long-standing, time-honored traditions; rather, it is integral to consumer culture. In our nation of aspirational shoppers, where purchases so often express envy or anxiety about social status, prestige almost always manifests itself as the aura around any expensive commodity: a house, a car, a watch, a pair of shoes, or, for my purposes, a college. Thus, though the concept of prestige may itself be ineffable, Americans who are conscious of prestige tend to want to assess it, put a price tag on it, brand it, and acquire it. This preoccupation with measuring prestige, in turn, leaves a host of traces that I can use to navigate the higher-education system.

That is, if we bracket those institutions, discussed in my last chapter, which advertise only their job-training capability, the rest of America's colleges and universities market themselves by establishing a relationship to prestige. Making sense of this commodified version of prestige allows us to sort out these institutions and predict where they are headed. One can similarly map academic areas, not only the humanities (my main focus), but also law schools, business schools, university medical centers, and even athletic programs, each of which establishes its own relationship to commodified prestige. Finally, while my treatment of prestige and prestige envy as an organizing category in higher education constitutes a new chapter, the model of college as occupational training remains a significant presence. It is now a ready-made, legitimate alternative mission for those colleges that choose not to compete in the prestige wars that I will shortly describe. As appealing as prestige may be as a potential measure of higher education, the notion of college as an investment in oneself and the means to one's professional self-actualization is a powerful force as well. Not only individuals, but also universities sometimes find themselves torn between the two.

The seeming incompatibility between the two messages—college as job training and college as a prestige marker—prompt an assortment of further questions. When for-profit universities renounce the quest for prestige, what exactly are they rejecting? At the other end of the spectrum, when an elite university bases its reputation and its claim to excellence on prestige, it would seem to be making a peculiar kind of circular argument. Why does such reasoning almost always go unchallenged? What motivates state universities without money or selective admissions to compete for prestige, a contest that they are bound to lose every time? I argued in chapter two that every professor has an individual investment in prestige, as marked by research, publication, and tenure. Professors also function, though, both as willing participants and as prizes in the institutional competition for prestige. Since the prestige wars show no signs of abating, any attempt to predict the future of higher education involves anticipating their outcome, the impact that they will ultimately have on the universities that wage them, and on the professors who work for those universities.

I will begin by examining two ingenious and heroic attempts to measure prestige. Neither is entirely successful, but they serve as a useful prelude to the crude banality of the most familiar prestige measure in higher education, the annual *U.S. News & World Report*'s college rankings issue, which I will discuss later. Those rankings are, as everyone knows, presented as a series of categorized lists without a rationale. *U.S. News* divulges the various metrics that it uses to evaluate schools, but owes its success to the fact that everyone focuses on the rankings themselves, not on the methodology used to devise them. By looking first at attempts to present theories of prestige in higher education, we can uncover the assumptions and the hopes that inform this all-important academic keyword.

Caroline Hoxby takes the ubiquitous comparison between the average lifetime earnings of a college graduate ($2.1 million) and those of a high school graduate ($1.2 million) one step farther, investigating the projected lifetime earnings of graduates from different *ranks* of colleges. Her comprehensive survey of data on "The Return to Attending a More Selective College: 1960 to the Present" focuses on the relationship between an education at a prestigious university and the recipient's subsequent earning power. She uses *Barron's* selectivity index, which is largely based on college and university acceptance rates, to sort the colleges and universities. *Barron's* divides academia into nine categories: Most Competitive, Highly Competitive Plus, Highly Competitive, Very Competitive Plus, Very Competitive, Competitive Plus, Competitive, Less Competitive, and Noncompetitive. Hoxby estimates that men who entered "Most Competitive" colleges between 1960 and 1982 would earn an estimated $2.9 million in their lifetimes, while those who entered "Less Competitive" or "Noncompetitive" colleges in the same year would earn $1.7 million. The difference is, in other words, larger than that separating the college-educated from the high school-educated. Moreover, that $1.2 million difference widened appreciably between the entering class of 1960 and 1982, the first and last years that Hoxby considers.[1]

The result is at least thought-provoking, but several major qualifications immediately suggest themselves. Hoxby cannot accurately weight an assortment of data—students' family backgrounds and relative wealth (in other words, what they themselves brought to the college experience), their majors, GPAs, and career ambitions—as factors in their lifetime earning power. Moreover, Hoxby excludes women from her study, operating on the assumption that they are more likely than men to defer their career plans after graduating and would thus complicate her averages. Clearly, though, this variable would have fluctuated from 1960 to 1982. Finally, an earlier study of a comparable time frame by economists Alan B. Krueger and Stacy Berg Dale contradicts Hoxby's basic conclusions. In 1995, Krueger and Dale reviewed the incomes of 14,000 adults who had enrolled in thirty different colleges in 1972. They sorted the colleges into two categories: those with average student SAT scores of greater than 1,200 and those with average student SAT scores of less than 1,200. Their study found that in 1995, the graduates of both the more and the less selective colleges were making identical salaries, $77,000 per year.[2]

Statistical outliers and outright contradictions notwithstanding, Hoxby's conclusions seem to confirm both the intuitions and the hopes of prestige-conscious consumers of higher education, namely, that there is a clear caste system in American higher education, and that going to an upper-caste college will enrich one's life not only symbolically, but also materially. Moreover, Hoxby's largely unstated starting assumptions expose two other rigid and closely connected dividing lines in higher education that will serve as focal points in this chapter. First, academic prestige is deeply interwoven with exclusivity, with decisions that each university makes about who gets admitted and who does not. She does not spell out all the implications of "More Selective" as a category, but they are pivotal to her argument. Second, and more important, prestige is the monopoly of America's richest private institutions of higher learning. Hoxby chooses *Barron's*, whose system foregrounds admissions selectivity as a means of distinguishing one school from another. By making exclusivity its chief criterion, *Barron's* implicitly and automatically privileges smaller schools over larger ones and thus, by extension, private universities over public universities. Indeed, the mission and often the state mandate of public universities entails *not* being especially selective in admissions; this in turn becomes a huge handicap in their competition for prestige.

Despite its emphasis on the single factor of selective admissions, *Barron's* list looks remarkably similar to those of its peers, and they're all overwhelmingly rich, very selective, and private. Among the 100 colleges and universities in *Barron's* top four categories in 2005 (Most Competitive through Competitive Plus), only four—the University of Virginia, the University of Michigan, the University of California–Santa Barbara, and New College of the University of South Florida—are public institutions. The other most popular published rankings, *U.S. News & World Report* and *The Princeton Review*, yield the same homogenous result. The 2006 edition of *U.S. News*'s discursive survey, *The Ultimate Guide to College*, lists 69 Most Selective universities and liberal-arts colleges, only nine of which are public. *The Princeton Review* rates colleges on a scale from 60 to 100 (100 is the highest, 60 is contemptuously assigned to any school that refuses to divulge its data). Of the 101 institutions that receive scores of 97 and higher, only 14 are public. The nomenclature varies slightly from one ranking scheme to the next, but the results are the same. Harvard, Yale, Princeton, Stanford, Amherst, and Williams all figure prominently, and even the placement of the public institutions is uniform: the University of Virginia, the University of Michigan, the University of North Carolina–Chapel Hill, and the University of California (both Berkeley and UCLA) make it onto every list, but never break into the top ten.[3]

Those prospective students intent on finding their place in that top tier can take comfort, then, in the clear consensus about which schools they ought to consider. Hoxby's study, however flawed, adds the reassurance that these elite universities enhance the earning power of their graduates as well and thus make good investments. Her logic is reminiscent of the message of the for-profit universities that college is an investment in one's professional future. In this case, though, one's money is invested in an exotic collectible. Like a Tiffany lamp or a Fabergé egg, a Harvard B.A. will appreciate over time.

Is there no difference among these high-end luxury items, nothing that lifts a prestigious college degree above the level of a commodity? Robert Frank, in "Higher Education: The Ultimate Winner-Take-All Market?" says that there is, arguing that in the higher-education market, prestige ultimately transcends commodification. He contrasts admission to a prestigious (and thus, necessarily, highly selective) college with another familiar luxury item manufactured by Porsche:

> When excess demand arises in the market for an ordinary private good or service, it is almost always fleeting. Thus when Porsche recently introduced its new Boxster, each new delivery was sold out more than a year in advance, yet anyone who really wanted this car could find one at a price. Not so in the upper reaches of the academic market. Despite the persistence of excess demand in this market, universities continue to turn qualified students away, while charging those they admit only about one-third of what it costs to serve them.[4]

Like Hoxby's conclusions, Frank's are easy to unravel, but nevertheless instructive. While it is true that the size of the entering classes at the Most Competitive colleges and universities remains fixed regardless of the demand for admission, money figures far more importantly than Frank acknowledges. With enough money, the right connections, and an early start, one can buy one's way into the upper reaches of the academic market just as easily as one could have bought a Boxster in 1996, "at a price." One could prepare to do so by going to an elite prep school, such as Phillips Andover, where tuition, room, and board for 2007–8 is $37,200, and signing up for the *Princeton Review*'s deluxe SAT preparation package for $7,000. Such measures, while hardly routine, are becoming increasingly common. Samuel G. Freedman reports that "the undergraduate test-prep business now has revenue of $726 million a year, up 25 percent from just four years ago." Growing in popularity even faster is the admissions counseling business. "The Independent Education Consultants Association, which represents private academic counselors, claims about 3,500 members, up from 200 only a decade ago. About 100 more consultants apply for membership each month." These counselors charge an average of $3,300 for their services, but if money is no object, the consulting company IvyWise charges $10,000 to $30,000. IvyWise offers several levels of service for high-schoolers aiming for highly ranked colleges, the top of the line being the "Junior/Senior Platinum Package."[5] The high-ranking universities also do their part in guaranteeing access to the very rich. Joseph A. Soares, in *The Power of Privilege: Yale and America's Elite Colleges*, used Yale's own data to show that 14 percent of the students attending in 2000 were "legacies," children of alumni. Daniel Golden, in *The Price of Admission: How America's Ruling Class Buys Its Way Into Elite Colleges—and Who Gets Left Outside the Gates*, looks at the benefits that accrue to Harvard's most generous donors and to the children of those who appear on the university's "Z List." As *Inside Higher Education* reports, the university's "Committee on University Resources . . . is generally restricted to those who have given at least $1 million. . . . Of the 340 committee members who have children who are college age or are past college age, 336 children are currently enrolled or have studied at Harvard—even though the university admits fewer than 1 in 10 candidates" overall. The Z List (on which Harvard refuses to comment), according to Golden, consists of 25 to 50 "well connected but often academically borderline applicants" who are told that they can enroll if they defer for a year.[6] The deferred admissions help Harvard line up prospective big donors. Thus, it is not true that admission to a selective college transcends price and is thus prestigious in a unique way. Rather, the price, when one combines both the cost of preparation and four years' tuition, exceeds that of even the most expensive cars.

In the end, then, both Hoxby and Frank's theories about prestige in higher education rest on unsubstantiated articles of faith. Hoxby articulates the belief that a degree from a prestigious college will lead to future prosperity; Frank asserts that something other than the forces of supply and demand (presumably merit in some idealized form) support academic prestige, making a degree from a school in "the upper reaches of the academic market" literally priceless. Both conclusions invite debate because they at least follow from thorough and accessible arguments. The *U.S. News & World Report* rankings, by contrast, appear every year as if carved into stone tablets. Their effect is immediate and far-reaching and is considerably more powerful, both inside and outside academia, than any discrete argument could be. The *U.S. News* rankings efface the complexity of evaluating and comparing colleges and simply showcase their lists. The magazine, whose ranking issue debuted in 1983, incorporates far more factors than Hoxby or Frank: peer evaluations by college presidents, acceptance rates, graduation rates, average SAT scores, percentage of students who graduated in the top 10 percent of their high school class, and alumni giving percentages. They then combine these factors in a formula that appears to yield a precise specification of academic prestige.

Decisions to emphasize other metrics can obviously produce different rankings. For example, as everyone knows, *U.S News* ranks individual departments as well as entire universities. The Faculty Scholarly Productivity Index, in its evaluation of departments, chose to weight faculty members' scholarly output and recognition—books, journal articles, journal citations, awards, honors, and grants received—more heavily than *U.S. News* does. Its top four English departments for 2005: Princeton, the University of Georgia, Penn State, and Washington University in Saint Louis. *U.S. News* perennials such as Columbia, Duke, Harvard, and Yale did not even make it into the Index's top ten.[7] *U.S. News* tinkered with its own recipe in 1997, deciding to emphasize dollars spent per student at each university. Caltech immediately shot to number one in its rankings, followed by MIT. The editors had apparently not recognized until too late that very expensive laboratories would tip the assessment balance in favor of science-oriented schools. The formula was immediately abandoned, and the list of top schools reverted to the usual uniform and predictable group the next year.[8] *U.S. News* also makes calculating errors. Its 2008 guide to graduate programs ranked Portland State University ninth in the country in electrical engineering, right behind MIT and Stanford. The magazine's director of data research, Robert J. Morse, admitted, "There was an error in data input," but not before Portland State had issued a chest-thumping press release, proclaiming itself "a national and international academic and research institution."[9]

There is currently a growing call to boycott *U.S. News*, led by Lloyd Thacker, whose book *College Unranked: Ending the College Admissions Frenzy* (2005) presented the first sustained critique of the nation's fixation on rankings. Thacker's foundation, the Education Conservancy, has organized a group of colleges (twenty-seven at this writing) to take a stand against *U.S. News*. Specifically, the presidents of these institutions have agreed not to fill out *U.S. News*'s "reputational surveys," impressionistic assessments of peer institutions that count as 25 percent of each school's score in the magazine's formula (by far the biggest component). These require no empirical support. As John Strassburger, president of Ursinus College, observes, "Very few people [college presidents], even those voting, could state which two colleges among Amherst, Swarthmore, Bucknell, Williams and Carleton have engineering. But they vote anyway." The college presidents who joined the boycott also agreed not to use *U.S. News*'s rankings in their schools' promotional materials. The early response to Thacker's call to arms is impressive, but Robert Oden Jr., president of Carleton College, which chose not to join the boycott, cautions, "I think some series of rankings are with us for now and for the future." Whether it is "best fly-fishing river" or best college, he says, "we seem as a nation to be given to rankings."[10]

Sadly, Oden may be right about the permanency of rankings, especially if so many universities, and even states, continue to use them as the basis for crucial policy decisions. Charles W. Quatt, co-author of *Dollars and Sense: The Nonprofit Board's Guide to Determining Chief Executives' Compensation*, reports that, increasingly, university presidents' compensation packages and bonuses are linked to some of the very metrics that matter most in *U.S. News*'s rankings formula: "increases in the applicant pool or in SAT averages, progress in recruiting faculty talent, growth in endowments . . . increases in graduation rate." The $60,000 in bonus pay for Arizona State University's president, Michael Crow, is tied to an improved rating from *U.S. News*. Matthew Quirk tells the story of Eugene Trani, the president of Virginia Commonwealth University, a Tier 3 school in the *U.S. News & World Report* rankings. Trani "carries a laminated card in his pocket to remind him of the school's strategic goal of making it to the next tier. For every year the school stays in the higher tier he will receive a $25,000 bonus."[11] Like Oden, Quatt sees these kinds of trends as a given: "the rankings are a fact," he says. "The magazine is published. It's a way the public is going to think about your institution."[12] Economists Ginger Zhe Jin and Alex Whalley look at the problem at the level of state education budgets. In a working paper for the National Bureau of Economic Research entitled, "The Power of Information: How Do U.S. News Rankings Affect the Financial Resources of Public Colleges?" they classified the colleges covered by *U.S. News* into three categories: those that were in the rankings before 1990 ("previous-ins"), those that were first added in 1990 ("added-ins"), and those that were never in before 1995 ("never-ins"), when the rankings expanded to include far more institutions. They found that "state funding increased 58 percent from 1987 to

1995 for colleges that first appeared in the rankings in 1990. By comparison, state funding increased 49 percent for colleges that were never ranked and 48 percent for those already on the list." Moreover, most of the funding increases went to merit scholarships and instruction, a clear if not deliberate affirmation of *U.S News*'s points of emphasis (student grades and SAT scores, student-faculty ratio). Thus their results "suggest that, in addition to a consumer response, the publication of quality rankings may influence the provision of quality through a political channel."[13]

The *U.S. News* rankings can even have a palpable psychological effect on students and alumni alike, and this too can influence policy. Peter Cohl, a graduate of Cornell, reacted to his university's slip in the rankings (it is currently thirteenth) by asserting that "my value as a human being feels like it's dropping." He joined other Cornell alumni to form an "image committee" that began a strategic attempt to improve the university's position. The committee "persuaded the bookstore to stock a line of vintage hats and sweatshirts that decidedly emphasized Cornell's Ivy League roots." They then concluded that "if Cornell could diminish the number of classes with more than 50 students, and increase the number with fewer than 20, it could significantly improve its U.S. News & World Report standing"; as Cohl sums it up: "If Cornell can reduce class size, they can be a top 5 school."[14]

Cornell is hardly alone in retooling itself specifically to conform to the *U.S. News* metrics and thus enhance its chances of moving up in the rankings. As Harvard economist David J. Collis points out, though, these policy moves, all made with the same goal in mind, are having the unintended effect of making "all institutions look like each other," thus posing a secondary problem for college administrators: how to avoid becoming a "homogenous multiversity."[15] Some schools have addressed this problem by hiring marketing specialists and focus groups in an effort to distinguish themselves, all the while competing in exactly the same *U.S. News*-dictated categories of excellence. The results include name changes and slogans. Beaver College gave itself a more dignified name, Arcadia University, in 2000; Case Western Reserve University is now referred to simply as "Case," after their consultant concluded that "all great universities have single-word names."[16] The University of Kentucky's logo now features a silhouette of a horse and the slogan, "Unbridled Spirit." Ohio State tried out the slogan, "Do Something Big," but went back to its focus groups and refined that ambiguous exhortation to "Do Something Great." After

consulting with Mark Edwards, a Massachusetts-based marketing special-
ist, in 2005, Oberlin College is promoting an image of fearlessness. Edwards felt that "a 'fearless' messaging campaign will help Oberlin stand
out and encourage students to take a look at what's different about the
college." As *Inside Higher Education* reports, students and faculty seem reluctant to take the campaign seriously: "One student joked, 'I guess I fear-
lessly go to class everyday.' One professor said that he didn't see anything
wrong with the college's image. 'If it's not broke, why mess with it?' he
asked. 'I guess I'm fearful.'" However, Oberlin *is* broken, having slipped
to twenty-third on *U.S. News*'s list of top liberal-arts colleges, so the messaging campaign was adopted as part of the college's new "strategic plan."
The front page of its admissions Web site now features a banner that
states, "We are Oberlin: Fearless."[17] This relatively new development, the
urgent quest for distinctiveness as a brand, follows directly from the fact
that so many colleges and universities are side by side in the same race,
the parameters of which are dictated by *U.S. News and World Report*. The
magazine's rankings have come to stand as the emblem of commodified
prestige in American higher education.

Let me move past the apparently unavoidable influence of the rankings
themselves to consider their two most important components, exclusivity
and money, both of which are already balkanizing academia. As it bears
on the future, undergraduate admissions policy is perhaps *the* crucially
important distinction in prestige between public universities and elite private schools. Selectivity in admissions is alluring to administrators and
potential students alike because it appears to be precisely measurable in
readily understandable ways: number of applicants, percentage admitted,
average SAT scores, and so on. In addition to the general critiques of
ranking schemes, many objections have been raised to the ways that colleges manipulate these numbers in order to appear to be more selective
than they actually are. Early decision policies and the practice of rejecting
highly qualified applicants solely because they are unlikely to attend are
the most notorious strategies that schools use to fix the percentages in
their favor.

Even so, the contrast on this point between the elite universities and
state institutions remains obvious. Without exception, state research universities are far less selective and have far less stringent admissions criteria
than do their Ivy League counterparts (along with the Amhersts, Stan-
fords, and MITs of the academic world). Indeed, a public university's
admissions criteria often guarantee that a certain percentage of the best

in-state high school students gain entrance. This requires the state universities to be flexible when it comes to the size of their entering classes. As we head into the future, the state universities are thus likely to continue to grow. I have already noted a migration to public colleges over the last half century: in 1947, 50 percent of undergraduates attended state institutions, now 80 percent do. Several states in 2003–4 infused large amounts of their higher-education budget into scholarship programs aimed at increasing enrollments. Arizona State University plans a 56 percent increase in its enrollment, from 61,000 to 95,000, by the 2020.[18] The selective universities, because they believe in the connection between exclusivity and elite status, will grow in size far more slowly or not at all.

In *Branded Nation*, James Twitchell labels these two distinct types of institutions "brand-name universities" and "mass-provider universities." He elaborates on this classification, since it is central to his argument about how higher education is marketed. He comments on the brand-name campuses that:

> These are the highly selective, high-status schools whose allure is that they are . . . names to conjure with. They are separated not by Ivy League or by conference, but by depth of story. . . . The value is not intramural but extramural, not in the experience but in the shared perception of others about the experience. Acceptance is crucial, yes, but denial is more important because the value of these schools is in exclusivity.

He goes on to note about the mass-provider campuses:

> Here are the hundreds of schools enrolling millions of students granting diplomas in factory fashion. . . . Second-tier state universities and perpetually anxious private schools keep one eye on the bottom line and the other eye on generating flow-through. . . . Commonality is the key to efficiency. Students are FTEs (full-time equivalents), and acceptance is usually determined by some kind of numerical system, such as being in the top 10 percent of your graduating high school class. [19]

Very selective undergraduate admissions, in Twitchell's terminology, helps the elite schools to protect their brand value. As he explains, they have to produce "an entering class that is not just the best and the brightest they can gather, but one that will demonstrate an unbridgeable quality gap between themselves" and the mass-provider universities. "They need this entering class because it is precisely what they sell to the next crop of consumers. . . . At the point of admissions, the goal is not money. . . . The goal is to publicize who is getting in. That's the product."[20] The money will come later in the form of gifts, endowments, and possibly government funding. So, as we have seen, when "the product" is expertly packaged and ranked in *U.S. News & World Report*'s annual America's Best Colleges issue, the ranking itself has the force of a rational declaration based on empirical data. It is taken as such not only by prospective students, but also by many administrators. Dominic J. Brewer, Susan M. Gates, and Charles A. Goldman, the authors of a recent RAND report on prestige in higher education, seem perplexed that "administrators could point to few measures of success beyond the rankings," but this circular reasoning makes perfect sense given Twitchell's theory of the "peer effects" of highly selective admissions: "The person who sits next to you generates [your] value" and vice versa.[21]

Driven by their different attitudes toward exclusivity and consequently adopting different admissions policies, the brand-name universities and the mass-provider universities are evolving toward very distinct futures. Collis even predicts that the exclusive universities will extend their dominance into the online higher-education marketplace, each capitalizing on its brand's name-recognition as a prestige marker in a way that the University of Phoenix (or any public university) cannot. A limited number of top institutions, he says, will "get the best of both worlds, reigning supreme in their own domain" of traditional, brick-and-mortar universities, while earning revenue from their online subsidiaries." He predicts that "the richer institutions will pull away from the poorer institutions" even more than they already have and will "form their own tier at the apex of higher education." He even speculates that these top universities, made all the richer by capitalizing on their brand names to market "basic lectures and courses" online, could then "shift back to the tutorial system to differentiate their on-campus education" experience.[22] They will, in other words, offer convenience to one market of students and prestige to another.

A few brand-name universities (most notably NYU, Columbia, Stanford, and Yale) have already taken ambitious, albeit unsuccessful steps in this direction. David Noble offers revealing details about Columbia's high-profile project to found a for-profit online campus called Fathom. In the mid-1990s, the university invested $18.7 million in its start-up, a deal orchestrated by former junk-bond king, Michael Milken. It then invested an additional $10 million to keep the struggling program running before deciding to close it down in 2003. Fathom's failure, though, ultimately illustrates the chasm between wealthy, elite private universities and their budget-conscious public counterparts. In the business world, Fathom's inability to generate money was perceived as the part of the normal risk in any venture capitalist undertaking.[23] As Columbia Business School dean Meyer Feldberg (a friend of Milken's) admitted to the *Wall Street Journal*, "I was less interested in the income stream [that Fathom promised to provide to Columbia] than in the capitalization. The huge upside essentially is the value of the equity in the IPO."[24] For Feldberg, in other words, the primary benefit of Fathom was not direct educational enhancement or even revenue for Columbia that could be channeled back into its traditional classrooms, but rather the potentially enormous profit on the stock exchange for those qualified to invest in Fathom at its initial public offering. Any revenue for Columbia would be a by-product of that profit. The fact that Fathom never did well enough to be brought public merely means that Feldberg and others speculated on the possibility of a huge return on their investment and lost. The setback has not deterred Columbia or its potential financial backers. According to Noble, even as Fathom struggled, Columbia became "party to an agreement with yet another company that intends to peddle its core arts and science courses."[25]

The story of Fathom's failure suggests that Collis's prediction—that the elite universities will adopt Oxford-style tutorial systems subsidized by vast online educational fiefdoms—is not likely to materialize soon. These institutions have yet to solve the problem of how to preserve their aura of exclusivity while at the same time expanding the market for their brand names. This is evident from the defensive press release in which Stanford announced its partnership, in 1999, with the Internet education company UNext.com (whose board of directors includes Milken) to offer a business education curriculum online. Geoffrey Cox, Stanford's vice provost and dean for institutional planning, seemed especially anxious about the possibility of cross-contamination. He makes clear that the UNext courses "will be targeted primarily through corporations at students overseas" and that "they will not compete with Stanford's existing educational opportunities." He added that "while Stanford faculty would help develop UNext's curriculum, they would not be interacting with students. . . . UNext plans to engage professors from other universities to serve in a support role for students taking the Internet courses."[26] As Twitchell and Collis make clear, though, the elite schools have only recently discovered their potential for marketing themselves on a grand scale, and online education still represents largely unexplored territory for them. Institutions as rich as

Columbia and Stanford, with permanently valuable brand names, can re-peatedly try and fail to expand and market themselves online until they eventually hit on the right advertising formula. Their challenge is to create an academic version of the distinction between Giorgio Armani and Arm-ani Emporium. The mass-provider institutions will never be in a position to explore such options.

Money is an equally tangible component of academic prestige and it helps to create a hierarchy not only of schools, but also of disciplines. One often hears the oversimplification that all of higher education is facing a funding crisis. It is more accurate, though, to say that funding for higher education is being reapportioned to the benefit of a handful of institutions to the exclusion of all others and reapportioned to the benefit of practical disciplines at the expense of the humanities. Not counting state funding, a diminishing and precarious source of revenue during the past two dec-ades, here are the top sources of support for higher education in 2003–4: federal government support for research ($21 billion), alumni donations ($6.7 billion), non-alumni individual donations ($5.2 billion), foundations ($6.2 billion), and corporations ($4.4 billion). Only the corporate support is distributed among a fairly mixed group of private and public, selective and non-selective universities. Cornell, Harvard, MIT, Stanford, and Yale receive $760 million, or 11.3 percent of the total alumni contributions. Stanford, Cornell, Harvard, Columbia, and the University of Southern California receive $540 million, or 10.2 percent of the total non-alumni donations. A staggering 5 percent (more than one billion dollars) of the federal research money goes to a single institution, The Johns Hopkins University.[27]

The lists of top recipients of all sources of research funding, though, consist entirely of elite private universities and the flagship institutions of a few states. Take my state, Ohio, as an example. The Ohio State Univer-sity ranks very high as a fund-raiser, drawing especially generous sums from state-located corporations eager for the affiliation. (Ohio State ranks sixth in the country in corporate donations received.) Yet it is the only institution from the state to rate highly on any of the lists. Second place in overall fund-raising in the state goes to the University of Cincinnati, which brings in only one quarter of the amount that Ohio State does. The other twenty-four, public, four-year universities in the state's system get minuscule amounts of money by comparison. Additionally, Ohio is home to the largest number of private, non-profit colleges in the country. With the exception of a few high-profile schools—Denison, Kenyon, and the now fearless Oberlin—these seventy institutions also get by with virtually no significant outside research money.

The inequitable funding trends are unlikely to change as we advance toward the future. In fact, as the National Association of College and University Business Officers suggests, the richest universities will continue to get richer. In 2006, universities with an endowment greater than $1 billion saw their investments increase an average of 15.2 percent, while universities and colleges with endowments of less than $25 million saw increases of only 7.8 percent.[28] As a result of this wealth gap, a great many of the underfunded colleges and universities are choosing to present themselves to the public in a very different way than the research universities do. Some try to stretch beyond their traditional commitment to the liberal arts. Marietta College, founded when Ohio was still part of the Northwest Territory, was initially charged with educating youth in "all the various branches of the liberal arts and sciences." It still does so, but its Web site now presents the liberal arts as the best preparation for "professional life." Others go further. Thomas More College, a poor, nonselective, Catholic school in Cincinnati, touts its "accelerated degree format that enables you to actively promote your career." It is "convenient and designed to fit into your busy schedule." The University of Northwestern Ohio's Web site announces in one of three rotating banner headlines: "Make your move to a great career . . . in the College of Distance Learning."[29] As we have seen, these are precisely the messages of the for-profit universities: utility, convenience, expedited degrees, and online learning options. Any traditional college that adopts these messages is, in effect, crossing a marketing Rubicon, setting itself up as a player in the game of higher education as job training. At the same time, it is conceding the race for prestige to its richer peers.

As James Engell and Anthony Dangerfield note, even some of the well-known, but still poor state university systems are adopting the rhetoric perfected by the for-profits. The state system in Massachusetts advertises "immediate economic utility not only as their chief but as their *only* asset for applicants to consider." When, too, in the late 1990s, then governor Tom Ridge of Pennsylvania advertised his state's universities on national television, he said that the schools "graduated thousands of students each year in computer science and various engineering fields, 'ready for the workforce.'" He mentioned "no other fields and no other conceivable purposes of higher education" beyond immediate job training.[30] This is an unmistakably desperate decision. If they mean what they say, these institutions are opting out of research culture and the intense competition for funding that it now entails and dropping out of the prestige race as well (though it is certainly not clear that this has actually happened at the University of Massachusetts–Amherst or Penn State). Such a surrender may indeed be inevitable, but the schools nonetheless retain, from a business perspective, the baggage of tenure and Byzantine organizational models. These place them at a big disadvantage if they now wish to compete with the for-profits. What will happen to these many colleges and universities? They could very well end up, however reluctantly, partnering with for-profit higher-education companies in what David Kirp predicts as the most likely scenario for the future. Twitchell is more pessimistic. He says flatly that even now, the poorer public and private colleges are "being crushed."[31]

The unequal concentration of outside funding that has stratified America's colleges and universities has also stratified its academic disciplines. Since the bulk of this money, including almost all of the federal resources, is dedicated to research in the sciences and engineering, the humanities has suffered everywhere. John Sommer, among others, worries that the "superenrichment of some fields of study over others" could lead to a "trolling of the leadership and curricula of higher-education institutions in those directions desired by the government elites" whose $21 billion is the largest pool of outside funding.[32] In practice, this means that only the most elite and richest of the brand-name universities will be able to fund their humanities programs generously. The rest, dependent on corporate, government, and private contributions that are earmarked for practical, applications-oriented disciplines will have no choice but to reshape themselves in line with those funding trends.

Steven Brint argues that this stratification of academic disciplines is slowly but surely taking effect, following the pattern of the shrinking of Classics, with which I began my last chapter. He notes that "employment conditions in the arts and sciences have not suffered as much as one might expect given the changing student enrollment pattern." From the late 1980s through the mid-1990s, "when three-fifths of undergraduate degrees . . . were awarded in professional programs, almost half of new hires continued to be in the arts and sciences fields." Hiring, though, is now beginning to conform to student preferences at all but America's richest universities. At underfunded state institutions in particular, "liberal arts faculty have in many cases become providers of distribution requirements for students in departments and schools of professional studies." Without the protection of these requirements, Brint adds, "arts and sciences faculty at institutions such as Central Michigan University, San Jose State University, Sam Houston State University, and the University of Massachusetts–Boston would shrink to a small cadre." By contrast, at the "great majority of the fifty leading research universities," the liberal arts reign supreme and "occupational and professional training is typically highly restricted for undergraduates."[33]

Brint offers a practical explanation of this phenomenon that is reminiscent of C. Wright Mills's theory of America's "power elite." Brint claims that "while public figures rely on technical experts drawn from a variety of fields to help develop and assess policies, they rely almost exclusively on liberal arts faculty and writers influenced by them to define broader themes and to suggest proper contexts for understanding."[34] In addition to this top-down theory, there is a bottom-up connection between the liberal arts and prestige that must be taken into consideration. As the RAND report notes, "those interested in the prestige that goes along with a degree from a specific institution generally do not have specific knowledge-based goals. Instead, they essentially trust that the education offered by the institution is 'good' and will be viewed as such by future employers and society in general."[35] In the context of the changing economics of higher education, however, fewer and fewer students can afford to place their trust in the intangible good that a liberal arts-based education offers and to forgo any specific professional training during their college years. Thus the liberal arts, with the humanities at its core, should continue to flourish only at the fifty or so research universities to which Brint refers. This is, though, an even shorter list than the one hundred most selective schools that Hoxby used as her research database and it represents only around one percent of the total number of higher-education institutions in the country.

In other words, the liberal arts and the humanities sit at the end of a chain reaction that begins with undergraduate admissions policies and ripples through to the very mission of every elite university. An exclusive admissions policy works, however irrationally, to build faith among administrators and students alike in the prestige of their institution. That shared sense of privilege, in turn, makes the university's ability to prepare its students for the workforce a less urgently important concern. It is, after all, the "signaling value" of the institution itself that matters most.[36] Absent the anxiety over offering practical professional training, these few universities continue to maintain a traditional curriculum, one that is favorable to the liberal arts and the humanities.

No humanist should take comfort in the notion of America's elite universities as a last refuge of the liberal arts, though, because those elite institutions' endorsement of the liberal arts is both insecure and tainted by ulterior motives. First, even for most of the elite universities, participating in the ranking schemes that determine their status is ultimately a losing game. In his argument that higher education constitutes the ultimate "winner-take-all market," Frank theorizes that in such markets, "small differences in performance (or even small differences in the credentials used to predict performance) translate into extremely large differences in reward" and that "the rewards tend to be concentrated in the hands of a few top performers."[37] The number of universities left in the highest tier of winners ought, then, to continue to shrink as consumers attach more and more significance to rankings distinctions. That is, the gulf between the top ten schools and numbers eleven through twenty will widen, as will the separation between the number-one-ranked university and all the rest.

Second, the fixation on prestige at the elite universities, while it may seem to work in favor of the humanities, renders the content of the curriculum irrelevant, almost trivial. Peter Drucker claims that the liberal arts survives only as an accessory to status. He argues that members of the older generation in America "still want a liberal arts education for their own children . . . though mainly for social status and access to good jobs. But in their own lives they repudiate such values. They repudiate the educated person of the Humanities."[38] There are subtler, sometimes tragicomic indications; Frank discloses that "respondents in one survey . . . listed Princeton as one of the ten best law schools in the country even though Princeton has never had a law school."[39] "Princeton" is simply a great name to conjure with.

Let us assume that the trends that I have described continue into the future as more and more of the poor colleges, both public and private, are forced to drop out of the competition for prestige, and "brand-name" colleges and universities continue to be very selective in admissions and protected against any pressure to change their mission and curriculum by their generous endowments. What will happen to the humanities and their professors, since I have suggested that neither the traditional disciplines of literature, history, and philosophy nor their scholars can survive if the humanities are supported by only a handful of exclusive institutions? I believe that the fate of the humanities in the next few generations hinges on the flagship state universities and university systems. For a century, they have formed the backbone of American higher education. As I have already noted, Duderstadt and Womack now locate them "beyond the crossroads." We need, then, to examine the relationship of those institutions to academic prestige and its components, exclusivity and wealth.

First, the inability of state universities to be very selective about the students they admit costs them the ability to generate prestige through their undergraduates. This fact rarely gets its fair share of attention, as those most concerned about the difference between elite private and flagship public universities tend to focus on financial issues. However, even if money were equally distributed between the two kinds of institutions, their vastly different admissions policies would still create a glass ceiling. Without the option of rejecting more applicants than they admit, state universities must abandon any claim to exclusivity and thus forego any dream of reaching the apex of the prestige scale. An open letter from Karen Holbrook, then president of Ohio State, to "alumni and friends" of the university puts a happy face on this predestination. She announces "I am pleased to report to you that *U.S. News & World Report*'s 2007 edition of America's Best Colleges, released today, ranks Ohio State among the nation's top 20 public universities. We made a significant move from 21st to a tie for 19th. Among all universities, public and private, Ohio State moved up from 60th to 57th." Holbrook's phrasing drives home the pathetic nature of the claims: she herself separates private from public universities, so as not to emphasize that Ohio State has moved *up* to fifty-seventh among all universities, and she characterizes the move from twenty-first to co-equal nineteenth as "significant." Reading the letter immediately sets one on the challenging task of naming all the universities that rank above Ohio State, the vast majority of them private, smaller, and thus in a position to be selective.[40]

If such testaments to the power of exclusivity seem nebulous and indirect, the evidence about the distribution of wealth across universities is abundant and compelling. Stories about declining state funding for higher education are by now familiar even to those outside the academy, but the extent of the hardship still deserves mention. A report by Illinois State's Center for the Study of Education Policy concludes that the country's state university systems have never really recovered from the four recessions that we have experienced since 1982. For example, as *Inside Higher*

Education reports, "Of the 44 states that cut funds, per full-time equivalent student, in the last recession (of 2001), only one state has seen funds restored so that—adjusting for inflation—spending per student is at least the same as it was pre-recession. Six states have yet to reach the levels they had before the recession of 1990–1."[41] This in turn has led to a widening gap in faculty salaries at public versus private universities and concomitant difficulties for public institutions trying to hire and retain talented professors. Duderstadt and Womack point out that in the early 1970s, public and private faculty salaries were fairly even. Now, the differences are striking, even if we restrict our comparison to doctoral-granting universities. The AAUP lists the following private and public averages for 2006–7: Professor, $136,689 versus $106,495; Associate Professor, $87,512 versus $74,075; Assistant Professor, $75,155 versus $63,131.[42]

How do the flagship state universities pursue prestige even though they are deprived of its most important sources, selective undergraduate admissions and an abundance of money? The answer is that such universities act according to a wholly different logic than their exclusive counterparts.[43] As state funding for public universities has declined, those institutions have been forced to raise their own funds. This implicitly places them in competition with private universities and threatens to alter both the institutional character and the traditional mission of state schools. However, these strictly economic and bureaucratic conclusions must be coupled with an account of how prestige and branding will figure in the increasingly privatized state university.

For a long time, public universities sought branding power through football. High-profile football programs have the advantage of being inexpensive, since ticket and concession sales and merchandising make such programs self-funding (thus state universities can afford them). They also galvanize a big following, as current students, alumni, and ordinary state citizens (who wish they were alumni) come together to root for the Buckeyes, the Fighting Illini, the Golden Gophers. Deprived of the means to enroll only an exclusive cadre of undergraduates or to lavish money on faculty, the flagship state universities competed for prestige by virtue of their sheer gargantuan presence, which gave them great advantages in NCAA sports and still does. Since 1990, only two private universities have won the NCAA championship in football.[44]

Football, though, has now become only one means for a large state university, unable to rely on exclusivity or unlimited money, to promote

its brand name. Now, the flagship state research universities most prominently display *all* aspects of themselves likely to receive extracurricular
publicity, public support, and possible private funding. At Ohio State, this
means the University Hospitals (in particular the James Cancer Research
Institute), the Fisher College of Business, and the Buckeye football team.
Former University of Florida president John Lombardi offered a similar
short list in response to the question of what generates brand value for his
school: "the medical center, the Fighting Gators football team, and the
idea of the school." This last, "the story that the school tells about itself,"
is closely tied to the football program. The campus's University of Florida
Foundation oversees the collection and distribution of $130 million a year
in alumni and non-alumni donations. In front of the Foundation's building, Twitchell reports, "where a statue of some illustrious donor or be-
loved professor would stand at an elite school, is a bronze statue of the
athletic department's trade-marked mascots, Albert and Alberta Alliga-
tor."[45] That football, M.B.A.s, and cures for cancer are unrelated to one
another typifies the confused message of most large state universities and
it reflects their ambiguous mission as well.

Duderstadt and Womack elaborate on this problem: "the new missions
that public universities are pressured to undertake are almost invariably
distant from their core activities. This 'mission creep' is one of the greatest
challenges to the public university."[46] Mission creep or mission multiplication requires the management of university resources across a vast array
of areas, as the flagship state universities increasingly attempt to be all
things to all their citizens and to establish a national reputation as well.
The creep extends to the undergraduate curriculum, as the flagships seek
to offer its heterogeneous student body two choices: the kind of traditional
liberal arts education they might find at an elite university and the kind
of focused professional training that would prepare them for immediate
entrance into the workforce. The result of this mission multiplication is an
amorphous institution that Bill Readings has ridiculed as "the university of
excellence," a concept that he associates with Ohio State president, Gordon Gee. He explains that "as an integrating principle, excellence has the
singular advantage of being entirely meaningless, or to put it more precisely, non-referential." It is thus the ideal umbrella term for a university
whose functions are so scattered. "Its very lack of reference allows excellence to function as a principle of translatability between radically different idioms: parking services and research grants can each be excellent, and

their excellence is not dependent on any specific qualities or effects that they share."[47]

The hyperdiversification of flagship state universities, accomplished despite significant budgetary constraints, all but forces them to operate in a fundamentally different way from their elite counterparts. The flagships, which still educate a large percentage of the country's undergraduates, do not have an exclusive, predominantly wealthy student body and thus the luxury of maintaining a steady focus on the traditional liberal arts. As a consequence, these institutions have come not only to operate, but also to think of themselves as businesses rather than social institutions. The transformation of America's state universities differs importantly from the emergence of the for-profit higher-education industry: the latter sprung up *as* businesses, while the former are now completing a fundamental changeover. That change also marks a step beyond the monetary influence that established corporations have on universities in the form of endowments, directed grants, and other kinds of subsidies. These have been in place for a century. The current transformation is a matter of organizational behavior.

Patricia Gumport, former director of the National Center for Postsecondary Improvement, elaborates on this changeover. She summarizes the traditional logic of the university as social institution:

> Historically, the logic of social institutions has encompassed a wide array of educational and social functions, from instruction to credentialing, to enhancing social mobility and socializing citizens. Over time, this logic has been elaborated into expectations that universities would fulfill a multiplicity of social goals. . . . Foremost among them were beliefs that the university would promote liberal education, protect freedom of inquiry, foster the preservation and advancement of knowledge, and cultivate intellectual pluralism by providing a social space for intelligent conversation, social criticism, and dissent.[48]

Only in fairly recent times have these beliefs and goals drawn heavy criticism as impractical, even undesirable. The attacks on professors that began in the late 1980s, along with the entire conservative side of the Culture Wars in the early 1990s, form a single argument. The mission of the university as a social institution has become diluted and confused, the argument goes, leaving the university divided against itself and unable to benefit the society that it supposedly serves.

This argument always concludes with the call for a return to "traditional" academic values as embodied in the liberal arts and the humanities.

The elite universities have been able to withstand this challenge; though they may have expanded the scope of their inquiry beyond the boundaries of Western culture, they have never deviated from a commitment to the liberal arts in any meaningful way. The great state universities, by contrast, *have* diluted their mission and have had to adopt a different logic in the process. Gumport explains this "industry logic" as large state universities have begun to employ it:

> In contrast to . . . liberal ideals, the industry logic has focused upon vital resources and dynamic markets. . . . Primary goals for public research universities include providing skill training that corresponds to labor market needs and developing knowledge applications that enhance the economy. In their management, universities are expected to attend to the harsh realities of market forces and adopt strategies such as scanning their competitive environments, planning, cutting costs, and re-engineering for efficiency and flexibility. . . . Students tend to be viewed as consumers rather than as members of a campus community.[49]

George Keller, an educational consultant and former president of the University of Maryland system, predicted the shift from social institution logic to industry logic in 1983 in his book *Academic Strategy*. Specifically, he anticipated that the shift would take the form of a "management revolution in higher education." Keller noted when he wrote that "alone among the major institutions in the United States, colleges and universities have steadfastly refused to appropriate the procedures of modern management." However, he observed that a "new era of conscious academic strategy is being born" in direct response to the rising costs of college. Keller declares that "higher education has entered a long period of consumer sovereignty, one which will require a great many adjustments in institutional behavior."[50] Gumport lists the major adjustments: "changing product lines, substituting technology for labor, and reducing fixed costs through such means as outsourcing and privatizing as well as increasing the proportion of part-time and temporary personnel."[51] The new management style goes by names such as Total Quality Management or Responsibility Based Budgeting.

Though no one seems to recognize it as an especially acute problem for the humanities, the management revolution now energetically pursued by public research universities is strikingly at odds with the desire for prestige. Public research universities, I contend, are either unable to choose between these two poles of efficiency and prestige or uncertain that a choice needs to be made. Their paralysis threatens their very future. Here are the terms of their dilemma: flagship state universities are deprived of the status benefits of exclusivity through selective undergraduate admissions, and they are chronically underfunded as well, yet they are eager to vie with their elite counterparts in all areas of higher learning. They can only hope to generate academic (as distinct from athletic or public-service) prestige through their faculty. This means that the flagship state institutions actually have the greatest incentive to pursue prestige through scholarship, academic programs, and faculty hiring. Yet the efficiency-first industry logic they have widely adopted stands philosophically opposed to the quest for prestige and to the notion that the individual accomplishments of professors will somehow contribute to the "signaling power" of the institution as a whole.

So what happens when Total Quality Management clashes with prestige envy? The answer, I believe, is that industry logic subsumes research culture, turning even the quest for prestige into yet another demonstration of efficiency. This in turn determines the whole atmosphere in which state university professors work. Two examples illustrate the crudeness by which state university management now imposes business values on the academic workplace. In 1997, the vice chair of Ohio State University's Research Commission, a thirteen-member unit created by the provost, claimed, without a trace of self-consciousness, "people have accepted the idea that our football team has to be in the top 10, that we want to be No. 1. . . . Academically, though, they've been satisfied with us being a very good university, and few have demanded that we be one of the best universities in the country."[52] The thinking of the Research Commission took the form of the "20/10 Plan," a scheme with the goal of seeing ten of Ohio State's academic departments ranked in the top ten nationally and another twenty ranked in the top twenty by 2010. No one stopped to ask: Why thirty total programs? Why 2010 rather than 2013? Why the top ten and top twenty rather than simply the top fifteen? The bewildering arbitrariness of the plan (appropriately, some might say, propped up by a football analogy which all Ohioans can appreciate) inaugurated an era of preoccupation with national rankings that continues at Ohio State to this day. Undergirding it all are two assumptions: (1) that only businesslike metrics of assessment reflect a university's true quality and (2) that this level of quality can only be determined competitively, with all of the university's academic departments vying for their place in national rankings.

Gumport provides a more detailed example of recent changes at the University of Illinois–Chicago. She quotes extensively from UIC planning documents that detail the university's efforts to upgrade itself as a research institution. The university begins with the assumption, surprisingly unexamined, that prestige through research is the universal goal: "'Everyone wants to be Research I'; we are 'in competition for the research dollars, stellar faculty, and top graduate students. Have we got the ingenuity and resources to successfully compete?'" Pursuing this goal, the UIC administration determines, will require "a coordinated program/unit evaluation linked with budgetary and other planning processes. . . . It is important to keep a scorecard, track progress, and make changes when necessary." They hope, in other words, to gain prestige in research by transforming their university into a model of competitive efficiency. They formalize their ambitions in the terms of industry logic, in which "excellence" and sustained growth figure as the proof of their success:

> *Goal*: Develop Ph.D. programs of distinction which reflect the interdisciplinary nature of modern inquiry, and which parallel the growth of UIC research activity. The rapid growth of our research enterprise . . . suggests that we set a goal of developing one to two new Ph.D. programs per year over the next ten years.[53]

Readings argued that the all-purpose use of "excellence" lends itself to marketization, and these examples reveal university administrators openly embracing the notion that faculty research, regardless of field, takes place in a market setting. The consequences for professors at public research universities may seem subtle, but are in fact far-reaching. Industry logic dictates that success is measured by growth and increased productivity. University administrators who are guided by this logic are far more likely to trust quantitative rather than qualitative assessment and to assume that more is always better. This means not only setting goals such as increasing the number of Ph.D. programs, but also reconceiving of faculty research as an output that must not only constantly be increased, but also be constantly and methodically measured.

In the face of the trends that I have described here, it seems to me that professors of humanities can resist their extinction only by shifting the focus of their attention in two important ways. First, rather than merely opposing the corporate assumptions that threaten their disciplines, humanists must challenge those assumptions along different lines. If we constantly meet the corporate model of higher education with skepticism, we might keep its most precious tenets from becoming articles of faith for everyone: students, society at large, even disempowered humanists. Central among these tenets is the assumption that a practical, occupation-oriented college education leads to a secure job and thus is crucial to improving one's quality of life. As I have described, over the past thirty years, more people than ever are going to college; more of them are choosing to major outside the liberal arts in fields that promise them immediate entry into growing professions with high employer demand. More students than ever are also opting to attend institutions that are wholly devoted to such professional preparation. As James Traub, former president of the University of Phoenix puts it, "the people who are our students don't want an education. They want what the education provides for them—better jobs, moving up in their careers."[54] Yet during this latest pronounced shift toward vocationalism, the claim that postsecondary education guarantees economic benefits seems never to have been evaluated critically. Most centrally, why, during the last thirty years, when more and more Americans have enrolled in college, are median wages—even for college graduates— declining? Can one make the case that America is increasingly becoming an economy of service work in which the value of all kinds of formal education is bound to diminish? John Aubrey Douglass, a Senior Research Fellow at the Center for Studies in Higher Education at Berkeley, frames his answer as follows: "As the global production of scientists and engineers grows, the rise of new high-technology industries and research clusters outside of the traditional hegemony is altering the flow of talent. Some worry that the US's ability, as well as that of Europe, to attract global talent will, in relative terms, decline."[55] Moreover, the global talent pool is not limited to scientists and engineers, but extends to every discipline covered in America's universities. If Douglass's predictions come true, the role of higher education in the global economy will be to level standards of living across the world. Thus the promise of the for-profits, now adopted by many traditional universities—college will train you for the high-skills–high-tech economy of the future, and set you on the road to prosperity—will be far shakier than is currently advertised.[56]

Yet many of the most insightful studies of the future of American higher education stop well short of the macroeconomic considerations that Douglass takes into account. For example, the lead story of the November 25, 2005 issue of *The Chronicle of Higher Education* looks ten years out at "Higher Education 2015." The article focuses on ten evolving topics that the authors see as the keys to its title question, "How Will the Future

Shake Out?": "Can Small Colleges Survive?", "The Future of Student Aid," "Tapping Boomers for Bucks" (that is, shifting from the government to alumni as the chief source of funding), "Research Inc." (the growing influence of corporations on university research agendas), the "For-Profit Outlook," "The State of Tenure," "Boom States: South and West," "The Shrinking States: Northeast and Midwest," and "America's Brand in the Global Market." The article fails to acknowledge that the last of these issues decisively overrides the nine that precede it, rendering topics like tenure and the fate of small colleges provincial by comparison. In its discussion of American higher education in the global market, the article also takes a narrow focus, emphasizing the problems caused by visa restrictions on foreign students since 9/11, and on theocratic objections to stem cell research as a handicap to American scientists.[57] There is no mention of the Bologna Process, by which forty-five European countries have agreed to shorten the undergraduate degree to three years and make degrees and university course credits transferable across national borders. There is no appreciation, either, for the growing global talent pool that Douglass analyzes, or the likelihood that the talent will concentrate in China, India, and emerging markets, not in the United States.

Most attempts to divine the future of American higher education are, in other words, economically myopic. As a group, humanists seem unwilling to acknowledge how powerless an increasingly global economy and an increasing transnational concentration of wealth actually make them. Their reluctance to do so goes beyond the traditional aversion that academic humanists have always shown toward all things financial. Minimizing the economic realities of higher education represents a desperate attempt by professors to retain some power over its future direction. My point all along has been that if we ever had that kind of power, we do not anymore. At the same time, though, there is ample room for pointing out the fallacies and gross oversimplifications in positions like "The hope of professional success is the best reason to go to college" or "An educated citizenship is good for the nation's economy."[58] We humanists need to keep pointing out the hollowness of such promises, but not in terms that suggest that we have something superior to offer our students, a transcendently "true higher learning" such as Aronowitz envisions.

The second, corollary action that humanists will have to take in order to stave off their disappearance from the university of the future is to balance their commitment to the content of higher education with a thorough familiarity with how the university works. That phrase, the title of

Marc Bousquet's study of higher education, advocates a perspective on academic labor that most humanities professors have been reluctant to adopt.[59] Not only do we need to resist the tendency to romanticize our work, but we also need to locate that work in an assortment of unfamiliar contexts. Many of the developments that I have discussed here—the hyperprofessionalization of academic careers, the rapid erosion of tenure, the rise of for-profit higher education, and the prestige race—seem to have caught professors by surprise, leaving them unprepared to deal with the very phenomena that directly affect their jobs. We seem to have forgotten what C. Wright Mills called "the first lesson of modern sociology": "that the individual cannot understand his own experience or gauge his own fate without locating himself within the trends of his epoch, and the life-chances of all the individuals in his social layer."[60] For professors to do this, and thus forestall their own extinction, they must first become not only sociologists but also institutional historians of their own profession. That is, only by studying the institutional histories of scholarly research, of tenure, of academic status, and, perhaps most important, of the ever-changing college curriculum, can we prepare ourselves for the future.

PREFACE

1. Derek Bok, *Universities in the Marketplace: The Commercialization of Higher Learning* (Princeton, N.J.: Princeton University Press, 2003). David L. Kirp, *Shakespeare, Einstein, and the Bottom Line: The Marketing of Higher Education* (Cambridge, Mass.: Harvard University Press, 2003).

2. J. Wall, *Andrew Carnegie* (New York: Oxford University Press, 1970; rpt. Pittsburgh: University of Pittsburgh Press, 1989), 837; Richard Teller Crane, *The Utility of all Kinds of Higher Schooling* (Chicago: H. O. Shepard, 1909), 106.

3. See Stanley Aronowitz and William DiFazio, *The Jobless Future: Sci-Tech and the Dogma of Work* (Minneapolis: University of Minnesota Press, 1994); and Jeremy Rifkin, *The End of Work: The Decline of the Global Labor Force and the Dawn of the Post-market Era* (New York: Putnam, 1995).

4. David Horowitz, *The Professors: The 101 Most Dangerous Academics in America* (Washington, D.C.: Regnery, 2006).

5. Robert Zemsky, Gregory R. Wegner, and William F. Massy, *Remaking the American University: Market-Smart and Mission-Centered* (New Brunswick, N.J.: Rutgers University Press, 2005).

6. The best explication of this pattern remains Paul J. DiMaggio and Walter W. Powell, "The Iron Cage Revisited: Institutional Isomorphism and Collective Rationality in Organizational Fields," *American Sociological Review* 48 (1983): 147–60.

7. For a rich series of case studies in curricular change, see Elizabeth Renker, *The Origin of American Literature Studies: An Institutional History* (Cambridge: Cambridge University Press, 2007).

8. *New York Times*, May 18, 2007, A16.

9. Eric Jacobs, *Kingsley Amis, A Biography* (London: Hodder and Stoughton, 1995), 143.

CHAPTER I
Rhetoric, History, and the Problems of the Humanities

1. Hayward Keniston, "We Accept our Responsibility for Professional Leadership," *PMLA* 68 (1953): 23.

2. Stanley Aronowitz, in *Will Teach for Food: Academic Labor in Crisis*, ed. Cary Nelson (Minneapolis: University of Minnesota Press, 1997), 188; J. Hillis Miller, "Literary Study in the Transatlantic University," *Profession* 1996, 11.

3. Bill Readings, in *The University in Ruins* (Cambridge, Mass.: Harvard University Press, 1996), 135–49, extends the crisis backward, but only to the student revolts of the late 1960s.

4. Three important exceptions are Christopher Newfield, *Ivy and Industry: Business and the Making of the American University, 1880–1980* (Durham, N.C.: Duke University Press, 2003); Evan Watkins, *Work Time: English Departments and the Circulation of Cultural Value* (Stanford, Calif.: Stanford University Press, 1989); and Clyde Barrow, *Universities and the Capitalist State: Corporate Liberalism and the Reconstruction of American Higher Education* (Madison: University of Wisconsin Press, 1990).

5. U.S. Department of Commerce, *Historical Statistics of the United States, Colonial Times to 1970*, Part 1 (Washington, D.C.: U.S. Department of Commerce, 1976), 255, 383.

6. Quoted in J. Wall, *Andrew Carnegie* (Pittsburgh: University of Pittsburgh Press, 1989; New York: Oxford University Press, 1970), 834–35.

7. Wall, 835, 837.

8. Clarence F. Birdseye, *Individual Training in Our Colleges* (New York: Macmillan, 1907), 156.

9. Richard Teller Crane, *The Utility of all Kinds of Higher Schooling* (Chicago: H. O. Shepard, 1909), 3.

10. J. A. Garraty and M. C. Carnes, *American National Biography* (New York: Oxford University Press, 1988), 674.

11. Crane, *The Demoralization of College Life* (Chicago: H. O. Shepard, 1911), 12.

12. Crane, *Utility*, 107.

13. Crane, *Demoralization*, 5.

14. Crane, *Utility*, 106.

15. Crane, *Demoralization*, 14.

16. Frederick W. Taylor, *The Principles of Scientific Management* (Norwood, Mass.: Plimpton Press, 1911; rpt. Harper and Brothers, 1916), 7.

17. Taylor, 125, 126.

18. Drucker, *Post-capitalist Society* (New York: Harper Business, 1993), 38.

19. David F. Noble, *America by Design: Science, Technology, and the Rise of Corporate Capitalism* (New York: Alfred A. Knopf, 1977), esp. 268–77.

20. Taylor, *Principles*, 128.

21. Drucker *Post-capitalist Society*, 36.

22. Newfield, *Ivy and Industry*, 34.

23. Morris Llewellyn Cooke, *Academic and Industrial Inefficiency: A Report to the Carnegie Foundation for the Advancement of Teaching* (Boston: Merrymount Press, 1910), 22, 24–25.

24. Cooke, 31.

25. Cooke's recommendations, perhaps too far ahead of their time, had no immediate effect on academia beyond a flurry of efficiency studies. See Barrow, 156–57.

26. See in particular James Hulme Canfield, *The College Student and His Problems* (New York: Macmillan, 1902); and Clayton Sedgwick Cooper, *Why Go to College?* (New York: Century, 1912).

27. Wall, 835–36.

28. Allan Nevins, *A Study in Power: John D. Rockefeller, Industrialist and Philanthropist* (New York: Scribner, 1953), 194.

29. Richard Hofstadter, *Anti-Intellectualism in American Life* (New York: Vintage, 1962), 260–61.

30. For the continued influence of this set of assumptions, indeed, an argument nearly identical to Crane's, see Caroline Bird, *The Case Against College* (New York: David McKay, 1975).

31. Thorstein Veblen, *The Higher Learning in America* (1916; New Brunswick, N.J.: Transaction, 1993), 3.

32. Veblen illustrates this claim with an anecdote about "one of the larger, younger and more enterprising universities [clearly Stanford], which built a commodious laboratory, well appointed and adequately decorated" for its biology department. Then, to conserve heating costs, the university administration, "in consultation with a suitable janitor," boarded up the ventilation outlets, leading to a buildup of sewer gas that poisoned (though not fatally) several biology professors (102).

33. Watkins, *Work Time*, 18.

34. Upton Sinclair, *The Goose-Step: A Study in American Education* (Pasadena, Calif.: published by the author, 1923), 164.

35. William Oxley Thompson, "The Spirit of the Land-Grant Institutions," in *The Spirit of the Land-Grant Institutions* (Chicago, 1931), 59–60.

36. This latter reference is to James Garfield's nostalgic look back on his alma mater, Williams College, where Hopkins was president from 1836 to 1872.

37. Aronowitz, in *Will Teach for Food*, 187–88.

38. Sonya Huber, "Faculty Workers: Tenure on the Corporate Assembly Line," in *Campus, Inc.: Corporate Power in the Ivory Tower*, ed. Geoffrey D. White (Amherst, N.Y.: Prometheus Books, 2000), 123.

39. David Damrosch, *We Scholars: Changing the Culture of the University* (Cambridge, Mass.: Harvard University Press, 1995), 86.

40. Aronowitz, in *Will Teach for Food*, 190–91.

41. This sentiment thrives today. Ivar Berg, in his introduction to *The Higher Learning in America*, ridicules a "massive and energetic cornerback" from Texas A&M, whose major is "Recreation, Parks and Tourism" (xlvii).

42. *Commission on the Humanities, Report* (New York; Amer. Council for Learned Soc., 1964), 4; Robert Scholes, "Presidential Address 2004: The Humanities in a Posthumanist World," *PMLA* 120 (2005): 733.

43. For an insightful history of the origins of the Culture Wars, see Mary Burgan, *Where Have the Faculty Gone?: Drift and Decision in Higher Education* (Baltimore: The Johns Hopkins University Press, 2006), 52–65. Burgan also unearths the fact that Lynn V. Cheney, a leader in the conservative attack on higher education in the 1980s and 1990s, wrote her Ph.D. dissertation at the University of Wisconsin on Matthew Arnold (63n.)

44. Charles Sykes, *Profscam: Professors and the Demise of Higher Education* (New York: St. Martin's Press, 1988), 6–7. See also Kimball, *Tenured Radicals*, and D'Souza, *Illiberal Education*.

45. An important exception to professors' general lack of awareness is the work of Gary Rhoades and Sheila Slaughter. See their "Academic Capitalism, Managed Professionals, and Supply-Side Higher Education," in *Chalk Lines: The Politics of Work in the Managed University*, ed. Randy Martin (Durham, N.C.: Duke University Press, 1998), 33–68; also Rhoades, *Managed Professionals: Unionized Faculty and Restructuring Academic Labor* (Albany: State University of New York Press, 1998).

46. Fish, *Professional Correctness: Literary Studies and Political Change* (Oxford: Clarendon Press, 1995), 118.

47. Fish concludes that "the public justification of academic practices is too important a task to be left to academics." He also fantasizes that we should hire lobbyists, "experts at thinking of ways to grab huge hunks of newspaper space or air time and fill it with celebrations of the university so compelling that millions of Americans will go to bed thankful that the members of the Duke English Department are assuring the survival and improvement of Western civilization" (126).

CHAPTER 2

Competing in Academia

1. Calvin Trillin, "U.S. Journal: Manhattan. Thoughts on Changing the Rules," *The New Yorker*, 7 March 1977, 84, 86.

2. Ben Morreale, *Down and Out in Academia* (New York: Pitman, 1972), 233.

3. Both Breneman's dissertation and Kerr's remarks are discussed in Gary North, "The Ph.D. Glut Revisited," http://www.lewrockwell.com/north/north.427.html, 24 January 2006 (accessed February 2006).

4. John H. Raleigh, "The Function of the English Department Placement Officer," *ADE Bulletin* 3 (October, 1964): 5–6.

5. Quoted in Kathy M. Newman, "Poor, Hungry, and Desperate? or Privileged, Histrionic, and Demanding? In Search of the True Meaning of 'Ph.D.,'" in *Will Teach for Food: Academic Labor in Crisis*, ed. Cary Nelson (Minneapolis: University of Minnesota Press, 1997), 81. Wolfe's recent academic novel, *I Am Charlotte Simmons* (New York: Farrar, Straus and Giroux, 2004), focuses exclusively on the undergraduate experience.

6. Michael T. Nettles and Catherine M. Millett, *Three Magic Letters: Getting to Ph.D.* (Baltimore: Johns Hopkins University Press, 2006), 7.

7. Doug Steward, "Report on Data from the 2004–2005 MLA Guide to Doctoral Programs in English and Other Modern Languages," *ADE Bulletin* 140 (2006): 65.

8. Nettles and Millett, 119.

9. Steward, "Report on Data," 64–65.

10. Doug Steward, "Report on the Survey of Earned Doctorates, 2004," *ADE Bulletin* 140 (2006): 83.

11. Nettles and Millett, 119–20. See Bernard Berelson, *Graduate Education in the United States* (New York: McGraw Hill, 1960); and Barbara Lovitts, *Leaving the Ivory Tower: The Causes and Consequences of Departure from Doctoral Study* (Lanham, Md.: Rowman and Littlefield, 2001).

12. Nettles and Millett, 184–85. Those students with higher GRE scores who remain in graduate school also tend on average to take longer to complete their Ph.D.s.

13. Chris Golde, "The Role of the Department and Discipline in Doctoral Attrition: Lessons from Four Departments," *Journal of Higher Education* 76 (December, 2005): 676–77.

14. Nettles and Millett, 95. Lovitts states plainly that "a student's relationship with her or his advisor is probably the single most critical factor in determining who stays and who leaves" (270).

15. Jody Nyquist et al., "On the Road to Becoming a Professor: The Graduate Student Experience," *Change* (May/June, 1999): 11. For an insightful meditation on this split, see Judith Fetterley, "Teaching and 'My Work,'" *American Literary History* 17, 4 (Winter 2005): 741–52.

16. Golde, "Should I Stay or Should I Go? Student Descriptions of the Doctoral Attrition Process," *Review of Higher Education* 23 (2000): 217; "The Role of the Department," 682, 688–89.

17. Golde, "Role of the Department," 684, 689.

18. Louise Mowder, "Time out of Mind: Graduate Students in the Institution of English," in *The Institution of Literature*, ed. Jeffrey Williams (Albany: State University of New York Press, 2001), 235. R. P. Blackmur, *The Lion and the Honeycomb: Essays in Solicitude and Critique* (New York: Harcourt, Brace,

1955), 25. Blackmur wrote this collection of essays after he had accepted a teaching position at Princeton, but he benefited from his outsider's perspective on higher education. He never received a college diploma, let alone a Ph.D.

19. Barbara E. Lovitts and Cary Nelson, "The Hidden Crisis in Graduate Education: Attrition from Ph.D. Programs," *Academe* 86 (November/December 2000), 3 (online version).

20. Golde, "Role of the Department," 693.

21. John Guillory, "Preprofessionalism: What Graduate Students Want," *ADE Bulletin* 113 (Spring, 1996): 4.

22. The most recent MLA survey places the average annual earned income of English graduate students at $13,200 (Steward, "Report," 75).

23. Cary Nelson and Stephen Watt, *Office Hours: Activism and Change in the Academy* (New York: Routledge, 2004), 53–69. Special thanks to Stephen Watt for elaborating on and updating this report for me. Watt's most ominous new detail is that between 1999 and 2004, graduate student debt increased by an average of 25 percent.

24. David Laurence and Doug Steward, "Placement Outcomes for Modern Language PhDs: Findings from the MLA's Surveys on PhD Placement," *ADE Bulletin* 138–39 (Fall 2005–Spring 2006): 103–22.

25. Marc Bousquet, "The Rhetoric of 'Job Market' and the Reality of the Academic Labor System," *College English* 66 (2003): 222.

26. William G. Bowen and Julie Ann Sosa, *Prospects for Faculty in the Arts and Sciences: A Study of Factors Affecting Demand and Supply, 1987–2012* (Princeton, N.J.: Princeton University Press, 1989), 118.

27. Bousquet, 219. The interview of Bowen that Bousquet discusses appears in Denis Magner, "Job Market Blues: Instead of the Anticipated Demand, New Ph.D.'s are Finding Few Openings," *Chronicle of Higher Education*, 27 April 1994, A 17.

28. Jack H. Schuster, "Speculating about the Labor Market for Academic Humanists: 'Once More Into the Breach,'" in *The MLA Guide to the Job Search*, ed. English Showalter et al. (New York: Modern Language Association of America, 1996), 118.

29. Cary Nelson, "What Hath English Wrought: The Corporate University's Fast Food Discipline," *Workplace* 1 (1998) http://workplace-gsc.com/fea tures/nelson.html, 3.

30. *MLA Final Report*, 28.

31. *MLA Final Report*, 34.

32. Karen Sowers-Hoag and Dianne F. Harrison, *Finding an Academic Job* (London: SAGE, 1998), xi, 3.

33. Haverty's essay appears in R. M. McLaren Sawyer et al., eds., *The Art and Politics of College Teaching: A Practical Guide for the Beginning Professor* (New

York: Peter Lang, 1992). The essay is cited in Eva Bueno's harrowing narrative of her various job searches, "On Piranhas, Interviews, and Crossing the River," *Minnesota Review* 45 (1997): 215–23, which illustrates that getting a college teaching job involves little politics and certainly no art.

34. Emily Toth, *Ms. Mentor's Impeccable Advice for Women in Academia* (Philadelphia: University of Pennsylvania Press, 1997), 18–19.

35. For an insightful critique of the academic self-help genre in general, and Ms. Mentor in particular, see Janet Badia and Jennifer Phegley, "Ms. Mentor and the Perils of Advice: (Re)Imagining Women's Authority in the Academy," *Professional Studies Review* (Spring, 2006): 1–15.

36. Terry Caesar, *Conspiring With Forms: Life in Academic Texts* (Athens: University of Georgia Press, 1992), 59.

37. "MLA Ad Hoc Committee on the Future of Scholarly Publishing," *Profession* 2002, 174.

38. Cathy Davidson, "Understanding the Economy of Scholarly Publishing," *Chronicle of Higher Education*, 3 October 2003, 2 (online version).

39. Jennifer Crewe, "Scholarly Publishing: Why Our Business is Your Business Too," *Profession* 2004, 26. Peter Givler, Executive Director of the American Association of University Presses, estimates the cost at $30,000 to $40,000 (Domna C. Stanton, "Working Through the Crises: A Plan for Action," *Profession* 2004, 40).

40. Derek Krissoff, "Interview with William Germano," *The Exchange* (Spring 2001): 2.

41. See Stanton, 37; and Lindsay Waters, "A Modest Proposal for Preventing the Books of the Members of the MLA from Being a Burden to Their Authors, Publishers, or Audiences," *PMLA* 115 (2000): 316. Stanley Fish unapologetically defends the practice. In his former capacity as Dean of Humanities at the University of Illinois, Chicago, he writes to Waters, "I understand your argument against giving over tenure-judgments to university presses, but as a dean I use the process as a gate-keeping device. I trust presses and their readers more than I trust departments. I hope you are well and that the Harvard Press flourishes so I can too." Lindsay Waters, *Enemies of Promise: Publishing, Perishing, and the Eclipse of Scholarship* (Chicago: Prickly Paradigm Press, 2004), 26–27.

42. See Davidson, 5, who suggests that the subsidies come out of dues paid by universities to national organizations such as the Association of American Universities. An MLA committee, chaired by Cary Nelson, recommended that universities provide the money (*MLA Newsletter*, Fall 2002, 17); as does Judith Ryan, both in an individual essay, "Publishing and Purchasing: The Great Paradigm Shift," *Profession* 2004, 8, and in the "Report of the MLA Ad Hoc Committee" (*Profession* 2002, 184), which she chaired; and Stanton, 35–36. For the counterargument, see Crewe, 26–27.

43. Endorsements of electronic publishing, admittedly more cautious than the proposals for subsidies, include *MLA Newsletter* Fall 2002, 17 and "The Future of Scholarly Publishing," *Profession* 2002, 180–81. See also Crewe, 25, 29.

44. Davidson, 6.

45. Ryan, 11.

46. Robert Markley, "Stop the Presses: A Modest Proposal for Sa(l)vaging Literary Scholarship," *The Eighteenth Century: Theory and Interpretation* 29 (1988): 76.

47. Jeffrey J. Williams, "Editorial Instinct: An Interview with William P. Germano," *Minnesota Review* n.s., 48–49 (1998): 5 (online version).

48. Willis Regier with Jeffrey J. Williams, "In Defense of Academic Publishing: An Interview with Willis Regier," *Minnesota Review* n.s., 61–62 (2004): 3. Actually, the comment is unintentionally complimentary: most professors would be thrilled to hear that their monograph was being stocked at a chain bookstore.

49. Markley, 77.

50. Waters, "A Modest Proposal," 315, 316.

51. Crewe, 27.

52. Davidson, 2; Philip Lewis, "The Publishing Crisis and Tenure Criteria: An Issue for Research Universities?" *Profession* 2004, 19; *MLA Newsletter* Fall 2002, 17; R. Stephen Humphreys, "Why Do We Write Stuff that Even Our Colleagues Don't Want to Read?" in AAUP Symposium, *The Specialized Monograph in Crisis*, September 11–12, 1997, 2, 3 (online proceedings).

53. Regier with Williams, 10.

54. Quoted in Ryan, 7.

55. Zelda Gamson, "The Stratification of the Academy," in *Chalk Lines: The Politics of Work in the Managed University*, ed. Randy Martin (Durham, N.C.: Duke University Press, 1998), 109.

56. Markley, 77.

57. Greenblatt's letter can be found at http://www.mla.org/resources/doc uments/rep_scholarly_pub/scholarly_pub.

58. *MLA Task Force on Evaluating Scholarship for Tenure and Promotion* (2006), 29.

59. Deborah C. Rohde, *In Pursuit of Knowledge: Scholars, Status, and Academic Culture* (Stanford, Calif.: Stanford University Press, 2006), 29. Rohde cites David P. Hamilton, "Research Papers: Who's Uncited Now?" *Science* 251 (January, 1991): 25

60. Philip Lewis, 21.

61. Martin Anderson, *Imposters in the Temple: A Blueprint for Improving Higher Education in America* (Stanford, Calif.: Hoover Institute, 1996), 84, quotes from a speech by Kennedy given on March 3, 1991. See also, Kennedy, *Academic Duty* (Cambridge, Mass.: Harvard University Press, 1997).

62. *MLA Task Force Report*, 17–18.

63. Russell Jacoby, *The Last Intellectuals* (New York: Basic Books, 1987), 7. Anderson, 118.

64. Ernest Boyer, *Scholarship Reconsidered: Priorities of the Professoriate* (Princeton: Carnegie Foundation for the Advancement of Teaching, 1990), 24. Robert Scholes, "Learning and Teaching," *Profession* 2004, 123.

65. Rohde, 50. Other recent discussions of this topic include Thomas J. Tighe, *Who's in Charge of America's Research Universities?: A Blueprint for Reform* (Albany: State University of New York Press, 2003), 90–106; James Axtell, *The Pleasures of Academe: A Celebration and Defense of Higher Education* (Lincoln: University of Nebraska Press, 1998), 3–68; and Phillip C. Wankat, *The Effective, Efficient Professor: Teaching, Scholarship, and Service* (Boston: Allyn and Unwin, 2002), 210–35.

66. Lionel S. Lewis, *Scaling the Ivory Tower: Merit and Its Limits in Academic Careers* (Baltimore: Johns Hopkins University Press, 1975; rpt. Transaction, 1997), 4, 7. Lewis's first chapter, "Higher Education and the Principle of Merit" (1–18), is a gold mine of information on the early decades of research culture in American higher education. The argument of his book, that merit as a norm is subject to all kinds of professional and personal influences, is still highly relevant today.

67. Quoted in Lionel Lewis, 3.

68. Quoted in Boyer, 4.

69. Quoted in Lionel Lewis, 5.

70. Lionel Lewis, 31–32, quotes *College and University Faculty: A Statistical Description*, American Council on Education Research, Report 5, no. 5 (Washington, D.C., 1970).

71. Boyer, 11.

72. Robert M. Diamond, "Changing Priorities and the Faculty Reward System," in *Recognizing Faculty Work: Reward Systems for the Year 2000*, ed. Diamond Adam and Bronwyn E. Adam (San Francisco: Jossey-Bass, 1993), 21. See also James S. Fairweather, *Faculty Work and Public Trust: Restoring the Value of Teaching and Public Service in American Academic Life* (Boston: Allyn and Bacon, 1996), xi–xv, 191; Gamson, in *Chalk Lines*, 108.

73. The classic theoretical discussion of this phenomenon is Paul S. DiMaggio and Walter W. Powell, "The Iron Cage Revisited: Institutional Isomorphism and Collective Rationality in Organizational Fields," *American Sociological Review* 48 (1983): 147–60.

74. Boyer, 12; Magali Sarfatti Larson, *The Rise of Professionalism: A Sociological Analysis* (Berkeley: University of California Press, 1977), 227.

75. Gamson, in *Chalk Lines*, 105, 106.

76. The Carnegie classification system organizes universities by kinds and varieties of degrees granted. Research I universities offer Ph.D.s in 50 or more

disciplines, Research II universities offer Ph.D.s in 20 or more disciplines, Master's degree universities offer the M.A. as the highest degree, and so on. Since the classification system is presented, at least implicitly, as a hierarchy based on graduate education and advanced degrees, it supports the proliferation of research culture.

CHAPTER 3
The Erosion of Tenure

1. AAUP, "Trends in Faculty Status, 1975–2003, http://www.aaup.org/AAUP/pubsres/research/trends1975–2003.htm (accessed August 2005). The survey counts graduate students teaching at colleges and universities other than their home institutions as non-tenure-track faculty.

2. Department of Education Web site, National Study of Postsecondary Faculty. Useful digests of this information can be found in *NEA Higher Education Resource Center* 7 (2001): 1–8 and John Lee and Sue Clery, "Key Trends in Higher Education," *American Academic* 1 (2004): 30–33.

3. Michael Dubson, ed., *Ghosts in the Classroom: Adjunct Faculty and the Price We All Pay* (Boston: Camel's Back Books, 2001), 36.

4. Roger G. Baldwin and Jay L. Chronister, "What Happened to the Tenure Track?" in Richard Chait, *'The Question of Tenure* (Cambridge, Mass.: Harvard University Press, 2002), 129. See also http://insidehighered.com/news/2006/12/11/aaup (accessed December 2006).

5. Gary Rhoades and Sheila Slaughter, "Academic Capitalism, Managed Professionals, and Supply-Side Higher Education," in *Chalk Lines*, ed. Martin, 47.

6. Wesley Schumer and Jonathan T. Church, "Above and Below: Mapping Social Positions within the Academy," in *Cogs in the Classroom Factory: The Changing Ideology of Academic Life*, ed. Deborah M. Herman and Julie M. Schmid (Westport, Conn.: Praeger, 2003), 30.

7. *St. Petersburg Times*, http://www.sptimes.com/2005/12/09/news_pf/Worldandnation/Battered_by...Kat rina (accessed May 2007); http://www.aaup.org/AAUP/pubsres/academe/2006/MA/kat.htm. Under the direction of its president, Cary Nelson, the AAUP conducted an expansive investigation into the Katrina-related layoffs, and on June 9, 2007, placed Loyola University, Southern University at New Orleans, University of New Orleans, and Tulane on its censure list. http://insidehighered.com/news/2007/06/11/aaup (accessed June 2007). The full AAUP report can be found at http://www.aaup.org/AAUP/protect/academicfreedom/investrep/2007/katrina/htm.

8. In a development that is, at least nominally, unrelated to the layoffs prompted by Katrina, the main campus of Antioch University, one of the oldest progressive liberal-arts colleges in the country (founded in 1852), announced on June 13, 2007 that it was closing due to financial exigency until

2012. Forty faculty members lost their jobs, and when the university reopens, it will likely be staffed entirely by adjuncts, as are Antioch's other campuses around the country. http://insidehighered.com/news/2007/06/13/antioch and http://insidehighered.com/news/2007/06/26/antioch (accessed June, 2007).

9. Judith Gappa and David Leslie, *The Invisible Faculty: Improving the Status of Part-Timers in Higher Education* (San Francisco: Jossey-Bass, 1993), 105.

10. AAUP Report. See also http://insidehighered.com/news/2006/12/11/aaup (accessed December 2006).

11. Gary Rhoades, *Managed Professionals: Unionized Faculty and Restructuring Academic Labor* (Albany: State University of New York Press, 1998), 136.

12. Chait, ed., *The Question of Tenure*, 19.

13. Stefano Harney and Frederick Moten, in *Chalk Lines*, ed. Martin, 155. Marc Bousquet, "The Waste Product of Graduate Education: Toward a Dictatorship of the Flexible," *Social Text* 20, no. 1 (2001): 81–104.

14. For summaries of the three plans, see http://insidehighered.com/news/2006/09/13/aaup (accessed September 2006), http://insidehighered.com/news/2007/03/05/adjuncts (accessed March 2007), and http://insidehighered.com/news/2006/11/30/fulltime (accessed November 2006). For recent hiring trends, see National Center for Educational Statistics, "Employees in Postsecondary Institutions, Fall 2005, and Salaries of Full-Time Instructional Faculty, 2005–06" (Washington, D.C.: U.S. Department of Education). The report is summarized in http://insidehighered.com/news/2007/03/28/faculty (accessed March 2007).

15. Stanley Aronowitz, "The Last Good Job in America," in *Chalk Lines*, ed. Martin, 202–24. Henry Rosovsky, *The University: An Owner's Manual* (New York: W. W. Norton, 1990), 186.

16. Terry Caesar, *Writing in Disguise: Academic Life in Subordination* (Athens: Ohio University Press, 1998), 113. See also Caesar's "On Teaching at a Second-Rate University," in *Conspiring With Forms: Life in Academic Texts* (Athens: University of Georgia Press, 1992), 145–66. Davidson's memoir is *36 Views of Mount Fuji: On Finding Myself in Japan* (New York: Plume, 1994).

17. Martin Scott, "Pagers, Nikes and Wordsworth: Teaching College English in a Shopping Mall," *Profession* 2001, 93–94.

18. Valerie M. Conley and David W. Leslie, *1993 National Study of Postsecondary Faculty and Staff: Who They Are, What They Do, and What They Think*, NCES 2002–193 (Washington, D.C.: U.S. Department of Education, National Center for Education Statistics, 2002), 20–21.

19. Dubson, ed., *Ghosts*, 36. Caesar, *Writing in Disguise*, 124–25.

20. Ben Hamper, *Rivethead: Tales from the Assembly Line* (New York: Warner Books, 1991), 74.

21. Dubson, ed., *Ghosts*, 10, 16, 38.

22. Dubson, ed. *Ghosts*, 10, 29; Scott, in *Profession*, 96.

23. Ross, "The Mental Labor Problem," *Social Text* 18, no. 2 (2000): 1–31.

24. Micki McGee, "Hooked on Education and Other Tales from Adjunct Faculty Organizing," *Social Text* 20, no. 1 (2001): 64, 65.

25. McKee, 67, quoting New York University's adjunct faculty handbook.

26. Rhoades, *Managed Professionals*, 4.

27. Schumer and Church, 33.

28. Gary Rhoades, *Managed Professionals: Unionized Faculty and Restructuring Academic Labor* (Albany: State University of New York Press, 1998), 134.

29. In addition to *The Invisible Faculty* and *Ghosts in the Classroom*, already mentioned, see the Web site *The Invisible Adjunct*, http://www.invisibleadjunct.com.

30. Caesar, *Conspiring with Forms*, 146.

31. Burton Clark, "Faculty Differentiation and Dispersion," in *Higher Learning in America, 1980–2000*, ed. Arthur Levine (Baltimore: Johns Hopkins University Press, 1993), 170, 175.

32. Elliott Krause, *Death of the Guilds: Professions, States, and the Advance of Capitalism, 1930 to the Present* (New Haven, Conn.: Yale University Press, 1996), 33, 22.

33. Steven Brint, *In An Age of Experts: The Changing Role of Professionals in Politics and Public Life* (Princeton, N.J.: Princeton University Press, 1994), 7. Brint quotes R. H. Tawney, *The Acquisitive Society* (1921; rpt. London: Fontana, 1961), 94–95.

34. JoAnne Brown explains this phenomenon somewhat differently as a measure of self-preservation. She argues that all professions seek to monopolize their knowledge "so that it is incomprehensible" in order to make it marketable. At the same time they try to popularize their contribution to society. "In the course of solving this dilemma, professionals create special forms of argument that explain the profession to its clients without revealing its secrets." See "Professional Language: Words that Succeed," *Radical History Review* 34 (1986): 33–51. Brown's work draws on Paul Starr, *The Social Transformation of American Medicine* (New York: Basic Books, 1982).

35. James Engell and Anthony Dangerfield, "Humanities in the Age of Money," *The Harvard Review* (May-June, 1998), 52.

36. Derek Bok, *Universities in the Marketplace: The Commercialization of Higher Learning* (Princeton, N.J.: Princeton University Press, 2003), 5.

37. See Annette Kolodny, "'60 Minutes' at the University of Arizona: The Polemic Against Tenure," *New Literary History* 27 (1996): 679–704. Kolodny refers to a tape cassette in which Leslie Stahl reveals that "60 Minutes" "had come to the University of Arizona expecting to film a polemic against tenure" (682).

38. Louis Menand, ed., *The Future of Academic Freedom* (Chicago: University of Chicago Press, 1996), 4. Fritz Machlup, quoted in Lionel S. Lewis,

Scaling the Ivory Tower: Merit and Its Limits in Academic Careers (Baltimore: Johns Hopkins University Press, 1975; rpt. Transaction, 1997), 25. Walter Metzger, *Dimensions of Academic Freedom* (Urbana: University of Illinois Press, 1969), 1.

39. The brochure can be found at http://www.nea.org/he/tenure.html.

40. For interesting reflections on this point, see Gerald Graff, *Clueless in Academe: How Schooling Obscures the Life of the Mind* (New Haven, Conn.: Yale University Press, 2003).

41. These examples from the earliest AAUP investigation are collected in *Professors on Guard: The First AAUP Investigations*, ed. Walter Metzger (New York: AMS Press, 1977).

42. Metzger, in *Freedom and Tenure in the Academy*, ed. William Van Alstyne (Durham: Duke University Press, 1993), 65.

43. The 1915 *Declaraton* can be found at http://www.campus-watch.org/article/id/566. Page numbers refer to this online version.

44. Metzger, in Van Alstyne, 15.

45. Metzger, in Van Alstyne, 12. The 1940 *Statement* can be found at http://www.aaup.org/statements/Redbook/1940stat.htm. Page numbers refer to this online version.

46. Though the phrase seems to have been coined by Roger Kimball, *Tenured Radicals: How Politics Has Corrupted Higher Edcucation* (New York: Harper and Row, 1990), Cary Nelson takes it as a compliment in *Manifesto of a Tenured Radical* (New York: New York University Press, 1997).

47. John C. Livingston, "Tenure Everyone?" in Bardwell L. Smith and Associates, *The Tenure Debate* (San Francisco: Jossey-Bass, 1973), 69.

48. Jon Huer, *Tenure for Socrates: A Study in the Betrayal of the American Professor* (New York: Bergin and Garvey, 1991), 12, 32.

49. See also, Zachary Karabell, *What's College For? The Struggle to Define American Higher Education* (New York: Basic Books, 1998), 94–95; and Rosovsky, 136. It is worth noting that Huer states in his acknowledgments that "this book could not have been written (unless I were insane) without the . . . protection of tenure."

50. Jeffrey J. Williams, "Smart," *Minnesota Review* n.s., 61–62 (2004): 3, http://www.theminnesotareview.org/ns61/williams.htm.

51. Bruce Wiltshire, *The Moral Collapse of the University: Professionalism, Purity, and Alienation* (Albany: State University of New York Press, 1990), 252.

52. Chait, *Question of Tenure*, 9, 6.

53. Chait, 9, 12, 13, 15.

54. Martin Anderson, *Imposters in the Temple: A Blueprint for Improving Higher Education in America* (Stanford: Hoover Institute, 1996), 121. Donald Kennedy, *Academic Duty* (Cambridge: Harvard University Press, 1997), 131.

55. Kennedy, 138–39, 2–3. Anderson, 39.

56. Richard Huber, *How Professors Play the Cat Guarding the Cream: Why We're Paying More and Getting Less in Higher Education* (Fairfax, Va.: George Mason University Press, 1992), 30.

57. Anderson, 50. See also 70.

58. Gideon Lewis-Kraus, "In the Penthouse of the Ivory Tower," *Believer* (July 2004): 3.

59. Caesar, noted earlier, and James Phelan, *Beyond the Tenure Track* (Columbus: Ohio State University Press, 1996), are two exceptions, though their vast differences from each other stymie any attempt to draw general conclusions.

60. Quoted in *Chalk Lines*, ed. Martin, 189.

61. Richard Ohmann, "Accountability and the Conditions for Curricular Change," in *Beyond English Inc.: Curricular Reform in a Global Economy*, ed. David A. Downing, Claude Mark Hurlbert, and Paula Mathieu (Portsmouth: N.H., Boynton/Cook, 2002), 71.

CHAPTER 4
Professors of the Future

1. Francis Wayland, *Thoughts on the Present Collegiate System in the United States* (1842), quoted in Richard Hofstadter and C. DeWitt Hardy, *The Development and Scope of Higher Education in the United States* (New York: Columbia University Press, 1952), 24–25.

2. Wayland neatly anticipates Marxist critiques of formal education, especially Ivan Illich, *Deschooling Society* (London: Marion Boyars, 1970); and Samuel Bowles and Herbert Gintis, *Schooling in Capitalist America: Educational Reform and the Contradictions of Economic Life* (New York: Basic Books, 1976).

3. The phrase "educational passport," originally from Illich (14), is used in Arthur E. Levine's provocative essay "The Future of Colleges: 9 Inevitable Changes," *Chronicle of Higher Education*, October 27, 2000 (online version).

4. Mary Burgan, *What Ever Happened to the Faculty?: Drift and Decision in Higher Education* (Baltimore: The Johns Hopkins University Press, 2006), xvi.

5. On the latter, see J. Hillis Miller, *Black Holes*, especially "Literary Study in the Transnational University" (Stanford, Calif.: Stanford University Press, 1999), 3–184.

6. For the debate about the free elective curriculum, see W. B. Carnochan, *The Battleground of the Curriculum: Liberal Education and the American Experience* (Stanford, Calif.: Stanford University Press, 1993), 9–21.

7. Robert Scholes, *The Rise and Fall of English: Reconstructing English as a Discipline* (New Haven, Conn.: Yale University Press, 1998), 2.

8. Victor David Hanson and John Heath, *Who Killed Homer?: The Demise of Classical Education and the Recovery of Greek Wisdom* (San Francisco: Encounter Books, 2001), 3.

9. Hanson and Heath claim that "at the two institutions [Rollins College and California State University at Fresno] where we each created Classics programs *ex nihilo* in the mid-1980s, Classics is now essentially moribund." They detail budget cuts that eliminated all tenure-track Classics appointments at Rollins, and that reduced the number of full-time Classics positions at Cal State Fresno from four to two. *Who Killed Homer?* 4.

10. *Who Killed Homer?*'s predecessor, *The Closing of the American Mind* (New York, 1987), by classicist Allan Bloom, falls into this category, as do Darryl J. Gless and Barbara Herrnstein Smith, eds., *The Politics of a Liberal Education* (Durham, N.C.: Duke University Press, 1992).

11. Stanley J. Aronowitz, *The Knowledge Factory* (Boston: Beacon Press, 2000), 161.

12. Hofstadter and Hardy, 103.

13. Dominic J. Brewer, Susan M. Gates, and Charles A. Goldman, *In Pursuit of Prestige: Strategy and Competition in U.S. Higher Education* (RAND report, June 2001), http://www.rand.org/pubs/drafts/DRU2541, 15. The RAND report is a companion piece to the authors' *In Pursuit of Prestige: Strategy and Competition in U.S. Higher Education* (New Brunswick, N.J.: Transaction Press, 2001).

14. A recent iteration appears in financial guru Suze Orman's best-selling book, *The Money Book for the Young, Fabulous, and Broke* (New York: Riverhead Books, 2005), 119.

15. C. Wright Mills discusses much smaller income inequities between college graduates and high-school graduates in *White Collar* (New York: Oxford University Press, 1951), 269–70.

16. James Duderstadt and Farris W. Womack, *The Future of the Public University in America: Beyond the Crossroads* (Baltimore: Johns Hopkins University Press, 2003).

17. College Board's Annual Survey of Colleges, http://www.collegeboard .com/prod_downloads/pres/cost05/trends_college_ pricing_05.pdf (accessed May 2007).

18. U.S. Department of Education, National Center for Education Statistics, *The Condition of Education, 2002,* 195. Moffatt estimates that "one-eighth [of the undergraduates that he studies] work at jobs between one and four hours a day." *Coming of Age in New Jersey: College and American Culture* (New Brunswick, N.J.: Rutgers University Press, 1989), 32.

19. Duderstadt and Womack, 37. College Board's Annual Survey of Colleges, www.collegeboard.com/prod_downloads/pres/cost05/trends_college (accessed April 2007).

20. *Wall Street Journal* online, July 19, 2005.

21. Brewer et al., *In Pursuit of Prestige,* 15, quoting a GAO survey. The RAND report also raises the troubling possibility that a great many people

simply *assume* that college is unaffordable. A 1996 survey by the American Council on Education found that "of 1000 adults, all overestimated the actual average price of college" (16).

22. Alexander W. Astin, et al., *The American Freshman: Thirty-Five-Year Trends, 1966–2001* (University of California, Los Angeles: Higher Education Research Institute Graduate School of Education & Information Studies, 2002), 58–59.

23. For the history of community colleges, see Steven Brint and Jerome Karabell, *The Diverted Dream: Community Colleges and the Promise of Educational Opportunity in America, 1900–1985* (New York: Oxford University Press, 1989).

24. David W. Breneman, Brian Pusser, and Sarah E. Turner, eds., *Earnings from Learning: The Rise of For-Profit Universities* (Albany: State University of New York Press, 2006), 60–61.

25. See Ross Gregory Douthat, *Privilege: Harvard and the Education of the Ruling Class* (New York: Hyperion, 2005); Jerome Karabell, *The Chosen: The Hidden History of Admission and Exclusion at Harvard, Yale and Princeton* (New York: Houghton Mifflin, 2005); and Jacques Steinberg, *The Gatekeepers: Inside the Admissions Process at a Premier College* (New York: Penguin, 2003).

26. "Status" is admittedly a loose term. For the contexts in which I use it here, see Mills, *White Collar*, especially 239–58.

27. http://sports.espn.go.com/nfl/news/story?id = 2603052 (September 26, 2006, accessed September 2006). For a historical account tying the for-profits to correspondence schools, see David F. Noble, *Digital Diploma Mills: The Automation of Higher Education* (New York: Monthly Review Press, 2001).

28. Kirp, 243.

29. John Sperling, *Rebel With a Cause: The Entrepreneur Who Created the University of Phoenix and the For-Profit Revolution in Higher Education* (Hoboken, N.J.: Wiley, 2000), 79.

30. Breneman, Pusser, and Turner, eds. *Earnings from Learning*, 7.

31. *Chronicle of Higher Education*, May 11, 2001, A32.

32. Columbine Capital Services, analyst report on Laureate Education.

33. http://insidehighered.com/news/2006/03/07/edmanagement (accessed June 2006).

34. http://ittesi.com/ireye/ir_site.2html?ticker = esi8script = 2100; http://www.strayereducation.com/profile.cfm; http://www.devryinc.com/corporate_information/mission_values.jsp; http://www.apollogrp.edu/AnnualReports/2005pdf (all accessed May 2007).

35. *Earnings from Learning*, 72.

36. David J. Collis, "New Business Models for Higher Education," in *The Future of the City of Intellect: The Changing American University*, ed. Steven Brint (Stanford, Calif.: Stanford University Press, 2002), 191.

37. Ana Marie Cox, "None of Your Business: The Rise of the University of Phoenix and For-Profit Education—and Why It Will Fail Us All," in *Steal This University: The Rise of the Corporate University and the Academic Labor Movement*, by Benjamin Johnson et al. (New York: Routledge, 2003), 19.

38. Kirp, 244–45.

39. Ruch, 17.

40. Ruch, 119.

41. David L. Kirp, *Shakespeare, Einstein, and the Bottom Line: The Marketing of Higher Education* (Cambridge, Mass.: Harvard University Press, 2003), 248.

42. Ruch, 116, 14.

43. Ruch, 88, 118.

44. Dan Carnevale, "Kaplan U. Professors Seek Faculty Union," *Chronicle of Higher Education*, March 24, 2006, A37.

45. Washburn and Press, "Digital Diplomas," *Mother Jones*, January 1, 2001, p. 1.

46. Apollo Group, Inc., *2000 Annual Report*, 2.

47. Goldie Blumenstein, "Boom in Online Programs Will Drive Growth of For-Profit Education, Analysts Predict," *Chronicle of Higher Education*, December 13, 2005, http://chronicle.com/temp/email.php?id=zqtgg5obnl4 kcnn5rd1hiblsmawghmk (accessed December 2005).

48. William F. Massy and Robert Zemsky, "Using Information Technology to Enhance Academic Productivity," http://www.educause.edu/ir/library/html/nli0004.html, 2.

49. Carol A. Twigg, "Improving Learning and Reducing Costs: New Models for Online Learning," *Educause Review* (September/October 2003), 30, 38.

50. Twigg, 30.

51. Carol A. Twigg and Diana G. Oblinger, "The Virtual University," A Report from a Joint Educom/IBM Roundtable, Washington, D.C.: November 5–6, 1996, http://www.educause.edu/nlii/vu.html, 16 (accessed December 2004).

52. Massy and Zemsky, 9–10, 7.

53. Noble, *Digital Diploma Mills*, 32. Washburn cites the accounting firm Coopers and Lybrand on this point.

54. Massy and Zemsky, 3.

55. Clyde W. Barrow makes the point that pressure to phase out instruction in the liberal arts because they were "inefficient areas of investment" began in the early twentieth century. See *Universities and the Capitalist State: Corporate Liberalism and the Reconstruction of American Higher Education* (Madison: University of Wisconsin Press, 1990), 159.

56. *Wall Street Journal*, September 11, 2000.

57. *Investor's Business Daily*, July 25, 2000.

58. *Chicago Sun Times*, November 20, 2000.

59. James P. Miller, "Career Education names new CEO," *Chicago Tribune* online, March 3, 2006. Standard & Poor's stock report on Career Education Corp., May 5, 2007.

60. *Chronicle of Higher Education*, May 21, 2005, A9.

61. *Chronicle of Higher Education*, July 1, 2005, A26.

62. Apollo Group Inc., *2005 Annual Report*.

63. Sam Dillon, "Troubles Grow for a University Built on Profits," *New York Times*, Februrary 11, 2007, http://www.nytimes.com/2007/02/11/educa tion/11phoenix.html?ei=d486046f49 (accessed February 2007).

64. Stephen Burd, "Promises and Profits," *Chronicle of Higher Education*, January 13, 2006, A23.

65. *Chronicle of Higher Education* online, October 29, 2004 (accessed April 2006).

66. http://insidehighered.com/2005/10/13/merger (accessed May 2007).

67. Yahoo Finance, May 18, 2007, http://biz.yahoo.com/seekingalpha/ 070518/35952 (accessed May 2007); *The Motley Fool*, February 9, 2007 and May 4, 2007, http://www.fool.com/investing/small-cap/2007/02/09/black board-gets-high-marks. aspx; http://www.fool.com/investing/small-cap/2007/ 05/04/blackboards-lessons-in-mono polism.aspx.

68. http://insidehighered.com/news/2006/08/18/patent (accessed May 2007).

69. The letter is quoted in its entirety at http://insidehighered.com/news/ 2006/10/27/educause (accessed May 2007).

70. http://www.insidehighered.com/news/2007/02/07/blackboard (accessed May 2007).

71. Carol Twigg, "Academic Productivity: The Case for Instructional Software," http://www.educause.edu/ir/library/html/nli0002.html (accessed May 2005).

72. http://insidehighered.com/news/2007/04/16/aacc (accessed May 2007).

CHAPTER 5
Prestige and Prestige Envy

1. Caroline Hoxby, "The Return to Attending a More Selective College: 1960 to the Present," in *Forum Futures: Exploring the Future of Higher Education, 2000 Papers*, ed. Maureen Devlin and Joel S. Meyerson (San Francisco: Jossey-Bass, 2001), 13–42.

2. "Stacy Berg Dale and Alan B. Krueger, "Estimating the Payoff to Attending a More Selective College: An Application of Selection on Observables and Unobservables," *The Quarterly Journal of Economics* 117 (November, 2002): 1491–527.

3. *Barron's 2005 Guide to the Most Competitive Colleges* (Hauppauge, N.Y.: Barron's Educational Series, 2005); *U.S. News & World Report, Ultimate Guide to College 2006* (Naperville, Ill.: Sourcebooks, Inc., 2005); *Princeton Review, Complete Book of Colleges, 2005* (N.Y.: Random House, 2005).

4. Robert Frank, "Higher Education: The Ultimate Winner-Take-All Market?" in *Forum Futures*, ed. Devlin and Meyerson, 3.

5. Samuel G. Freedman, "In College Frenzy, A Lesson Out of Left Field," *New York Times*, April 26, 2006. See also IvyWise.com.

6. Soares, *The Power of Privilege: Yale and America's Elite Universities* (Stanford, Calif.: Stanford University Press, 2007); Daniel Golden, *The Price of Admission: How America's Ruling Class Buys Its Way into Colleges—and Who Gets Left Outside the Gates* (New York: Random House, 2006), http://insidehigher ed.com/news/2007/04/11/soares, http://insidehighered.com/news/2006/09/05/admit.

7. Piper Fogg, "A New Standard for Measuring Doctoral Programs," *Chronicle of Higher Education*, January 12, 2007.

8. James B. Twitchell, *Branded Nation: The Marketing of Megachurch, College, Inc., and Museumworld* (New York: Simon and Schuster, 2004), 155.

9. http://insidehighered.com/news/2007/04/04/usnews.

10. *College Unranked: Ending the College Admissions Frenzy* (Cambridge, Mass.: Harvard University Press, 2005). See also Lloyd Thacker, ed., *College Unranked: Affirming Educational Values in College Admissions* (The Education Conservancy, 2004), http://insidehighered.com/news/2006/06/14/admit; http://insidehighered.com/news/2007/05/18/usnews; http://insidehighered.com/news/2007/05/07/usnews (accessed May 2007).

11. Matthew Quirk, "The Best Class Money Can Buy," *Atlantic Monthly*, November, 2005: 132.

12. http://insidehighered.com/news/2006/10/03/compensation (accessed October 2006); http://insidehighered.com/news/2007/03/19 (accessed March 2007).

13. Jin and Whalley, Working Paper 12941 (http://www.nber.org/papers/w12941), abstract. See also http://insidehighered.com/news/2007/03/02/us news (accessed March 2007).

14. Alan Finder, "Cornell's Worried Image Makers Wrap Themselves in Ivy," *New York Times*, April 22, 2006.

15. Paul Fain, "Competitive Pressure is Turning Research Universities Into Look-Alike Institutions, Economist Warns," *Chronicle of Higher Education* online (June 11, 2005).

16. Stephen Budinsky, "Brand U.," *New York Times*, April 26, 2006.

17. http://insidehighered.com/news/2006/03/09/oberlin (accessed March 2006. See also http://www.oberlin.edu/admissions.

18. John I. Pulley, "Raising Arizona," *Chronicle of Higher Education*, November 17, 2005, A28.

19. Twitchell, 132–33. Mass-provider universities chafe under the distinction. Ohio State symbolically resists it by insisting that every graduating senior march up to receive his or her diploma personally, thus stretching commencement ceremonies to epic length.

20. Twitchell, 156.

21. Brewer, Gates, and Goldman, *In Pursuit of Prestige*, 26; Twitchell, 156.

22. David J. Collis, "New Business Models for Higher Education," in *The Future of the City of the Intellect: The Changing American University*, ed. Steven Brint (Stanford, Calif.: Stanford University Press, 2002), 199; " 'When Industries Change' Revisited: New Scenarios for Higher Education," in *Forum Futures*, 114, 115.

23. Indeed, failure, which has always carried the most negative associations in all educational institutions, is not only understood as routine in business, but also even theorized as such. See Tom Peters's classic *Thriving on Chaos* (New York: Harper and Row, 1987).

24. Noble, *Digital Diploma Mills*, 22.

25. Noble, 23.

26. http://www.stanford.edu/dept/news/report/news/june30/unext 630.html (accessed December 2001).

27. *Chronicle of Higher Education, Almanac Issue*, 2005–6.

28. http://insidehighered.com/layout/set/print/news/2006/12/14/nacubo (accessed December 2006).

29. http://marietta.edu, http://www2.thomasmore.edu, http://www .unoh.edu.

30. James Engell and Anthony Dangerfield, *Saving Higher Education in the Age of Money* (Charlottesville and London: University of Virginia Press, 2005), 24–25.

31. Twitchell, *Branded Nation*, 117.

32. RAND report, 52, quoting John Sommer, ed., *The Academy in Crisis: The Political Economy of Higher Education* (Oakland, Calif.: The Independent Institute, 1995).

33. Brint, "The Rise of the 'Practical Arts,' " in *The Future of the City of the Intellect*, 239–240.

34. Brint, "The Rise of the 'Practical Arts,' " 241. See also C. Wright Mills, *The Power Elite* (New York: Oxford University Press, 1957).

35. RAND report, 11.

36. RAND report, 11.

37. Frank, "Higher Education," 5; *Winner-Take-All Society*, 24.

38. Peter F. Drucker, *Post-capitalist Society* (New York: Harper Business, 1993), 213.

39. Frank, *Winner-Take-All Society*, 149.

40. E-mail from Karen A. Holbrook, August 18, 2006.

41. http://insidehighered.com/news/2006/10/30/recession (accessed October 2006).

42. Duderstadt and Womack, 27, http://insidehighered.com/layout/set/ print/news/2007/04/12/salaries (accessed April 2007).

43. Katharine C. Lyall and Kathleen R. Sell, *The True Genius of America at Risk: Are We Losing Our Public Universities to De Facto Privatization?* (Praeger, 2006); and Edward P. St. John and Douglas M. Priest, eds., *Privatization and Public Universities* (Bloomington: Indiana University Press, 2006).

44. One could add the rule that, in a big state university's sphere of influence, the football coach's name comes more readily to mind that does that of the university president, and the coach makes a lot more money. See J. Douglas Toma, *Football U.: Spectator Sports in the Life of the American University* (Ann Arbor: University of Michigan Press, 2003).

45. Twitchell, 177, 115.

46. Duderstadt and Womack, 24.

47. Bill Readings, *The University in Ruins* (Cambridge: Harvard University Press, 1996), 22, 24.

48. Patricia Gumport, "Universities and Knowledge: Restructuring the City of Intellect," in *The Future of the City of Intellect*, ed. Brint, 54.

49. Gumport, 55.

50. George Keller, *Academic Strategy: The Management Revolution in American Higher Education* (Baltimore: The Johns Hopkins University Press, 1983), viii, 17.

51. Gumport, 55.

52. Ohio State University, *On Campus*, September 24, 1998, 1.

53. Gumport, 69–71.

54. Marilyn Kleinberg Neimark, "If It's So Important, Why Won't They Pay for It? Public Higher Education at the Turn of the Century," *Monthly Review*, October, 1999: 30.

55. John Aubrey Douglass, "The Waning of America's Higher Education Advantage: International Competitors Are No Longer Number Two and Have Big Plans in the Global Economy" (June, 2006); http//cshe.berkeley.edu (accessed December 2006).

56. For more on this topic, see Neimark; and Stuart Tannock, "Higher Education, Inequality, and the Public Good," *Dissent* (Spring, 2006): 45–51.

57. *Chronicle of Higher Education*, November 25, 2005, A1–A4, A11–A19.

58. Ohmann credits George H. W. Bush with making this second slogan "the official ideology of public education, noting that, in sending Congress his Educational Excellence Act of 1989, he "cited just four benefits of 'educational achievement': it 'promotes sustained economic growth, enhances the nation's competitive position in world markets, increases productivity, and leads to higher incomes for everyone.'" *Politics of Knowledge: The Commercialization of*

the University, the Professions, and Print Culture (Middletown, Conn.: Wesleyan University Press, 2003), 146.

59. Marc Bousquet, *How the University Works: Higher Education and the Low Wage Nation* (New York: New York University Press, 2008).

60. C. Wright Mills, *White Collar: The American Middle Classes* (New York: Oxford University Press, 1951), xx.

Anderson, Martin. *Imposters in the Temple: A Blueprint for Improving Higher-Education in America.* Stanford, Calif.: Hoover Institute, 1996.

Arnold, Matthew. *Culture and Anarchy.* 1869; rpt. New Haven, Conn.: Yale University Press, 1994.

Apollo Group, Inc. *2000 Annual Report.*

Aronowitz, Stanley J. *The Knowledge Factory.* Boston: Beacon Press, 2000.

Aronowitz, Stanley, and William DiFazio. *The Jobless Future: Sci-Tech and the Dogma of Work.* Minneapolis: University of Minnesota Press, 1994.

Astin, Alexander W., et al. *The American Freshman: Thirty-Five-Year Trends, 1966–2001.* University of California, Los Angeles: Higher Education Research Institute Graduate School of Education and Information Studies, 2002.

Badia, Janet, and Jennifer Phegley. "Ms. Mentor and the Perils of Advice: (Re)Imagining Women's Authority in the Academy." *Professional Studies Review* (Spring, 2006): 1–15.

Barron's 2005 Guide to the Most Competitive Colleges. Hauppauge, N.Y.: Barron's Educational Series, 2005.

Barrow, Clyde. *Universities and the Capitalist State: Corporate Liberalism and the Reconstruction of American Higher Education.* Madison: University of Wisconsin Press, 1990.

Berelson, Bernard. *Graduate Education in the United States.* New York: McGraw Hill, 1960.

Bird, Caroline. *The Case Against College.* New York: David McKay, 1975.

Birdseye, Clarence. *Individual Training in Our Colleges.* New York: Macmillan, 1907.

Blackmur, R. P. *The Lion and the Honeycomb: Essays in Solicitude and Critique.* New York: Harcourt, Brace, 1955.

Bloom, Allan. *The Closing of the American Mind.* New York: Simon and Schuster, 1987.

Bok, Derek. *Universities in the Marketplace: The Commercialization of Higher-Learning.* Princeton, N.J.: Princeton University Press, 2003.

Bousquet, Marc. *How the University Works: Higher Education and the Low-Wage Nation.* New York: New York University Press, 2008.

———. "The Rhetoric of 'Job Market' and the Reality of the Academic Labor System." *College English* 66 (2003): 207–28.

———. "The Waste Product of Graduate Education: Toward a Dictatorship of the Flexible." *Social Text* 20, no. 2 (2001): 81–104.

Bowen, William G., and Julie Ann Sosa. *Prospects for Faculty in the Arts and Sciences: A Study of Factors Affecting Demand and Supply, 1987–2012.* Princeton, N.J.: Princeton University Press, 1989.

Bowles, Samuel, and Herbert Gintis. *Schooling in Capitalist America: Educational Reform, and the Contradictions of Economic Life.* New York: Basic Books, 1976.

Boyer, Ernest. *Scholarship Reconsidered: Priorities of the Professoriate.* Princeton, N.J.: Carnegie Foundation for the Advancement of Teaching, 1990.

Breneman, David W., Brian Pusser, and Sarah E. Turner, eds. *Earnings from Learning: The Rise of For-Profit Universities.* Albany: State University of New York Press, 2006.

Brewer, Dominic J., Susan M. Gates, and Charles A. Goldman. *In Pursuit of Prestige: Strategy and Competition in U.S. Higher Education.* RAND report, June 2001.

Brint, Steven, ed. *The Future City of Intellect: The Changing American University.* Stanford, Calif.: Stanford University Press, 2002.

———. *In an Age of Experts: The Changing Role of Professionals in Politics and Public Life.* Princeton, N.J.: Princeton University Press, 1994.

———, and Jerome Karabell. *The Diverted Dream: Community Colleges and the Promise of Educational Opportunity in America, 1900–1985.* New York: Oxford University Press, 1989.

Brown, JoAnne. "Professional Language: Words that Succeed." *Radical History Review* 34 (1986): 33–51.

Burgan, Mary. *What Ever Happened to the Faculty?: Drift and Decision in Higher Education.* Baltimore: Johns Hopkins University Press, 2006.

Caesar, Terry. *Conspiring With Forms: Life in Academic Texts.* Athens: University of Georgia Press, 1992.

——— *Writing in Disguise: Academic Life in Subordination.* Athens: Ohio University Press, 1998.

Canfield, James Hulme. *The College Student and His Problems.* New York: Macmillan, 1902.

Carnegie, Andrew. *The Empire of Business.* New York: Doubleday, Page, 1902.

Carnochan, W. B. *The Battleground of the Curriculum: Liberal Education and the American Experience.* Stanford, Calif.: Stanford University Press, 1993.

Chait, Richard, ed. *The Question of Tenure.* Cambridge, Mass.: Harvard University Press, 2002.

Cooke, Morris Llewellyn. *Academic and Industrial Inefficiency: A Report to the Carnegie Foundation for the Advancement of Teaching.* Boston: Merrymount Press, 1910.

Commission on the Humanities, Report. New York: American Council for Learned Societies, 1964.

Cooper, Clayton Sedgwick. *Why Go to College?* New York: Century, 1913.

Crane, Richard Teller. *The Demoralization of College Life.* Chicago: H. O. Shepard, 1911.

———. *The Utility of all Kinds of Higher Schooling.* Chicago: H. O. Shepard, 1909.

Crewe, Jennifer. "Scholarly Publishing: Why Our Business is Your Business Too." *Profession* (2004): 25–31.

Dale, Stacy Berg, and Alan B. Krueger. "Estimating the Payoff to Attending a More Selective College: An Application of Selection on Observables and Unobservables." *The Quarterly Journal of Economics* 117 (November, 2002): 1491–527.

Damrosch, David. *We Scholars: Changing the Culture of the University.* Cambridge, Mass.: Harvard University Press, 1995.

Devlin, Maureen, and Joel S. Meyerson, eds., *Forum Futures: Exploring the Future of Higher Education, 2000 Papers.* San Francisco: Jossey-Bass, 2001.

Diamond, Robert M., and Bronwyn E. Adams, eds. *Recognizing Faculty Work: Reward Systems for the Year 2000.* San Francisco: Jossey-Bass, 1993.

DiMaggio, Paul, and Walter W. Powell. "The Iron Cage Revisited: Institutional Isomorphism and Collective Rationality in Organizational Fields." *American Sociological Review* 48 (1983): 147–60.

Douglass, John Aubrey. "The Waning of America's Higher Education Advantage: International Competitors Are No Longer Number Two and Have Big Plans In the Global Economy." http://cshe.berkeley.edu, June 2006.

Douthat, Ross Gregory. *Privilege: Harvard and the Education of the Ruling Class.* New York: Hyperion, 2005.

Downing, David, Claude Mark Hurlbert, and Paula Matthieu, eds. *Beyond English Inc.: Curricular Reform in a Global Economy.* Portsmouth, N.H.: Boynton/Cook, 2002.

Drucker, Peter. *The Post-Capitalist Society.* New York: Harper Business, 1993.

Dubson, Michael, ed. *Ghosts in the Classroom: Adjunct Faculty and the Price We All Pay.* Boston: Camel's Back Books, 2001.

Duderstadt, James, and Farris W. Womack. *The Future of the Public University in America: Beyond the Crossroads.* Baltimore: Johns Hopkins University Press, 2003.

Engell, James, and Anthony Dangerfield. "Humanities in the Age of Money." *The Harvard Review* (May–June 1998): 48–55, 111.

———. *Saving Higher Education in the Age of Money.* Charlottesville and London: University of Virginia Press, 2005.

Fairweather, James S. *Faculty Work and Public Trust: Restoring the Value of Teaching and Public Service in American Academic Life.* Boston: Allyn and Bacon, 1996.

Fish, Stanley. *Professional Correctness: Literary Studies and Political Change.* Oxford: Clarendon Press, 1995.

Frank, Robert H., and Philip J. Cook. *The Winner-Take-All Society: How More and More Americans Are Competing for Ever Fewer and Bigger Prizes, Encouraging Economic Waste, Income Inequality, and an Impoverished Cultural Life.* New York: Free Press, 1995.

Gappa, Judith, and David Leslie. *The Invisible Faculty: Improving the Status of Part-Timers in Higher Education.* San Francisco: Jossey-Bass, 1993.

Garraty, J. A., and M. C. Carnes. *American National Biography.* New York: Oxford University Press, 1988.

Gless, Darryl J., and Barbara Herrnstein Smith, eds. *The Politics of a Liberal Education.* Durham, N.C.: Duke University Press, 1992.

Golde, Chris. "The Role of the Department and Discipline in Doctoral Attrition: Lessons from Four Departments." *Journal of Higher Education* 76 (2005): 669–700.

———. "Should I Stay or Should I Go? Student Descriptions of the Doctoral Attrition Process." *Review of Higher Education* 23 (2000): 199–227.

Goldin, Daniel. *The Price of Admission: How America's Ruling Class Buys Its Way Into Colleges—and Who Gets Left Outside the Gates.* New York: Random House, 2006.

Graff, Gerald. *Clueless in Academe: How Schooling Obscures the Life of the Mind.* New Haven: Yale University Press, 2003.

———. *Professing Literature: An Institutional History.* Chicago: University of Chicago Press, 1987.

Guillory, John. "Preprofessionalism: What Graduate Students Want." *ADE Bulletin* 113 (Spring, 1994): 4–8.

Hamper, Ben. *Rivethead: Tales from the Assembly Line.* New York: Warner Books, 1991.

Hanson, Victor David, and John Heath. *Who Killed Homer? The Demise of Classical Education and the Recovery of Greek Wisdom.* San Francisco: Encounter Books, 2001.

Herman, Deborah M., and Julie M. Schmid, eds. *Cogs in the Classroom Factory: The Changing Ideology of Academic Life.* Westport, Conn.: Praeger, 2003.

Hofstadter, Richard. *Anti-Intellectualism in American Life.* New York: Vintage, 1962.

Hofstadter, Richard, and C. DeWitt Hardy. *Thoughts on the Present Collegiate System in the United States.* New York: Columbia University Press, 1952.

Horowitz, David. *The Professors: The 101 Most Dangerous Academics in America.* Washington, D.C.: Regnery, 2006.

Huber, Richard. *How Professors Play the Cat Guarding the Cream: Why We're Paying More and Getting Less in Higher Education.* Fairfax, Va.: George Mason University Press, 1993.

Huer, Jon. *Tenure for Socrates: A Study in the Betrayal of the American Professor.* New York: Bergin and Garvey, 1991.

Humphreys, R. Stephen. "Why Do We Write Stuff that Even Our Colleagues Don't Want to Read?" *The Specialized Monograph in Crisis*. AAUP Symposium, online proceedings, September 11–12, 1997. http://arl.org/scomm/epub/paper/humphreys.html.

Illich, Ivan. *Deschooling Society*. New York: Marion Boyars, 1970.

Jacobs, Eric. *Kingsley Amis, A Biography*. London: Hodder and Stoughton, 1995.

Jacoby, Russell. *The Last Intellectuals*. New York: Basic Books, 1987.

Johnson, Benjamin, et al. *Steal This University: The Rise of the Corporate University and the Academic Labor Movement*. New York: Routledge, 2003.

Karabell, Jerome. *The Chosen: The Hidden History of Admission and Exclusion at Harvard, Yale and Princeton*. New York: Houghton Mifflin, 2005.

Karabell, Zachary. *What's College For? The Struggle to Define American Higher Education*. New York: Basic Books, 1998.

Keller, George. *Academic Strategy: The Management Revolution in American Higher Education*. Baltimore: The Johns Hopkins University Press, 1983.

Keniston, Hayward. "We Accept our Responsibility for Professional Leadership." *PMLA* 68 (1953): 18–24.

Kennedy, Donald. *Academic Duty*. Cambridge, Mass.: Harvard University Press, 1997.

Kerr, W. J., Eugene Davenport, E. A. Bryan, and W. O. Thompson. *The Spirit of Land-Grant Institutions*. Chicago, 1931.

Kimball, Roger. *Tenured Radicals: How Politics Has Corrupted our Higher Education*. New York: Harper and Row, 1990.

Kirp, David L. *Shakespeare, Einstein, and the Bottom Line: The Marketing of Higher Education*. Cambridge, Mass.: Harvard University Press, 2003.

Kolodny, Annette. "60 Minutes at the University of Arizona: The Polemic Against Tenure." *New Literary History* 27 (1996): 679–704.

Krause, Elliott. *Death of the Guilds: Professions, States, and the Advance of Capitalism, 1930 to the Present*. New Haven: Yale University Press, 1996.

Krissoff, Derek. "Interview with William Germano." *The Exchange* (Spring 2001): 1–3.

Larson, Magali Sarfatti. *The Rise of Professionalism: A Sociological Analysis*. Berkeley: University of California Press, 1977.

Lee, John, and Sue Clery. "Key Trends in Higher Education." *American Academic* 1 (2004): 21–36.

Levine, Arthur. "The Future of Colleges: 9 Inevitable Changes." *Chronicle of Higher Education* online, October 27, 2000.

———, ed. *Higher Learning in America, 1980–2000*. Baltimore: Johns Hopkins University Press, 1993.

Lewis, Lionel S. *Scaling the Ivory Tower: Merit and Its Limits in Academic Careers*. Baltimore: The Johns Hopkins University Press; rpt. New Brunswick, N.J.: Transaction, 1997.

Lewis, Philip. "The Publishing Crisis and Tenure Criteria: An Issue for Research Universities?" *Profession* (2004): 14–24.

Lewis-Kraus, Gideon. "In the Penthouse of the Ivory Tower." *Believer* (July 2004), http://www.believermag.com/issues/july_2004/lewiskrauss.php.

Lovitts, Barbara, and Cary Nelson. "The Hidden Crisis in Graduate Education: Attrition from Ph.D. Programs." *Academe* 86 (November/December 2000). http://www.aaup.org/publications/Academe/2000/oond/NDooLOVI.HTM.

———. *Leaving the Ivory Tower: The Causes and Consequences of Departure from Doctoral Study.* Lanham, Md.: Rowman and Littlefield, 2001.

Lyall, Katherine C., and Kathleen R. Sell. *The True Genius of America at Risk: Are We Losing Our Public Universities to De Facto Privatization?* Westport, Conn.: Praeger, 2006.

MLA Ad Hoc Committee on the Future of Scholarly Publishing. Report. *Profession* (2002): 172–186.

Markley, Robert. "Stop the Presses: A Modest Proposal for Sa(l)vaging Literary Scholarship." *The Eighteenth Century: Theory and Interpretation* 29 (1988): 71–79.

Martin, Randy, ed., *Chalk Lines: The Politics of Work in the Managed University.* Durham, N.C.: Duke University Press, 1998.

Massy, William F., and Robert Zemsky. "Using Information Technology to Enhance Academic Productivity," http://www.educause.edu/ir/library/nliooo4.html.

McGee, Micki. "Hooked on Education and Other Tales from Adjunct Faculty Organizing." *Social Text* 20, no. 2 (2001): 61–80.

Menand, Louis, ed. *The Future of Academic Freedom.* Chicago: University of Chicago Press, 1996.

Metzger, Walter. *Dimensions of Academic Freedom.* Urbana: University of Illinois Press, 1969.

———, ed. *Professors on Guard: The First AAUP Investigations.* New York: AMS Press, 1977.

Miller, J. Hillis. *Black Holes.* Stanford, Calif.: Stanford University Press, 1999.

———. "Literary Study in the Transatlantic University." *Profession* 1996: 6–14.

Mills, C. Wright. *The Power Elite.* New York: Oxford University Press, 1957.

———. *White Collar.* New York: Oxford University Press, 1951.

Moffatt, Michael. *Coming of Age in New Jersey: College and American Culture.* New Brunswick, N.J.: Rutgers University Press, 1989.

Morreale, Ben. *Down and Out in Academia.* New York: Pitman, 1972.

Neimark, Marilyn Klein. "If It's So Important, Why Won't They Pay for It? Public Higher Education at the Turn of the Century." *Monthly Review* (October 1999): 21–31.

Nelson, Cary, and Stephen Watt. *Office Hours: Activism and Change in the Academy*. New York: Routledge, 2004.

Nelson, Cary, ed. *Will Teach for Food: Academic Labor in Crisis*. Minneapolis: University of Minnesota Press, 1997.

———. "What Hath English Wrought: The Corporate University's Fast Food Discipline." *Workplace* 1 (1998): www.workplace-gsc.com.

Nettles, Michael T., and Catherine M. Millett. *Three Magic Letters: Getting to Ph.D.* Baltimore: The Johns Hopkins University Press, 2006.

Nevins, Allan. *A Study in Power: John D. Rockefeller, Industrialist and Philanthropist*. New York: Scribner, 1953.

Newfield, Christopher. *Ivy and Industry: Business and the Making of the American University, 1880–1980*. Durham, N.C.: Duke University Press, 2003.

Noble, David F. *America By Design: Science, Technology, and the Rise of Corporate Capitalism*. New York: Alfred A. Knopf, 1977.

———. *Digital Diploma Mills: The Automation of Higher Education*. New York: Monthly Review Press, 2001.

Nyquist, Jody, et al. "On the Road to Becoming a Professor: The Graduate Student Experience." *Change* (May/June 1999): 18–27.

Ohmann, Richard. *English in America: A Radical View of the Profession*. New York: Oxford University Press, 1976; rpt. Middletown, Conn.: Wesleyan University Press, 1996.

———. *Politics of Knowledge: The Commercialization of the University, The Professions, and Print Culture*. Middletown, Conn.: Wesleyan University Press, 2003.

Orman, Suze. *The Money Book for the Young, Fabulous, and Broke*. New York: Riverhead Books, 2005.

Peters, Tom. *Thriving on Chaos*. New York: Harper and Row, 1987.

Phelan, James. *Beyond the Tenure Track*. Columbus: Ohio State University Press, 1996.

Princeton Review Complete Book of Colleges, 2005. New York: Random House, 2005.

Readings. Bill. *The University in Ruins*. Cambridge, Mass.: Harvard University Press, 1996.

Regier, Willis with Jeffrey Williams. "In Defense of Academic Publishing: An Interview with Willis Regier." *Minnesota Review*, n.s. 61–62 (2004), http://www.theminnesotareview.org/ns61/regier.htm.

Renker, Elizabeth. *The Origin of American Literature Studies: An Institutional History*. Cambridge: Cambridge University Press, 2007.

Rhoades, Gary. *Managed Professionals: Unionized Faculty and Restructuring Academic Labor*. Albany: State University of New York Press, 1998.

Rifkin, Jeremy. *The End of Work: The Decline of the Global Labor Force and the Dawn of the Post-market Era*. New York: Putnam, 1995.

Rohde, Deborah C. *In Pursuit of Knowledge: Scholars, Status, and Academic Culture*. Stanford, Calif.: Stanford University Press, 2006.

Rosovsky, Henry. *The University: An Owner's Manual*. New York: W. W. Norton, 1990.

Ross, Andrew. "The Mental Labor Problem." *Social Text* 18, no. 2 (2000): 1–31.

Ruch, Richard S. *Higher Ed. Inc.: The Rise of the For-Profit University*. Baltimore: The Johns Hopkins University Press, 2001.

Ryan, Judith. "Publishing and Purchasing: The Great Paradigm Shift." *Profession* (2004): 7–13.

Sawyer, R. M., et al., eds. *The Art and Politics of College Teaching: A Practical Guide for the Beginning Professor*. New York: Peter Lang, 1992.

Scholes, Robert. "Learning and Teaching." *Profession* 2004: 118–27.

———. "Presidential Address 2004: The Humanities in a Posthumanist World." *PMLA* 120 (2005): 724–33.

———. *The Rise and Fall of English: Reconstructing English as a Discipline*. New Haven, Conn.: Yale University Press, 1998.

Scott, Martin. "Pagers, Nikes and Wordsworth: Teaching College English in a Shopping Mall." *Profession* (2001): 92–98.

Showalter, English, et al. *The MLA Guide to the Job Search*. New York: Modern Language Association of America, 1996.

Sinclair, Upton. *The Goose-Step: A Study in American Education*. Pasadena, Calif.: published by the author, 1923.

Smith, Bardwell L. and Associates. *The Tenure Debate*. San Francisco: Jossey-Bass, 1973.

Soares, Joseph. *The Power of Prestige: Yale and America's Elite Universities*. Stanford, Calif.: Stanford University Press, 2007.

Sowers-Hoag, Karen, and Dianne F. Harrison. *Finding an Academic Job*. London: SAGE Publications, 1998.

Spenser, L. "The Perils of Socialized Higher Education." *Forbes*, May 27, 1991.

Sperling, John. *Rebel with a Cause: The Entrepreneur Who Created the University Of Phoenix and the For-Profit Revolution in Higher Education*. Hoboken, N.J.: Wiley, 2000.

Sperling, John, and Robert W. Tucker. *For-Profit Higher Education: Developing a World-Class Workforce*. New Brunswick, N.J.: Transaction, 1997.

Stanton, Domna C. "Working Through the Crises: A Plan for Action." *Profession* (2004): 32–41.

Steinberg, Jacques. *The Gatekeepers: Inside the Admissions Process of a Premier College*. New York: Penguin, 2003.

St. John, Edward P., and Douglas M. Priest, eds. *Privatization and Public Universities*. Bloomington: Indiana University Press, 2006.

Sykes, Charles. *Profscam: Professors and the Demise of Higher Education*. New York: St. Martin's Press, 1988.

Tannock, Stuart. "Higher Education, Inequality, and the Public Good." *Dissent* (Spring 2006): 45–51.

Taylor, Frederick W. *The Principles of Scientific Management*. Norwood, Mass.: Plimpton Press, 1911; rpt. New York: Harper and Brothers, 1916.

Tawney, R. H. *The Acquisitive Society*. 1921; rpt. London: Fontana, 1961.

Thacker, Lloyd, ed., *College Unranked: Affirming Educational Values in College Admissions*. The Education Conservancy, 2004.

———. *College Unranked: Ending the College Admissions Frenzy*. Cambridge: Harvard University Press, 2005.

Toma, J. Douglas. *Football U.: Spectator Sports in the Life of the American University*. Ann Arbor: The University of Michigan Press, 2003.

Toth, Emily. *Ms. Mentor's Impeccable Advice for Women in Academia*. Philadelphia: University of Pennsylvania Press, 1997.

———, and Diana G. Oblinger. "The Virtual University." A Report from a Joint Educom/IBM Roundable, Washington, D.C. November 5–6, 1996, http://www.educause.edu/nlii/vu/html.

Trillin, Calvin. "U.S. Journal: Manhattan. Thoughts on Changing the Rules." *The New Yorker*, March 7, 1977, pp. 84, 86.

Twigg, Carol. "Improving Learning and Reducing Costs: New Models for Online Learning." *Educausel Review* (September/October 2003): 28–38.

Twitchell, James B. *Branded Nation: The Marketing of Megachurch, College Inc., and Museumworld*. New York: Simon and Schuster, 2004.

U.S. Department of Commerce. *Historical Statistics of the United States, Colonial Times to 1970*, Part I. Washington, D.C.: U.S. Department of Commerce, 1976.

U.S. Department of Education, National Center for Education Statistics. *The Condition of Education*, 2002.

U.S. News & World Report Ultimate Guide to College 2006. Naperville, Ill.: Sourcebooks, 2005.

Van Alstyne, William, ed. *Freedom and Tenure in the Academy*. Durham, N.C.: Duke University Press, 1993.

Veblen, Thorstein. *The Higher Learning in America*. 1916; rpt. New Brunswick: N.J.: Transaction, 1993.

Wall, J. *Andrew Carnegie*. New York: Oxford University Press, 1970; rpt. Pittsburgh: University of Pittsburgh Press, 1989.

Washburn, Jennifer, and Eyal Press. "Digital Diplomas." *Mother Jones* 26 (January–February 2001): 34–42.

Waters, Lindsay. *Enemies of Promise: Publishing, Perishing, and the Eclipse of Scholarship*. Chicago: Prickly Paradigm Press, 2004.

————. "A Modest Proposal for Preventing the Books of the Members of the MLA from Being a Burden to Their Authors, Publishers, or Audiences." *PMLA* 115 (2000): 315–17.

Watkins. Evan. *Work Time: English Departments and the Circulation of Cultural Value*. Stanford, Calif.: Stanford University Press, 1989.

Wayland, Francis. *Thoughts on the Present Collegiate System in the United States*. Boston: Gould, Kendall and Lincoln, 1842; rpt. New York: Arno Press, 1969.

White, Geoffrey D. *Campus, Inc.: Corporate Power in the Ivory Tower*. Amherst, N.Y.: Prometheus Books, 2000.

Williams, Jeffrey. "Editorial Instinct: An Interview with William P. Germano." *Minnesota Review*, n.s. 48–49 (1998), http://theminnesotareview .org/ns48/germano.htm.

————, ed. *The Institution of Literature*. Albany: State University of New York Press, 2001.

Wiltshire, Bruce. *The Moral Collapse of the University: Professionalism, Purity, and Alienation*. Albany: State University of New York Press, 1990.

Wolfe, Tom. *I Am Charlotte Simmons*. New York: Farrar, Straus and Giroux, 2004.

Zemsky, Robert, Gregory R. Wegner, and William F. Massy. *Remaking the American University: Market-Smart and Mission-Centered*. New Brunswick, N.J.: Rutgers University Press, 2005.

AAUP. *See* American Association of University Professors
Academic and Industrial Inefficiency (Cooke), 8
academic freedom, 71–78, 80
academic labor hierarchy, 59, 64
Academic Strategy (Keller), 133
accountability, 80
adjuncts, 56–67
  at Harvard, 58
  at Stanford, 58
agribusiness, 16
America by Design (Noble), 7
American Association of University Professors (AAUP), 59, 71, 73–77, 130
  General Declaration of Principles, 75–77
  Statement of Principles, 76–77
American Council on Education, 52
American Federation of Teachers, 72
Amherst College, 53, 114, 118, 120
Amis, Kingsley, xix
Anderson, Martin, 50, 79, 80
Andover. *See* Phillips Academy, Andover.
anti-intellectualism, 13–114
Anti-Intellectualism in American Life (Hofstadter), 9
Antioch University, 148–49n8
Apollo Group, 94, 95–97, 99
Arizona State University, 118, 121
Armani Emporium, 124
Armani, Giorgio, 124

Arnold, Matthew, 20–22
Aronowitz, Stanley, 2, 19, 60–64, 71, 111, 137
  on academic unionism, 18
  on job search, 88
Associate's degree, 92
Association of American University Presses, 45
Association to Advance Collegiate Schools of Business, 103
Atkinson, Edward, 9

Bachelor's degree, xvii, 91, 92
Baptist Education Society, 9
Barnes and Noble, 45
Barron's, 84, 113–14
Barrow, Clyde, xiv, 155n55
Beaver College, 119
The Believer, 81
Bennett, William, xv
Bennington College, 57
Berelson, Bernard, 28
Berkeley. *See* University of California
Bérubé, Michael, xvi
Birdseye, Clarence F., 4–9, 10, 20, 21, 79
Blackboard, 105–8, 109
  WebCT and, 106
Blackmur, R. P., 30–31, 143–44n18
Bogel, F. V., 38
Bok, Derek, xi, 70
Bousquet, Marc, xvi, 34, 35, 40, 58–59, 137–38
Bowen, William G., 34–35, 37

Boyer, Ernest, 50–51, 53, 54
Branded Nation (Twitchell), 121–22
Brandeis, Louis, 13
Brandeis University, xii
Brand, Myles, 49
Breneman, David W., 25, 94
Brewer, Dominic J., 122
Brewster, James H., 74
Brint, Stephen, xiv, 68, 126–27
Brown, JoAnnne, 150*n*34
Brown, Laura, 38
Brown University, 83
Bucknell University, 118
Burd, Stephen, 113
Burgan, Mary, 142*n*43
Bush, George H. W., 159*n*58
Business principles, 5

Caesar, Terry, 38, 60–61, 62
Career Education Corp (CECO), 96,
    102, 104
Carleton College, 118
Carnegie, Andrew, xiii–xvi, 3–10, 20,
    53
Carnegie Foundation, 28, 52, 53,
    108,147*n*76
Carnegie Institute, 24
Carnegie Technical School, 5, 7
Case Western Reserve University,
    107, 119
Casper, Gerhard, 49
Castle, Terry, 38
CECO. *See* Career Education Corp
Center for Academic Transforma-
    tion, 100
Center for Studies in Higher Educa-
    tion, 136
Center for the Study of Education
    Policy, 129
Central Michigan University, 127
Chait, Richard, 78–79
Cheney, Lynn V., 142*n*43

Chronicle of Higher Education, 104,
    105, 136
City National Bank, 15
Civil War, 2, 51, 85
Clarion University, 66, 67, 71
Clark, Burton, 66–67
Coe College, 25
Cohl, Peter, 119
Cold War, xiv, 2
College of Distance Learning, 125
College standards, 5
*College Unranked: Ending the College
    Admissions Frenzy* (Thacker), 117
Collis, David, 97, 119, 122, 123
Columbia University, 51, 76, 84, 99,
    117
    corporate America and, 13–14
    Fathom and, 122–24
    press, 41
Columbine Capital Services, 96
Cooke, Morris Llewellyn, 8–9, 21,
    108, 141*n*25
Cooper, James Fenimore, xvii
Cornell University, 46, 47, 119
    funding, 124
corporate culture, 88–89
corporatization, 98–99
Corwin, Scott, 57
course management, 105
Cox, Geoffrey, 123
Crane Co., 5
Crane, Richard Teller, xiii–xvi, 9–10,
    12, 20, 79, 85
    research of, 5–7
Crewe, Jennifer, 41, 43–44, 46
crisis, xii–xiii, 1, 24, 36
Crow, Michael, 118
Culler, Jonathan, 38
Culture and Anarchy (Arnold), 20–21
Culture Wars, xv, 21, 132
CUNY (City University of New
    York), 60

Dale, Stacy Berg, 113
Damrosch, David, 19
Dangerfield, Anthony, 69, 125
Davidson, Cathy, 41, 44, 46, 47, 49,
    61, 62, 64, 145*n*42
deBolla, Peter, 38
Denison University, 124
Department of Education, 62, 71, 89,
    95
    on University of Phoenix, 102–3
Desire2Learn, 106–7, 109
DeVry, 94–98, 104, 105
Diamond, Robert, 52
Digital Diploma Mills (Noble), 101
Dillard University, 57
Dillon, Sam, 103
*Dollars and Sense: The Nonprofit
    Board's Guide to Determining
    Chief Executive's Compensation*
    (Quatt), 118
Douglass, John Aubrey, 136, 137
Dow Jones, 96
dropouts, 104
    Ph.D., 27–28
Drucker, Peter, 7, 128
D'Souza, Dinesh, xv
Dubson, Michael, 63–64
Duderstadt, James, 92–93, 129, 130,
    131
Duke University, 46, 47, 61, 117,
    142*n*47

*Earnings from Learning: The Rise of
    For-Profit Universities* (Brene-
    man, Pusser, and Turner), 94
eCollege, 107, 109
EdTechPost (blog), 106
Education Management Corpora-
    tion, 96
Educause, 100, 107, 108
Educom, 108
Eduventures, Inc., 99

Edwards, Mark, 120
efficiency, 79–81
Eisenhower, Dwight D., 84
electronic publication, 41, 43–44
Eliot, Charles W., 51, 85
Empire of Business (Carnegie), 6–7
Engell, James, 69, 125
Entrepreneurs, 9
Equal Employment Opportunity
    Commission, 72
ESPN, 93, 95
expert professionalism, 68–69

Faculty Scholarly Productivity Index,
    117
failure, 158*n*23
Fathom, 122–33
Feldberg, Meyer, 123
Fernandez, John J., 103
*Final Report of the MLA Committee on
    Professional Employment*, 36
financial reforms, 43
Financial Times, 107
Finding an Academic Job (Harrison
    and Sowers-Hoag), 37
Fisher College of Business, 131
Fish, Stanley, 22–23, 50, 142*n*47,
    145*n*41
Flint, 63
football coaches, 159*n*44
for-profit university, xvi, xvii–xviii, 8,
    52, 58, 82, 84, 87–88, 92, 93–
    106, 109, 115, 125, 126, 136
    online, 99–101
    prestige and, 111–12
    recruiting practices of, 104
Frank, Robert, 115, 116–17, 128
Freedman, Samuel G., 115–16
funding, 124–25
Future of Public Universities in America
    (Dudestadt and Womack),
    92–93

Gamson, Zelda, 47, 53
Gappa, Judith, 58
Garfield, James, 141*n*36
Gates, Susan M., 122
Gee, Gordon, 131
Geiger, Roger, xiv
General Declaration of Principles, 75–77
General Motors, 63
Georgetown University, 84
Germano, William, 42, 45, 47
Ghosts in the Classroom (Dubson), 62
Golde, Chris, 28–32
Golden, Daniel, 116
Goldman, Charles A., 122
Gonick, Lee, 107
Goose-step: A Study of American Education (Sinclair), xiii, 13, 17–18, 20
governing boards, 10, 11
graduate school, 25–33, 37
Graff, Gerald, xiv, 20
Grand Canyon University, 102–3
Great Depression, xiv, 67
Greek, 85–86
Greenblatt, Stephen, 48
Guide to the Job Search, 35
Guillory, John, 322, 39, 40
Gumport, Patricia, 132–33

Hamper, Ben, 63
Hanson, Victor David, 86–87, 153*n*9
Harney, Stefano, 58
Harper, William Rainey, 10
Harrison, Dianne F., 37
Hart-Scott-Rodino Anti-Trust Improvements Act, 106
Harvard University, xviii, 6, 7, 48, 51, 85, 90, 114, 115, 117
  adjuncts at, 58
  funding, 124
  presidents at, 70, 84, 85
  Press, 45
  Z List of, 116

Haverty, Linda, 37
Heath, John, 86–87, 153*n*9
Higher Ed. Inc. (Ruch), 94
Higher Education Research Institute, 91
"Higher Education: The Ultimate Winner-Take Market?" (Frank), 115
Higher Learning in America (Veblen), xiii, 10
Hill, Anita, 72–73
Hofstadter, Richard, 9–10, 89
Holbrook, Karen, 129
Hoover, Herbert, 15
Hopkins, Mark, 17, 20
Horowitz, David, xv
Houston, 61
Hoxby, Caroline, 113–17, 127
Huber, Richard, 79
Huber, Sonya, 18
Huer, John, 77
humanism, 87
humanities, xi–xviii, 1, 20, 25, 126–29, 137
  job market in, 34–40
  looking forward and, 87–88
  money in, 68–69
Humphreys, R. Stephen, 46, 47
Huntington, Collis P., 14
Hurricane Katrina, 57, 148*n*7, 148*n*8

Illinois State University, 129
Imposters in the Temple (Anderson), 79, 80
Independent Education Consultants Association, 115
Indiana University, 32, 49
Individual Training in Our Colleges (Birdseye), 4
Inside Higher Education, 96, 105, 116, 120, 129–30
Instructional Technology Council, 108

intellectual property, 70, 109–10
ITT Educational Services, 96
IvyWise, 116

Jacoby, Russell, 50
James Cancer Research Institute, 131
Jin, Ginger Zhe, 118
job market, 24–25, 33–40
job system, 40
job training, 94, 111–12
Johns Hopkins University, xii, 6, 51, 52, 76, 124
Jordan, David Starr, 74
J-STOR, 41
The Jungle (Sinclair), 13

Kaplan University, 98
Katherine Gibbs School, 102, 103
Keller, George, 133
Keniston, Hayward, 1
Kennedy, Donald, 49, 79
Kenyon College, 124
Kerr, Clark, 25
Killing the Spirit (Smith), 79
Kimball, Roger, xv, 151*n*46
Kirp, David, xi, 94, 97, 126
Knowledge Factory: Dismantling the Corporate University and Creating True Higher Learning (Aronowitz), 88
Krause, Elliott, 67
Krueger, Alan B., 113

labor colleges, 17
Land-Grant Act, 16
Larkin, Philip, xix
Larson, John M., 102
Larson, Magali S., 53
Latin, 85–86
Laureate Education (LAUR), 96, 99
law school, 27
Lederman, Doug, 96

Lerner, Elaine S., 98
Leslie, David, 58
Leslie, Scott, 106
Levine, Arthur, 99
Levin, Henry M., 103
Lewis-Kraus, Gideon, 81
Lewis, Philip, 46, 47, 48–49
liberal arts, 2, 3, 6, 10, 83–85, 91–92, 125, 126–28, 132–33
lifetime earnings, 84, 113
Listserves, 38
Livingston, John C., 77
loans, 90
Louisiana State University, 93
Lovejoy, A. O., 76
Lovitts, Barbara, 31
Loyola University (New Orleans), 57, 148*n*7
Lutheran Church, xi

Machlup, Fritz, 71
Marietta College, 125
market-model university, 69
Markley, Robert, 45, 47
Marquette University, 109
Massachusetts Institute of Technology, 8, 117, 120, 124
Massy, William, 100, 101
Master's degree, xvii
McGee, Micki, 64–65, 70
McKeon, Michael, 38
medical school, 27
Meek, Ed, 62
Menand, Louis, 71
mental labor problem, 64
meritocracy, 19, 63
Metzger, Walter, 71
Meyers, Patrick, 98
Mickleson, Manfred, 38–39, 42, 45
Midvale Steel Company, 7
Milken, Michael, 122, 123
Miller, J. Hillis, 2

Millett, Catherine M., 27, 28, 29
Mills, C. Wright, 127, 138
MIT. *See* Massachusetts Institute of
Technology
MLA. *See* Modern Language
Association
Modern Language Association
(MLA), 1, 20, 24, 25, 27, 35, 36,
46, 48, 50, 67, 145*n*42
Moffatt, Michael, 90
money
in humanities, 69
life goals and, 91
prestige and, 124
Moral Collapse of the University (Wilt-
shire), 78
Morgan, J. P., 13
Morreale, Ben, 25
Morrill Act, 85
Morse, Robert J., 117
Moten, Frederick, 58
Motley Fool (web site), 106
Mowder, Louise, 30
*Ms. Mentor's Impeccable Advice for
Women in Academia* (Toth), 37

NASDAQ, 95, 96
National Association of College and
University Business Officers,
125
National Bureau of Economic Re-
search, 118
National Center for Postsecondary
Improvement, 132
National Education Association, 71,
72
*National Labor Relations Board v. Ye-
shiva University* (court case), 18
NCAA, 130
Nearing, Scott, 74–75
Nelson, Cary, xvi, 31–32, 33, 69
Nettles, Michael T., 27, 28, 29

New College of the University of
South Florida, 114
Newfield, Christopher, xiv
New Orleans, 57
New Yorker, 24
New York University, 122, 150*n*25
Noble, David F., 7, 93–94, 101, 122,
123
North Central States Association, 98
Nussbaum, Felicity, 38
Nyquist, Jody, 29, 31

Oberlin College, 120, 125
Oden, Robert, Jr., 118
Office Hours (Nelson and Watt), 33
Ohio State University, xii, xix, 15, 16,
109, 124, 129, 131, 134, 158*n*19
Ohmann, Richard, xiv, 69, 82,
159*n*58
O'Neal, Shaquille, 93
online education, 93–94, 95, 99–101,
105–10, 122–25
Ore Trust, 13
organizational structure, 98
outsourcing, 42, 66, 133
Oxford University Press, 47

Paradiso, Nathaniel, 39
part-time employment, 56. *See also*
adjuncts
part-time students, 89
Pearson, 107, 109
Penguin Books, 107
Pennsylvania State University, 117,
126
Pesch, Pat, 102
Ph.D. degrees, xvi, 24–40, 45, 51, 67,
135
attrition rates, 27–28
job search and, 33–40
Phillips Academy, Andover, 115
Pierce College of Business, 4

Pope, Alexander, 73
Portland State University, 117
"Power of Information: How Do
U.S. News Rankings Affect the
Financial Resources of Public
Colleges" (Jin and Whalley),
118
*Power of Privilege: Yale and America's
Elite Colleges* (Soares), 116
*Practical Guide for the Beginning Pro-
fessor* (Haverty), 37
practicality, 12
preprofessionalism, 32, 37, 40
"Preprofessionalism: What Graduate
Students Want" (Guillory), 32
prestige
concept of, 111
for-profit universities and, 112
measuring, 112–13
money and, 121–23
public universities and, 129–32
*Price of Admission: How America's Rul-
ing Class Buys Its Way Into Elite
Colleges—and Who Gets Left Outside the Gates* (Golden), 116
Princeton University, xviii, 6, 34, 82,
90, 105, 114, 117, 128, 144*n*18
Princeton Review, 53, 114, 115
Principles of Scientific Management
(Taylor), 7
Pritchett, Henry S., 8
private universities, 18, 89, 90
productivity, 9
Professing Literature (Graff), xiv
professionalism
expert, 68
social-trustee, 68
professors
income of, 18
role of, 22
profitability, 11
Profscam (Sykes), 79

*Prospects for Faculty: A Study of Factors
Affecting Demand and Supply*
(Bousquet), 34, 35, 37
public universities, 18, 89, 90. *See also*
state universities.
prestige and, 129–32
publishing, 39, 40–49
electronic, 43–44
Pusser, Brian, 94

Quatt, Charles W., 118
Quirk, Matthew, 118

Raleigh, John H., 25
RAND, 122, 127
Readings, Bill, 131, 135
recessions, 96, 129–30
recruiters, 104
Regier, Willis, 45, 47
Rensselaer Polytechnic Institute, 100
*Report of the Commission of the Human-
ities*, 20
Responsibility Based Budgeting, 65,
133
"Return to Attending a More Selec-
tive College: 1960 to the Pres-
ent" (Hoxby), 113
Rhoades, Gary, 65–66, 81, 142*n*45
Richardson, Brent, 103
Ridge, Tom, 125
Rivethead: Tales from the Assembly Line
(Hamper), 63
Rockefeller, John D., 9
Rohde, Deborah C., 48, 51
Roman Catholic Church, xi
Rosovsky, Henry, 60
Ross, Andrew, 64, 69
Ross, Edward A., 74
Routledge, 38, 42
Ruch, Richard S., 94, 98
Rutgers, 90
Ryan, Judith, 44

Sakai Foundation, 107
salary, 18
  public v. private, 130
Sam Houston State University, 127
San Jose State University, 127
SAT scores, 113, 115, 117–20
Saudi Arabia, 61
Scholarship, 39
Scholes, Robert, 20, 50, 51
Schuster, Jack, 35, 36
Scott, Martin, 61, 62
Seligman, E. R. A., 76
Sevy, Milton, 74
Shakespeare, Einstein, and the Bottom Line (Kirp), xi, 94
Sinclair, Upton, xiii, 2, 13–22
  Veblen and, 17–19
60 Minutes (TV program), 71, 104
Slaughter, Sheila, 81, 141*n*45
Smith, Page, 79
Soares, Joseph A., 116
social-trustee professionalism, 68
Sommer, John, 126
Sosa, Julie Ann, 34, 35, 37
Southern University, 57
Soviet Union, xiv
Sowers-Hoag, Karen, 37
Specialized Scholarly Monograph in Crisis, 45
Sperling, John, 94, 97
standardized erudition, 10
Standard Oil, 13
Stanford University, xii, 49, 74, 79, 114, 120, 123–24, 141*n*32
  adjuncts at, 58
  corporate America and, 14–15
  funding, 124
Stanford, Leland, 14, 15, 74
Statement of Principles (AAUP), 71–77
state universities, 90, 92–93, 112, 121, 125, 129–34
  influence of, 159*n*44

St. Petersburg Herald, 57
Strassburger, John, 118
Strauss, Howard, 105
Strayer Education, 96
Students for Academic Freedom, xv
student transcripts, 11
Super Bowl, 93
Supreme Court, 18
Swarthmore College, 82, 84, 118
Sykes, Charles, xv, 21, 79
Sylvan Learning Centers, 99
systems of accountancy, 11

Taft, William Howard, 6
Tawney, R. H., 68
Taylor, Frederick Winslow, xv, 7–8, 9, 21
Taylor, Ronald, 102
teaching assistants, 81
Temple University, 109
tenure, 17, 45–46, 48, 49–53, 55–70, 106
  corporatization of, 77–78
  erosion of, 70–82, 109
  myths about, 72
tenure-track jobs, 24–26, 33–54
Thacker, Lloyd, 117–18
Thomas More College, 125
Thompson, James Oxley, 15, 16
Three Magic Letters: Getting to Ph.D. (Millett and Nettles), 27
To Reclaim a Legacy (Bennett), xv
Total Quality Management, 133, 134
Toth, Emily, 37–38
Touraine, Alaine, 81
training, 9, 10
Trani, Eugene, 118
Traub, James, 136
Trillin, Calvin, 24–25
tuition fees, 89–90
Tulane University, 57
Turner, Sarah E., 94

20/10 Plan, 134
Twigg, Carol, 100–101, 108–9
Twitchell, James, 121–22, 123, 126, 131

Ultimate Guide to College, 114
undergraduates, 85–86
undergraduate teaching, 29
"Understanding the Burden of Scholarly Publishing" (Davidson), 44
UNext.com, 123
uniform faculty profiles, 66
unionization, 17–19, 57, 70
United Gas Improvement, 13
universities, xi. *See also specific universities*
  American, 1
  corporate, 12
  for-profit, xvi, xvii–xviii, 8, 52, 58, 82, 84, 87–88, 92, 93–106, 109, 115, 125
  private, 89–90, 92
  public, 89–90
  as social institutions, 132–33
  societies and, 83–84
  state, 90, 92–93, 112, 11, 125, 129–34, 159n44
  Veblen on, 10–13
University in the Marketplace (Bok), xi, 70
University of Arizona, 90, 109
University of California, 14
  Berkeley, 25, 53, 114, 136
  Los Angeles (UCLA), 91, 114
  Santa Barbara, 46, 114
University of Chicago, 9 10, 13
University of Cincinnati, 124
University of Colorado, 74, 90
University of Florida Foundation, 131
University of Georgia, 72, 73, 117

University of Illinois, 51
  Champaign, 109
  Chicago, 135, 145n41
  Press, 45, 47
University of Iowa, 109
University of Kansas, 90
University of Kentucky, 119
University of Massachusetts
  Amherst, 126
  Boston, 127
University of Michigan, 114
University of Minnesota, 13, 51–52
  tenure at, 57
University of North Carolina, 114
University of Northwestern Ohio, 125
University of Oklahoma, 72–73
University of Pennsylvania, 13
University of Phoenix, 93–94, 95, 97, 103–5, 122, 136
  Department of Education and, 104
University of Southern California, 109, 124
University of Utah, 74
University of Virginia, 24, 114
University of Wisconsin, 109
university presses, 40–49
usefulness, 12
U.S. News and World Report (magazine), xviii, 53, 88, 112, 114, 116–20, 122, 129
Utility of All Kinds of Higher Schooling (Crane), 6

Valve World (journal), 6
Veblen, Thorstein, xiii, 2, 10–13, 14, 88, 95, 141n32
  Sinclair and, 17–20, 21
Virginia Commonwealth University, 118
vocationalism, xiii, xviii, 12, 82, 136

Walden University, 99
Wall Street Journal, 123
Washington Post Company, 102
Washington University, 117
Waters, Lindsay, xvi, 45, 47
Watt, Stephen, 33
Wayland, Francis, 83, 84, 87
WebCT, 105
    Blackboard and, 106
Web sites, 96, 120, 125
We Scholars (Damrosch), 19
Whalley, Alex, 118
Wharton School, 3, 75
Who Killed Homer? (Hanson and
    Heath), 86
Wilbur, Ray Lyman, 15
Wilde, Oscar, 45
Williams College, 114, 118, 141*n*36
Williams, Jeffrey, 78

Wilson, Woodrow, 6
Wiltshire, Bruce, 78, 79
Wolfe, Tom, 26
Womack, Farris W., 92–93, 129, 130,
    131
Woodruff, Neal, 25
workers colleges, 17
World War II, xiv, 3
"Writing Resignation" (Caesar), 61

Xavier University, 57
XML, 44

Yahoo Finance, 106
Yale University, xviii, 6, 52, 84, 86,
    114, 116, 117, 122
    funding, 124

Zemsky, Robert, xv–xvi, 100, 101
Z List, 116